Johann Christian Edelmann

Religion and Society 3

EDITORS

Leo Laeyendecker, *University of Leyden*

Jacques Waardenburg, *University of Utrecht*

Mouton · The Hague · Paris

Johann Christian Edelmann

From Orthodoxy to Enlightenment

by

WALTER GROSSMANN

Mouton · The Hague · Paris

ISBN: 90-279-7691-0

© 1976, Mouton & Co

Printed in Hungary

74-5470 — Szegedi Nyomda

For Maria

Preface

Johann Christian Edelmann was a major German radical thinker of the eighteenth century who lived in open conflict with most of the accepted philosophical and religious beliefs of his time. His intellectual development is characterized by a movement from orthodoxy to pietism and a combination of spiritualism with rationalism that was uniquely his own.

Edelmann's work has not been neglected by past scholarship, yet no entire book has been written about him. In important studies of the literature, philosophy, and theology of the eighteenth century by Hermann Hettner, Fritz Mauthner, Paul Hazard, and Emanuel Hirsch some excellent pages are devoted to his life and works.

Edelmann recorded the story of his own life, though only up to the year 1747. This autobiography was discovered among other manuscripts of his by C.R.W. Klose in the Hamburg City Library and published in 1849. Edelmann's works were printed in editions of five hundred copies, at most a thousand, and many of the copies were subsequently destroyed. For the first time since their original publication between the years 1735 and 1747 they are now being reprinted – by the publishing house of Frommann in Stuttgart under my editorship.

It is the purpose of this study to present Edelmann's life and work in the complex political and social environment of his time. The account of his formative years, of his attendance at various schools and at the University of Jena, and of contacts with major religious leaders is a rich chapter in the intellectual history of his time. The very nature of Edelmann's work provoked strong reaction, bringing the author fame and censure, loyal friendships and deep animosities.

Edelmann traveled his own road. Even more remarkable is the fact that, at a time when every preacher or teacher was attached to some office, he sought to be free from all such bonds. He was among the first German intellectuals who felt that, in order to fulfill the mission of the 'unattached intelligentsia,' one could not be in anybody's pay. Consequently his precarious economic position exemplifies the struggle of the writer in a society in which those in power are hostile.

The discussion of Edelmann's works leads into the center of the religious and philosophical debate of his age. I have tried to guide the reader to Edelmann's works and to portray the ardent struggle waged by this great iconoclast.

At Yankton College, South Dakota, I first became aware of a religious tradition and search which I feel prepared me for the study of Edelmann. In Yankton Wolfgang and Gertrud Liepe, and Friends Meeting in Cambridge, have helped me to appreciate varieties of religious expression.

Friendships with the late Waldo Emerson Palmer, the late Lois Smith, and with Marshall Smith have helped me to understand truly independent thinkers.

Edwin E. Williams has listened with a 'third ear' to my incessant talk on Edelmann. How much I thank him cannot be expressed in an acknowledgment.

Professor Ernst Benz's interest in my work has given me great encouragement.

I am deeply grateful to Professor Howard Mumford Jones for reading the manuscript and for innumerable comments and suggestions. James Tanis' informed enthusiasm has given me continuous support, and Henry Hatfield's friendly impatience has contributed to my completing the study. George H. Williams' historical understanding of religious movements has elucidated many problems with which this study is concerned. I appreciate greatly his continuing interest, and also that of Bernhard Blume.

Alice Goebell, who corrected my first attempts to write English, also applied her editorial skill to this manuscript. So did Mrs. Madeleine Gleason, with unrelenting care and patience. I also thank Molly Matson for assistance, particularly on bibliographical questions.

I thank Clemens Heller for having found a home for this study.

Alyce Curran and Ellie Riordan typed and retyped the manuscript, always with good humor, and I am very grateful to both of them.

Erwin Neweling, the steward of the local treasures at Berleburg, guided me to that rich archive. Heinz Lorenz and Ingo Bach showed me theirs and Edelmann's home town, Weissenfels. A visit to Herrnhut acquainted me with some of the Brethren's religious practices, and Richard Träger, of the Archiv der Brüder-Unität, Herrnhut, provided valuable information.

I am also grateful to the staff of the Universitätsbibliothek Marburg who greatly facilitated my work there in 1964/65 and in the summer of 1970. The Handschriftenabteilung of the Universitäts- und Staatsbibliothek Hamburg has kindly given me access to the Edelmann manuscripts and permission to film them. For difficult and excellent filming I am thankful to Fritz Meier, Rosen-Apotheke, Marburg. I thank Harold Jantz for providing me with a photocopy from the manuscript of Edelmann's *Die Andere Epistel Harenbergs* which is in his collection.

Fellowships from the John Simon Guggenheim Memorial Foundation, New York, and the Humboldt Gesellschaft, Bad Godesberg, have enabled me to pursue the research for this study, to visit most of the places where Edelmann lived, and to examine numerous local archives. I acknowledge also gratefully grants from the Clark Fund at Harvard University. This study could not have been written without such generous support.

The book was written in carrel 166 of Widener Library. From its window I could watch the Harvard Yard in the change of seasons and admire the loving care with which trees and grounds were attended. To these joys the use of the collection within the building walls and the use of the carrel were linked. For these privileges I am forever grateful.

University of Massachusetts at Boston   W. G.

Contents

Preface VII

1. Childhood and Education (1698–1724) 1

2. Tutor in Austria (1724–1731) 23

3. The Search for Christian Perfection (1731–1734) 43

4. First Publications (1734–1736) 61

5. Berleburg Years (1736–1740) 87

6. 'Moses mit Aufgedeckten Angesichte' (1740)................... 111

7. Confession of Faith (1741–1749) 141

8. Refuge in Berlin (1749–1767) 155

Conclusion 171

Notes 179

Sources and Selected Bibliography 199

Index 205

1. Childhood and Education
1698–1724

When the impressive castle 'Neu-Augustenburg' at Weissenfels was completed in the summer of 1680, Johann Adolf of Sachsen-Weissenfels (1640–97) moved his court from Halle to the town which gave the land and the ruling family its name. The establishment of the duchy of Sachsen-Weissenfels, like that of two others, Sachsen-Merseburg and Sachsen-Zeitz, resulted from the testament of the Elector Johann Georg I of Saxony, which divided the electorate into an Albertine Saxon main line and three secundogeniture lines; this division lasted for three generations until, in 1746, the last of the three, Weissenfels, returned to the main line.[1]

Music, which had had an important role in the lavish secular and religious festivities at the court in Halle, found in the new environment a rich and distinguished tradition. Johann Hermann Schein and Heinrich Schütz had lived at Weissenfels;[2] here 'in the eighth decade of his life, burdened by hopeless financial and courtly conditions, Schütz executed the three great Passion compositions in which the oratorios of Bach and Händel have their foundations'.[3] In 1672, only ten years after Schütz's death, the new castle's magnificent chapel built in ceremonial Renaissance style was inaugurated with a six-day celebration. For each day Johann Philipp Krieger had prepared new compositions calling for as many as sixty-six voices and instruments. It was also at the organ of this new chapel that the nine-year-old Georg Friedrich Händel made his debut in 1694.[4]

At Christmas 1695, Gottlob Edelmann, who came from a long line of organists and organ-makers,[5] joined the court orchestra; his elder brother Christian had entered the service of the count as organist and Kammer-composer in the early eighties.[6] Gottlob Edelmann undertook dual duties as a musician and tutor to the pages. This arrangement, which burdened the musicians with not inconsiderable administrative responsibilities, seems to have been peculiar to the Weissenfels; obviously it was financially advantageous to them.[7]

As a musician Gottlob Edelmann sang alto parts and played the flute.[8] The duties of the tutor to the pages are enumerated in a memorandum dated January 1711, which accompanied a letter of appointment to Edelmann's successor, Gottfried Wendebaum. What was expected of the new incumbent had certainly been asked of Gottlob Edelmann: he was to remain unwaveringly true to the pure Evangelical Augsburg Confession, the Apology, the Schmalkaldic Articles and the Formula of Concord. The first paragraph of the memorandum demands that the tutor, above all, take care that the pages are taught and admonished in true piety and obedience to God.[9] Thus Gottlob Edelmann's duty had been to educate them in the strict Lutheran faith of the land, which doubtless he diligently did. He also seems to have won the favor of his master by his pleasing voice and by his art in playing the flute.

A son was born to Gottlob and his wife, Dorothea Magdalena, on July 9, 1698. The Duke Johann Georg, his younger brother Duke Christian, and their wives became the child's godparents although they were not present at the actual ceremony in the chapel on July 11th, but were represented by the Stallmeister von Seidlitz, the Junker von der Mosel, and the Lady Winterfeld.[10] The name chosen for the Edelmanns' oldest son therefore became Johann Christian [for the two Dukes]. In later years he remarked that the noble godparents had been of no advantage to him and it would have been just as well if his parents had chosen his godparents from among their own kind.[11]

Indeed, the actual financial circumstances of the Edelmann family were precarious, as the salaries at court were small and, in addition, were paid irregularly, and often not at all. The visible splendor of court life contrasted with the economy of a land which had been ravaged and its population depleted in the Thirty Years' War and the ensuing Northern Wars. The indulgence of the Elector Johann Georg II of Saxony in luxury and entertainment was shared by his brother Johann Adolf and his son Johann Georg at Weissenfels in the years when the country needed a prudent policy of economic reconstruction.[12]

Duke Christian, already deeply in debt, established his own household at Sangerhausen in 1711, a year before he actually became the ruler of the Duchy. With him he took as his secretary, Gottlob Edelmann, whose family now included his wife and mother-in-law, three sons Johann Christian,

Heinrich Gottlob and Moritz Rudolph, and a daughter Dorothea Sophia. The family were together for the last time; a year later the seven-year-old Dorothea Sophia died, and Gottlob returned with Duke Christian to Weissenfels, leaving the family at Sangerhausen.

Edelmann attended the Sangerhausen public school for four years. This was a welcome change because his teacher at Weissenfels had tried to make up for his own ignorance by freely using the cane.[13] The Sangerhausen city school was in its most successful era, under the leadership of Rectors Schneemelcher (1705–1714) and Henneberg (1714–1721?). Religion, Latin, Rhetoric and Greek occupied the major part of the curriculum. Among the Latin authors studied were Cicero, Virgil, and Cornelius Nepos; grammar and syntax were taught; Greek instruction was confined to the New Testament.[14]

The religious instruction relied primarily on memorizing and repeatedly plowing through Leonhard Hutter's *Compendium Locorum Theologicorum*, a text which would stay with Edelmann, as with all other students, into his gymnasium years. Christian II had commissioned the Wittenberg theologian Leonhard Hutter to produce a Lutheran textbook for use in the Saxon schools. Hutter submitted it to his own faculty and to that of Leipzig University for approval; when first published it carried a letter by the Elector in which he expressed the hope that 'youth who drink in with their mother's milk the primary elements of pure Christian teaching ... will not deviate easily from the royal road of recognized truth'. Hutter was convinced 'that the theological compendium of the main articles of the Christian faith be drawn from the Formula of Concord and that, as far as possible, the exact words of the Formula be observed in order to accustom the school children from tender youth to the modes of healthy expression'.[15] The entire material is presented by Hutter in thirty-four articles ('*loci*') in the form of questions; those intended for the more advanced students carried a cross, and those for even more learned little scholars, an asterisk. The first (I) of the questions was on the Holy Scriptures and characteristically included questions (10–17, all with asterisks) on the ecumenic or catholic symbols, the three confessions of faith, the symbolic books of the Lutheran Church, the Augsburg Confession of 1530, the Apology, the Schmalkaldic Articles of 1537, the two Catechisms of Luther, and the Formula of Concord.[16] Further articles dealt with the Trinity (II),

Creation (IV), the image of man in God (VI), the good works (XIV), the Church (XVII), the sacraments (XIX), hell (XXXIII) – to mention only a few which give an idea of the structure of the compendium. In its commentaries it leaned most heavily on the Augsburg Confession and the Formula of Concord, the writings of Luther, Melanchthon, Martin Chemnitz (co-author of the Formula), and Aegidius Hunnius. It is difficult today to realize how deeply the youth of that time was imbued with an extensive body of theological instruction.

A statement by Henneberg written before Edelmann transferred to Lauban bears witness to the latter's abilities as a student. That he had a sense of pride and enjoyed showing off is evident from an incident when a candidate for a teaching post was being examined before the mayor and other officials. When the candidate revealed his poor Latin, Edelmann could hardly keep from correcting the older student and displaying his own knowledge. His self-confidence was nourished by Henneberg's lavish and frequent praise.[17] On the other hand he could become frightened like any other fourteen-year-old boy – as when a classmate, having induced him to go rowing in a tub in a quite deep canal, the Wege, engaged in all sorts of acrobatic jesting in his own wide and safe tub, urging Edelmann in his much narrower and higher one to imitate him. It did not take long before Edelmann's tub capsized, and, though he quickly got out from under it, he long remembered the scare.[18]

Edelmann was a promising student, and his father, recognizing the fact, was anxious to further his education. The choices of secondary schools for Edelmann show clearly the father's interest in the boy's education, choices that might well have been influenced by family relations and by the need for finding inexpensive and suitable living conditions. What Gottlob did not do with his son was to follow the prescribed pattern for an aspirant at the Weissenfels court – that of sending him, after the Sangerhausen school, to the Weissenfels gymnasium for two years. This requirement was initiated in 1666, and Duke Johann Adolf impressed it on the city council of Sangerhausen again in 1689. Another rather easy course apparently was also rejected, that of taking up one of the scholarships available at Schulpforta to the graduates of Sangerhausen school.[19]

Edelmann was sent to his uncle Gottfried Edelmann, pastor at Lauban, to attend the Lyceum for the years 1715 to 1717. During this period his evident self-confidence and eagerness to win attention and approval was reinforced. His fellow students were older than he and some were of the local nobility. They impressed Edelmann, who found them, in manners and education, superior to his classmates in Sangerhausen, and he worked hard to catch up and keep up with them. Although he was no born poet, Edelmann did not want to be held incompetent in verse-making (which was taught at the Lyceum) and therefore he mastered the art – at least to the point where he found that poems made to order could bring in some much-needed pocket money. Debate played an important role in the curriculum and although the questions and issues may have been worthless, as Edelmann observed in retrospect, the process sharpened his mind and tongue and he acquired facility in speaking Latin. A classmate of these years remembered Edelmann 'as a wide-awake youth, full of fire, who displayed his natural gifts to the great hopes of the teachers'.[20] The hopes of the teachers were that he would become a good clergyman worthy to join their ranks.

We have but few glimpses into Edelmann's inner life, but the story of the ambitious and self-demanding student during these years should not be ignored. In his uncle's house he shared a room with a theology student by the name of Flegel, whose undesirable name, meaning an impudent fellow, was, as it turned out, very appropriate. Flegel was obviously crude, but what Edelmann resented most was the older boy's flirtations with the maids in the stable and the kitchen. He even went so far as to denounce his roommate to his uncle, who, however, told him to mind his own business. It is not indulging in psychological speculation to interpret his resentment of sex as adolescent and his condemnation of what he was not yet ready to attain as an evil on which he could, self-righteously, pass judgment.[21]

These years at Lauban were not easy for Edelmann. Since he lived free of cost at his uncle's house, he felt under obligation; in school he was younger than most of the students and he put a great deal of pressure on himself to avoid being outdone; on occasion he preached in school; and he was poor among the well-to-do. He had already started to earn extra money as a tutor. He gave private instruction to Rector Heer's children and tutored a classmate, Wunsch, son of a Silesian aristocratic family, who was several years older and who would much rather 'have been his superior officer than subject pupil'.[22] When his roommate Flegel left, Edelmann succeeded him as tutor to Gottfried Edelmann's children. But Edelmann resented his uncle's permissiveness in his household and towards his children; the burden of tutoring lay heavy on him; and he certainly did not find it easy to command authority, particularly in a home where he was not supported by the parents. He asked his father to find a different place for him.

The two years at Lauban were important ones for Edelmann: he began his preparation for the ministry and his career as tutor, an occupation he was to pursue for many years to come. He also started the habit of copying passages which seemed significant in his reading. This habit, begun as a device to pad sermons devoid of personal experience, helped him in later years, when he had recourse to these notebooks filled with quotations and excerpts from books no longer accessible to him.[23]

Edelmann now went to Altenburg where an uncle, Moritz Wilhelm Haberland, was chancellor in the service of the Duke of Gotha. Haberland was willing to take his nephew as a tutor while he attended the local gymnasium. The period of over two years (approximately February 1717 to September 1719) in this uncle's house and in the new school were happy ones for Edelmann. He was, however, not greatly impressed at that time by the change of scenery – neither the slopes of the Harz over Sangerhausen nor the wide panorama of soft hills in the Upper Lausitz seemed to attract his attention. It was not until later that his eyes were opened to the beauties and variety of nature.

In the Haberland house he found an atmosphere of mingled discipline and kindness. Uncle and nephew were in such harmony that Edelmann later found it hard to realize that not everyone approved of his sternness as a tutor. Although his gymnasium years were fragmented, he was again fortunate in finding a school under the leadership of an able and erudite director, Christian Friedrich Wilisch (1714–1720).[24] Wilisch, a graduate of Leipzig University, had humanist interests in literature and history. His special concern was the unusually fine school library which had grown from modest beginnings to approximately 5000 volumes. It was founded through Georg Spalatin's initiative. In spite of its size and quality, remarkable for its time, it had been badly housed and was now neglected. Wilisch started a program of cleaning the dusty tomes, cataloguing them, refurbishing the library rooms, and setting up regular hours for the public to use the library. He did this with the help of the students, who became well acquainted with the collection and were thus motivated to use it for their orations and other papers.[25]

It is most likely that Edelmann attended Prima and Selecta (the last two years of the gymnasium) in order better to prepare for his academic studies. These special classes were intended to supplement and broaden the student's knowledge in the fields of logic, rhetoric, ethics, and also in physics, mathematics, astronomy, history and geography.[26] Despite these innovations the aim of education still was the 'exercitio pietatis'[27] and Latin was the foundation; the unavoidable *Compendium* of Hutter was still the standby, and Cicero and Virgil were read and re-read. Other classical authors like Tacitus, Ovid, and Plutarch were also on the reading list, besides textbooks for Hebrew. Students had the opportunity to discuss with their teachers, in evening sessions, the materials covered in their classes, as well as readings on local Saxon history, *jus gentium*, and natural history.

Natural history was especially well presented by a rather odd but learned man, Friedrich Friese (1668–1721), who had studied anatomy at Jena, had published books on the animal world and on folklore, and also had started a collection of specimens at the school.[28] Edelmann participated in disputations and, as he recalled long afterwards, he had benefited from having to endure the professor's censure of his cockiness.[29]

Director Wilisch lived to see the bicentennial jubilee of the Reformation. This was celebrated from October 31 to November 2 throughout the Duchy and was an impressive and memorable occasion at Altenburg. He skillfully made the Reformer's concern for the education of youth the theme of one of his major addresses.[30] In another oration he spoke on the Saxon princes' understanding of and concern for Luther's catechism, the most important work in the teaching of the faith. When the oration was printed, he dedicated it to Edelmann's uncle Moritz Wilhelm Haberland, among other government servants.[31] Inspired by the occasion, Edelmann was more eager than ever to teach the pure faith seriously and zealously.[32]

Edelmann had been at Altenburg less than two years when his uncle and family felt that it was time for him to leave a place of which he had become fond.[33] Upon his uncle Haberland's advice he decided to take an examination that had been given by the consistory since 1664 to local students who planned to continue their academic studies, and sometimes to foreigners like Edelmann.[34] His success in passing this examination later encouraged him to choose the career of a preacher in the Gotha-Altenburg duchy.

It is amusing to see how Edelmann's admittedly choleric temperament misled him when, after leaving town, he received from Wilisch what was intended to be a favorable report and a letter of recommendation. He was surprised and indignant to find that the letter started with a picture of an indolent and slothful student. Feeling himself unjustly condemned, he was about to tear it up, but he restrained the impulse and was happily rewarded by finding himself described as a virtuous and ardent pupil – in sharp contrast, indeed, to the common type first cited.

Edelmann was ready to move on. The logical step was to start at a university, but the financial situation of the family had never been worse. Edelmann's mother with her youngest son and the grandmother were still at Sangerhausen, while his father was at Weissenfels. The Duke owed him eight years of salary; in addition, Gottlob had even lent money to the Duke out of his own meager reserves. Edelmann's autobiography[35] gives a glimpse of what went on behind the splendid facade of a courtly household, with its staff of 117 persons employed solely for the personal services of the family. For example, it took eleven of them to assist the Duke while hunting and twenty to run the kitchen, not counting the three pastry cooks and the Duke's private chef.[36] We do not know how they fared, but, if their salaries were more promptly paid than poor Gottlob's, it was at the expense of the long-suffering peasantry.[37]

The appalling poverty of the Edelmanns was cruelly evident when an opportunity arose for Gottlob to enter a new position at Eisenach – he found that he did not have enough money to travel. Johann Christian had to add a couple of thalers towards Gottlob's traveling expenses because his father could not get even this paltry amount from the ducal accounting office. It was a catastrophe almost leading to an emotional crisis when an ink bottle was spilled over Johann Christian's only suit. The father's effort to find a tailor who skillfully patched the spot pathetically illustrates the miserable life in the Weissenfels' service. Of the dukes Edelmann bitterly remarks 'that they made the Edelmanns blessed, because blessed are the

poor, but the state of bliss is not easily appreciated by those in such circumstances of want and oppression'.[38]

The year at the Weissenfels Gymnasium Augusteum Illustre, however
praiseworthy that institution may have been, was for Edelmann a frustrating
one. He meditated that it might have been wiser for his parents to let him
learn a decent trade, rather than allow him, at twenty-one years of age, to
reach a point in his education where his developing talents and acquired
skills seemed doomed to a premature death. Reluctantly he acted in one of
the many comedies produced for the entertainment of the court, yielding to
the pleading of his father, who feared that a refusal would offend Princess
Wilhelmine, the sister of the Duke. Edelmann did gain her favor and the
promise of a new suit and ten thalers a year towards his future university
education; this promise was kept.

Edelmann's tenacity in realizing his plans to attain a university education
helped him to overcome all obstacles. He appealed to his uncle at Altenburg, who had appreciated him and who now succeeded in getting for
his nephew a purse of twenty Meissen thalers from the Consistory. Professor
Johann Michael Schumann, a man of reputation and weight, wrote a
letter on Edelmann's behalf, testifying in moving words to the need of
the deserving young scholar. With this recommendation Edelmann started
early in May for Jena.[39] His father walked with him for an hour beyond
the city gate; when they parted Johann Christian gave his father a gulden
from his own pocket, and amid his father's tears and blessings, took his
leave.

To study at the university was Edelmann's ambition and it seems that
by 'the university' Jena was unquestionably understood. According to
Pratje, the great reputation of Jena's theological faculty determined Edelmann's choice.[40] A statement by Pratje, as such, would not carry much
weight, were it not for the fact that Edelmann did not dispute its truth
as he had done, sometimes in pedantic detail, whenever he thought Pratje
to be wrong. It should also be noted that Edelmann, though a foreigner in
the Ernestine Gotha land, had taken an examination at Altenburg with the
hope that it might later win for him a small scholarship. It seems probable
that the scholarship was more readily granted to students who aspired to
go to the University of Jena, of which Gotha-Altenburg was one of the

sustaining duchies. On May 4th he matriculated at Jena, followed by his brother Heinrich Gottlob six months later.[41]

Although Jena's theological faculty had declined towards the end of the seventeenth century, during the years when Edelmann was preparing to become a student there it had experienced a great period of deserved prestige. This was mainly due to the impressive personality, the fine human qualities, and scholarly breadth of Johann Franz Buddeus (1667–1729).[42] When Edelmann refers in his recollections to his 'beloved teacher Buddeus' with a certain tone of irony, it is perhaps belated self-mockery rather than an indication that he had not, as a student, felt admiration and loyalty towards his teacher. In Edelmann's four years at Jena he admittedly 'stuck as close as possible to Buddeus and Johann Georg Walch (1693–1775)',[43] his son-in-law. Walch had come to Jena in 1719 as professor 'philologiae et antiquitatum' and had transferred to the theological faculty in 1724. Edelmann's concentration on studies in church history is corroborated by the fact that Buddeus was lecturing in this field throughout the years from 1721 to 1725.[44] In the following pages an attempt will be made to describe the theologian Buddeus and especially some of his concepts as a teacher of church history; the focus is on his activity during the years when Edelmann was among his students.

Buddeus was one of the two professorial appointments made to raise the level of the theological faculty and at the same time to secure the teaching of Orthodox Lutheranism against the danger threatening from Pietism. The latter derived its name from Philip Jakob Spener's slender but consequential book *Pia Desideria* (1675), which outlined and defined the program and concept of Pietism. Fear of Pietism beset those ruling German Protestant families not carried away by its religious message. As a religious movement it threatened the frozen formalism and scholasticism of seventeenth-century orthodox Protestantism and, by emphasizing new modes of religious devotion, undermined the conventional church practices. As any threat to the austerity of the established church was also a threat to political power, Pietism often appeared to be a direct danger to the secular authority. The inward-directed quietistic character of Pietism did not favor any social or political rebellion. Rather, it fostered a warm, emotionally rich religious life which offered more to the socially oppressed than zealous harshness and theological righteousness. The stress on responsible conduct as the true sign of belonging to Christ brought great comfort to many in the miserable decades following the Thirty Years' War, years of extreme human cruelty and princely rule that too often indulged in pomp and licence. The implied high moral standards of Pietism and its stress on active social service as the true practice of Christian charity made complacent clergy and self-indulgent princes uncomfortable. But even when the individual conscience was troubled, the princes did not feel that they could tolerate any weakening of a church for which they were responsible and whose authority rested in them.

In 1696 the five sustaining powers of the University of Jena – the Ernestine Saxon principalities Coburg, Meiningen, Weimar, Eisenach, and Gotha – appointed a committee to investigate the extent to which Pietism had infiltrated faculty and students.[45] The fear of Pietism seems to have been greater than its actual impact, but that fear continued and played a part when appointments were made at the turn of the century. Among the candidates considered were the famous arch-conservative professor Gottlieb Wernsdorf from Wittenberg and that uncompromising foe of Pietism, Valentin Ernst Löscher.[46] Buddeus, however, was the final choice. The hope of finding a man of real stature was indeed fulfilled, but if Buddeus was expected to be a bulwark against Pietism, such expectations were unrealistic and destined to be disappointed.

In 1705 Buddeus had come to Jena from Halle, where August Hermann Francke had developed a large complex of institutions, all aimed at realizing the ideas and ideals of Pietism. Buddeus had not been entirely successful there as a philosophy professor, and the pietistically oriented theological faculty remained cool towards him; yet he felt in sympathy with the spirit of Halle. Correspondence with Francke and frequent personal meetings testify to the continuation of Buddeus' feelings of real friendship. And Francke entrusted Buddeus with his son, who lived in Buddeus' house at Jena until Francke's successful disputation (February 12, 1720), when he left Jena, shortly before Edelmann's arrival.[47] At Halle the son of Philip Jakob Spener, the originator of Pietism, had also been a pupil of Buddeus.

The sympathy that Buddeus felt with the religious attitudes and endeavors of Spener and Francke is best understood in terms of Buddeus' own earlier religious educational experiences. Buddeus' ideal was Luther, the Luther who had purified theology of scholasticism. In his introduction to a collection of Luther's letters he laments that 'our life and our Christianity harmonize so little with the sense and meaning of Luther'.[48] Luther, he felt, was not caught up in speculation and unnecessary controversy but expounded a living faith that nourished the souls of men. He felt that Luther's exegesis of the Scriptures was sustained not by mere pedantic scholarship but by a spirit in keeping with its message. Thus Buddeus was moved to include among his many lecture series a presentation of theology arranged according to Luther's Catechism.[49] Addressing himself to university students, his purpose was to demonstrate how theological knowledge, the teachings and rules of the faith, should be transmitted to an audience of most varied education; he chose the Lutheran Catechism as a point of departure because he could assume that his audience, brought up in the Lutheran Church, had been familiar with it since childhood. Moreover Buddeus again and again emphasized Luther's demand 'on every Christian heart that it should with greatest trust in faith assimilate all truth to the work of redemption'. To a new Leipzig edition of Johann Christian Arndt's *Wahren Christentum* he wrote a preface in which he praises Arndt's ability to present instruction in practising blessed obedience to God ('die Lehre von der Übung der Gottseligkeit') thoroughly, perfectly and forcefully.[50]

It was the emotional power of this theology that drew Buddeus to Luther and to Johann Christian Arndt; it also made him appreciate Spener and Francke. He was by no means an enthusiast, and his theological exegesis always remained within the faith circumscribed by his church. Buddeus accepts the *Symbolic Books* as providing the right definition of the teachings of his church and the right of the state ('Obrigkeit') to require its servants to be committed to the books by oath. It is characteristic of Buddeus that in his discussion of the *Symbolic Books* (at the very beginning of his lectures on the religious controversies) he chooses to quote 'the most worthy blessed' Spener's commentary which gives no weight to their historical prestige but accepts them solely for the truth of the faith they expound.

Before embarking on the account of the religious controversies that form part of the lectures of 1721/23 Buddeus carefully sets down sixteen points that show the superiority of the Evangelical-Lutheran faith over Socinianism, Roman Catholicism, and the Evangelical Reformed. Point eight well reflects Buddeus' own moderate temperament and at the same time his strict adherence to tradition. 'We prove the truth of our religion because it poses correct and definite limits to will and reason. We teach that reason is only to be esteemed as a means of recognizing Divine Truth. The principle of knowledge remains the Holy Scriptures alone.'[51]

In the course of his studies and teaching experience, Buddeus became convinced that the most satisfactory manner of presentation was to divide the material into its two essential aspects: dogmatic theology and polemic theology. When Buddeus first began his lectures he followed Friedman Beckmann (1628–1703) in discussing controversial theological issues with little attention to their historical background. Buddeus found this method confusing and he began, during the years when Edelmann was among his students, to develop the history of religious controversies through 'an accurate idea of origin, growth, and other historical circumstances', treating each individual sect and its system.[52] In executing this plan Buddeus had the help of Walch, who, in the final printed form, continued and supplemented his work. The presentation itself was to be restrained and not to indulge in bitter language. Buddeus did not advocate indifferentism or failure to expose differences and errors, but he wished to avoid twisting and misquoting the adversary's words and indulging in insults, accusations, and maledictions. Observing the divine laws of love and the rule of decency and modesty,[53] Buddeus applied his method of historical penetration to his lectures on the Old Testament and the Apostolic period. The mastery of his material through a historical approach and the division of Protestant history into periods constitute an important contribution to the methodology of the writing of church history.[54]

In his lecture series on church history that began in 1721, Buddeus used as a textbook the *Institutiones Historiae Ecclesiae* by the Württemberg theologian Christian Mattheus Pfaff. Pfaff held a position in theological matters similar to his own. Pfaff's little book was a most useful compendium, breaking down the history of the Christian church from its origins to modern times according to centuries. Over and above this division, he introduced a major periodization into four Epochs: the first, from Augustus to Constantine, the time of propagation of faith and persecution, when the image of the Church most purely reflected its founder; the second, from Constantine to Charlemagne; the third, to the Reformation;

and the fourth, to the present. Thus Pfaff put the development of the Church solidly into the frame of political history, in accordance with the idea expressed in the preface that political history is the basis for the understanding of ecclesiastical history.[55] He provided a handy table for each century, offering the important dates in appropriate divisions. In the tables for the seventeenth century, for instance, he placed in the column headed 'Heretics': Quakers, Fanatics, Weigelianers, Behmenists, Rosicrucians, and Socinians; but he put Pietism, Jansenism, Molinism in the separate column 'Memorabiliae'.

When Pratje claims that Edelmann became imbued at that time with Gottfried Arnold's *Kirchen und Ketzer Historie*, Edelmann corrects him and emphasizes that not until many years later did he become acquainted with the work of Arnold. He is probably telling the truth unless his memory deceives him, but it certainly would have been proper for him to have read Arnold since he would only have been following Pfaff's advice to read and reread the works by Caves and Friedrich Spanheim as well as Arnold's *Kirchen und Ketzer Historie*. Edelmann's idea of his own development is that of slow growth, and linked to that is the intimation that, had he become acquainted earlier with writings like Arnold's, the effect on him would have been so explosive that he would then and there have abandoned his theological studies.[56]

It is difficult to reconcile Edelmann's account with the fact that in Buddeus' lectures on church controversies, which he undoubtedly attended, the teachings and writings of the 'Fanatics', namely, Anabaptists and Mennonites, Quakers, Weigelianers, Behmenists and Rosicrucians, and 'Inspirierte' were discussed at length. Buddeus does not fail to mention Arnold as an important source, 'although Arnold according to his own inclination took the part' of the heretics.[57] Furthermore, not only did Buddeus discuss 'left wing' radical sects of the Reformation and the seventeenth century, he also devoted an entire book to the discussion of atheism and superstition. The second edition of this book was published at Jena in 1723. It gives a comprehensive exposition of the history, principles and impact of atheism. This takes up about the first half of the book and is followed by chapters repudiating atheism. In the later chapters Buddeus discusses superstitions, which he thinks were often an unfortunate and extreme reaction against atheism. Buddeus' own position is symbolized by the frontispiece which shows a straight path leading to a temple, presumably the way of wisdom; on either side are winding roads, each skirting an abyss and leading to the Wild Mountains. On the one road, apparently signifying the way to atheism, there gallops a wild unbridled horse, and on the other walks a man holding a rosary, an 'Alraune', and a scroll with astrological scribblings, signifying superstitious religious practices and obscurantism.

Thus the thoughts of heretics and atheists were put before Edelmann and even sympathetically presented, as Arnold's great history recommended. Edelmann could well have gathered information on Spinoza, whom Buddeus regarded as the foremost atheist of his time.[58] Indeed, he would not have found it necessary to get information on the ideas of Hobbes and Bayle from fellow students. It was Edelmann's own narrow understanding that made him intolerant: 'I could not bear it when my comrades brought up doubts derived from Bayle and Hobbes.'[59] We might also suspect that the future rebel may have been afraid of his own readiness to doubt. To his teacher Buddeus, the honest examination of atheism and Christian doctrines other than his own Lutheran faith did not mean a deprecation of Scriptures and Creed.

While the moderates felt themselves threatened by atheism and the orthodox feared Pietism and practically every aberration from dogma and creed, a new controversy over the philosophy of Christian Wolff (1679–1754) began to shake faculties and students of all German universities. Edelmann was drawn into it only peripherally and, at that, only as a loyal disciple of Buddeus. Though he was later to launch an attack in the name of reason on all established religions, he was far from catching fire from Wolff's *Vernünfftige Gedancken von Gott der Welt und der Seele des Menschen* (1720). It is revealing that Wolff's philosophy, which could have served Edelmann as a philosophical basis for the radicalization of his thinking, had no such effect on him. On the contrary, we find him debating a fellow student, Johann Kaspar Heimburg (1702–1773), who denied, in the name of Wolff, that the soul moves the body.[60] Edelmann admits that his rejection of the Wolffian philosophy was prompted by his devotion to Buddeus rather than by his own understanding.

In the winter of 1723 Wolff became the victim of a united front of denunciation. Friedrich Wilhelm of Prussia lent his ear to the absurd accusation that Wolff's deterministic philosophy excused desertions from the King's army; that is, it exonerated the deserting soldier because he was only ful-filling his destiny. In harsh mid-winter, upon royal order and on threat of death by hanging, Wolff was forced to leave Halle within forty-eight hours. Even late in life, when he wrote his autobiography (1750), Edelmann lacked a true appreciation of Wolff as a man of enlightenment who had helped prepare the way for the dissolution of traditional religious concepts. Edel-mann, who himself suffered persecution, seems to have learned no better than to refer to Wolff's shameful expulsion from the University of Halle in a sarcastic allusion to his deterministic philosophy. In fact, he was only repeating a cynical joke of Wolff's great enemy, Joachim Lange (1670–1744), the pietist professor of theology at Halle.[61]

In January 1724 Buddeus lashed out against Wolff with *Bedencken über die Wolffianische Philosophie*, a pamphlet slight in weight and content. The pamphlet, probably not even intended to be published, demonstrated Bud-deus' sympathies with his Halle friends, who may have suggested it. The attack is directed against Wolff's determinism, his idea of God as the source of both good and evil, his denial of the acting of the soul upon the body – in short, against the concept of pre-established harmony which he considers the *summa* of the Leibniz–Wolff philosophy. Buddeus, like Lange, holds that this concept of necessity excludes freedom and chance and therefore endangers morality and religion. He continues to argue that the extent to which Wolff agreed or disagreed with Spinoza is irrelevant since there are different types of atheism, and one can well be an atheist without being a follower of Spinoza. Alluding to Wolff, Buddeus concludes, 'a person may hold corrupting ideas and propositions that lead to atheism, though he might differ on one or another issue from Spinoza'.[62] The ugly spectre of atheism by innuendo thus raised a form of slander with which we are well acquainted today in its secularized political forms.

If Edelmann's antipathy toward Wolff stemmed originally from imita-tion of Buddeus, it also had deeper and lasting causes. Wolff's modes of thinking were thoroughly attuned to mathematics. He revived the neo-scholastic tendency to develop a metaphysical system, yet one that was to incorporate the knowledge of exact science and philosophical speculations (in particular, those of Descartes, Leibniz and Thomasius). Pure thinking and rationalization, the basis of this voluminous work, remained alien to Edelmann long after he had moved completely away from Buddeus. Edelmann was not a historian of ideas, looking backward and trying to find the proper place for Wolff;[63] rather, he was a contemporary like Voltaire, to whom the Leibniz–Wolff idea of a world deduced from maxims as the best of all possible worlds, seemed strange if not ridiculous.[64] His failure to understand the far more important aspects of Wolff's thought or to sympathize with Wolff is important for our comprehension of Edelmann.

The senses of the students were tempted as well as their minds. Edelmann's admiration for Buddeus, his poverty, and surely a certain priggishness that we have already noticed, kept him well in the path of 'Sittsamkeit'.[65] Buddeus sought to apply his teachings to the daily life of the students. That the exertion of such influence was called for is obvious from all contemporary descriptions. In a population of about 4000 at Jena, some 1500 were students, a fact which demonstrates the extent to which this was a university town.[66] To identify the students with the 'Renomists' is probably an exaggeration, but that this type was conspicuous and often dominated the scene can be conceded. A description of 'Renomists' written in 1716, just a few years before Edelmann's arrival on the scene, reads:

They are always ready to draw their swords and greet nobody except their acquaintances. They reek of tobacco, beer and brandy. They roam around by day and night, and often carry on their banquets openly in the market. As soon as they start to drink, the heroic spirit possesses them; they draw their long daggers and beat and stab around, as if they had the most valid reason to break each other's necks.[67]

Edelmann seemed to have been well acquainted with the type and felt that, in view of his own choleric temperament, he was fortunate in being able to apply to himself the familiar saying, 'Who returns from Jena without scars is to be congratulated as fortunate'.[68]

The rowdiness of the students became so serious that Proctor Johann Reinhard Rus (1679–1738), professor of Oriental languages, vigorously undertook to curtail and if possible eradicate the 'nationalities' and their banquets. The 'nationalities', modeled on the 'German Nations' at the universities of Paris and Bologna, were associations of students from the same geographical area. Such societies functioned as mutual aid organizations and then developed into fraternities with their code of honor and their prejudices. They were really small pressure groups.[69] When on May 1st, 1724, such a fraternity held a feast in the market, contrary to the warning of the Proctor, it ended like most of these occasions in drunken fights, riotous yelling, and a demonstration against Rus. At the subsequent investigation by the Senate on May 4th, students burst into the courtyard of the building demanding immediate cessation of the action in the name of ancient student liberties. Buddeus addressed the students in a sermon the following day, but to no avail. Student rioting continued and, after a strong interdict against the 'nationalities' and the banquets was issued on June 23rd, an attempt was made to storm the home of Rus.[70] Edelmann reports having heard 'that Rus opened the door with the words "Gentlemen, here I am, do what you want with me, my job is to do my duty." Upon which words the students departed, leaving the house unmolested'. Edelmann adds: 'an example that God helps a just cause against wanton violence, and supports authority if it acts for the benefit of its subjects'. The riots, however, did not end with the courageous stand of the Proctor but finally had to be quelled by a company of grenadiers. Edelmann, amused, watched the spectacle: 'Indeed it was something to see how these heroes took to flight. They had hardly seen the soldiers when they started to run while valiantly crying, "Stand fast, stand fast, brother!" Nobody heeded the admonition and the field was empty before any of the grenadiers arrived.'[71]

Edelmann did not abstain from all student frolics. He enjoyed playing cards, especially the hazardous ombre game that was forbidden by the university authorities; it apparently did not get him into as much trouble as it did many others who were obliged to pawn their meagre belongings in order to pay off their gambling debts.[72] It did, however, keep him up to the small hours, especially on Saturday nights when he gathered with a circle of friends. That he slept the next morning and missed the Sunday service is not surprising. Moreover, Sunday church services do not seem to have been serious or appealing. Edelmann writes:

> One has to admit that very few of the students attend Church as a place of devotion. It would be even impossible for those who wish to worship there to do so, because of the continuous walking in and out of church by students who hardly stay long enough for the Lord's Prayer. Groups of women with children and often suckling babes beleaguer the church door, raising such a clamor that the minister's sermon becomes inaudible. While the service goes on, students walk down the aisles reading the

newspapers and chatting with each other. In short the Jena church was like a pigeon house.[73]

Edelmann enjoyed the 'collegium musicum', a cheerful weekly gathering of some of his colleagues in a room at the 'Rosenkeller', where musical instruments, including a piano, were kept. He had a good background himself, having been brought up in a family of professional musicians, and could play the piano, flute, and flute travers quite skillfully. Above all he appreciated and loved music, praising it as 'the soul of poetry'.[74]

The Edelmann brothers benefited from an old institution, the 'convictorium',[75] where meals were served to stipendiaries free of charge or very cheaply. Edelmann does not mention that he suffered on account of belonging to the underprivileged, although he probably was aware of 'a certain condescension shown by Jena students toward those of their comrades who depend on the convictorium'.[76] Retrospectively at least, Edelmann felt that poverty helped him to avoid certain follies; thus necessity became a virtue.

The family's fortunes were slightly improved now. It became possible after the grandmother's death for the mother to join her husband at Eisenach. To make ends meet, Edelmann, through most of the time he studied at Jena, shared his modest room with some comrade: the first was Stisser, who later became court secretary in the Braunschweig service, 'an honest soul, who, however, had many cronies who feasted in our room, messing it all up so much that it looked more like a pigsty than student quarters'. It was worse still when Edelmann's brother moved in with him, and distractions often made learning difficult. When, in his last year at Jena, Edelmann shared the room with his good friend Hasserodt from Eisenach, he had become used to this rather convivial student life and enjoyed it.[77]

For half a year Edelmann was employed as tutor in the house of the French teacher and secretary of the Weimar Court, Roux. The four hours of teaching in addition to his six or seven hours of classes proved to be too much for him, and he became over-tired and irritable. Roux, who was an understanding and kind person, noticed this and attempted to make it easy for Edelmann to resign voluntarily. He explained that the children were unruly in Edelmann's absence and needed more supervision than he was able under present circumstances to provide. Instead of appreciating the chance Roux gave him to quit honorably, Edelmann was insulted. He gave up tutoring the children, rented a room in their house, and took his French lessons from Provansal, Roux's greatest antagonist. Heaping insult on injury, he ordered Augsburg beer from a nearby inn, ignoring Roux's cellar, from which he used to buy it regularly. Edelmann confesses that in a blind rage he insulted a man who had shown him nothing but kindness and who was to continue to do so generously, in spite of Edelmann's misbehavior to him. Like Rousseau, Edelmann did not forget insults he had unjustly inflicted on others; the feeling of shame and repentance remained with him even as years later he described the incident in the autobiography.[78]

His last year at Jena brought grief, joy, and disappointment. With his brother he decided to visit his parents at Eisenach; his mother had been ailing for many years, and her health now had become more precarious. The two brothers started out on foot, and Johann Christian, who had not been well, was soon cured by the exercise and the lovely spring air. At Gotha they visited relatives of their mother, and the harmonious atmosphere of the household impressed them most agreeably. Edelmann also 'thought he sensed ... that the oldest of the daughters of the house took a liking to him', and he did not feel indifferent towards her. Such inclination 'he could well notice, as no such emotions had been raised in him by the presence of any other fair female', and Edelmann sums it up: 'I do not deny that, if I had then been in a position to make a place for love in an honest manner, I would have talked on a more intimate basis to her. But love had to cede to reason and our intercourse remained within the bounds of politeness and conventional frolic.'[79] With regret, and with many signs of mutual affection, Edelmann left his newly won friend, to spend a fortnight with his parents. His mother, who had placed her hopes on Edelmann's becoming a minister, would have liked him to give a sermon, but, inexperienced in that art, he did not dare to try it. Edelmann's brevity in recording the days at Eisenach is in significant contrast to the detail with which he describes his return visit to Gotha.

An excursion to nearby Erfurt to watch the Roman Catholic celebration and procession of Corpus Christi day promised to bring Edelmann every opportunity to enjoy the close company of his lady. The proper and sober reflection upon his first visit gives way to avowed disappointment when circumstances made it impossible to realize this hope.

Never have I experienced greater sorrow than that night, when our entire party went to sleep in the hayloft. I managed to lie down next to my friend, but another woman got on the other side and acted as a kind of sentinel, preventing us from exchanging any caresses. In such a position the short night seemed to last an eternity, and I was glad when day dawned and allowed me to leave the place of my torments, since I had no pleasure there.[80]

Back in Jena, his emotions still in a state of turmoil, he received the news of his mother's death. He had just experienced his first and – as it apparently was to be – his only infatuation for a woman. The knowledge of his mother's illness had made him feel uneasy and the puritan in him tried to convince him that his frustrations were justly deserved. He tried to tell himself that the pleasures of betrothal and marriage which circumstances prevented him from aspiring to could now wait for several years. Actually, at one and the same moment, Edelmann had lost a tender mother and the girl with whom he had fallen in love. He was never to have a close relationship with a woman.

It was at this point also that Edelmann was confronted with the question of his future. He was still aiming at a theological career, but a decision had to be made concerning the kind he would choose. During these last months at Jena he tested himself in the neighboring villages as a preacher. Although he felt that he performed to the satisfaction of his audience and the local ministers, he became aware that he did not possess the ability to speak extemporaneously. He was good at delivering a carefully prepared text which his excellent memory helped him to retain, but not at delivering a sermon on the spur of the moment. He thought that this inability would likewise block the career of a teacher for him, or at the least make it most difficult and wearing. The latter path appeared closed to him in view of the lack of funds necessary to attain the 'Magister' degree. The cost of approximately 160 thaler for graduation was very high if one considers that a student who was not a stipendiary needed on the average 250 thaler a year for all his living expenses. It also appears that exemption from these fees was granted only to the indigenous stipendiaries of the dukes.[81] In this period, formal conclusion of studies was not as usual as it later became; the more well-to-do concluded their university studies with the grand tour rather than with examinations. Edelmann seems to have entertained similar desires but, being poor, he had to find some other course that would make it possible for him 'to look around the world'.[82]

First, however, in May 1724, he joined his father, who hoped to find a place for him at the Eisenach Theological Seminary. But Edelmann soon tired of waiting, since there was little for him to do except to deliver an occasional sermon in the local churches. Therefore, it was with gratitude that he received a letter from his former roommate Hasserodt telling of an opening for a tutor in the household of an aristocratic Austrian family. The bitter drop mixed with the good news was that a recommendation from the French teacher Roux, whom Edelmann had treated with such insolence, was required. The good Hasserodt, however, made the request and Roux, after receiving a letter of explanation from Edelmann, generously furnished the recommendation. On this occasion, Edelmann also procured from his great teacher Buddeus a letter testifying to his knowledge, industry, and honesty.[83] Finally he succeeded in more or less begging his not inconsiderable travel expenses, the larger part being contributed by his future employer. Then, without delay, Edelmann parted from his father and took the coach to Gotha, where he once more stayed with his cousin and her parents. The parting was not easy for the young lovers, but Edelmann had chosen his path, and with the excitement of youth he set out for the world and his destiny.

2. Tutor in Austria
1724–1731

The coach took a speedy route through Arnstadt, Ilmenau, Eisfeld, Coburg, and Bamberg, to Nürnberg. The gentle landscape passed swiftly by Edelmann as he traveled. He recorded little except the threatening mobs of beggars on the outskirts of Bamberg. His reflection on the contrast between their misery and the wealth of silver and gold that adorned the statues of the dead dignitaries and the saints in the churches can certainly be construed as an afterthought. The landscape was thick with gallows and crosses from which hung the bodies of the condemned – a cruel punishment and a gruesome sight such as he and his fellow travelers never expected to see.[1]

Among his companions in the coach he enjoyed one in particular, a musician by the name of Meussel, who was on his way from Hamburg to Venice. The feeling was mutual, and Meussel decided to stay with Edelmann in Nürnberg. At the 'Weissen Ross' in the Heumarkt they found comfortable quarters, and Meussel even asked the willing servant to put a piano in their room. For eight days they roamed – sightseeing through the town, admiring the city hall and the armory, touring the imperial castle, and wandering in the Johannis cemetery among the magnificently wrought brasses which marked the graves of distinguished Nürnberg artists and patricians. Some of the legends attached to relics and images in the churches baffled the young Protestant, hitherto unacquainted with expressions of Catholic piety. In Meussel Edelmann had found a good companion, considerably more experienced in travel than he was and an artist open to the beauty of the works of nature and man. Meussel told him of the poem 'Irdisches Vergnügen in Gott' by the Hamburg poet Barthold Heinrich Brockes, who, like the great Baroque painters, brought heaven and earth, the divine and the terrestrial, nearer to each other than Edelmann would ever have dreamed. As presented by Meussel, the poem served as the fine start of a journey that was to open his eyes to new beauties. When the coach for Vienna was ready, Edelmann and Meussel made their adieux. Arriving at Regensburg, Edelmann embarked for Melk.

The voyage down the Danube had been a joy to travelers for hundreds of years. The hilly banks with their castles and towns such as Passau and Linz, their villages nestled between river and slopes, presented a picturesque landscape the unique beauty of which had inspired many a poet and artist. Moreover, the river already had the distinction of having given its name to a whole school of painters of the early sixteenth century, the 'Donauschule'. When Lucas Cranach first encountered this landscape (around 1500), a new mode of painting developed that was continued in the works of Albrecht Altdorfer, Erhard Altdorfer, Wolf Huber, and many others.[2] Naturally, Edelmann also came under the almost mysterious Danubian spell and, although he had paid for private quarters on the boat, he spent his time on deck, anxious not to miss a moment of the passing panorama. Never before had he 'seen such beauty of nature displayed before him at once and in such continuing variety'.[3] His mood was that of awed astonishment at the beauty of Creation, and he remembered Meussel's telling him of Brockes. He wished to become acquainted with the poet's works, a wish which in the near future was fulfilled. On this voyage a new world of experience began to open up for Edelmann, which would have a lasting impact on his life and work.

Not uncharacteristic of Edelmann's impulsiveness and desire to show off was his decision to stay on board as the only passenger, while the boat took its perilous course near Grein, through the 'Strudel' – a combination of dangers caused by a narrowing of the river bed[4] and the presence of a stony island called 'Hausstein' below the village of Struden. The adventure frightened him and he recalled that twice before, at Sangerhausen and again on the Saale in Jena, he had narrowly escaped drowning. He was relieved when the boat came into quiet waters again and he was joined by his fellow passengers (who had walked around the steep hills), whose crude company he did not usually enjoy.[5]

More somber thoughts appeared to trouble him as the boat neared the end of its trip, for he began to doubt his great qualification as a teacher of French. At Melk he disembarked and soon found transportation to St. Pölten. There at the 'Goldenen Löwen' further instruction awaited him on how to reach his final destination, the estate of Count Kornfeil at Würmla.

The Kornfeils had come in the middle of the fifteenth century from Weinfelden in the Thurgau in Switzerland to the region around St. Pölten known as the Ober-Wiener-Wald. Johann, who had distinguished himself in the defense of St. Pölten against the Turks (1529), had inherited from his second wife's family the estate of Würmla, where the Kornfeils lived when Edelmann joined their household. Their son, Andreas III von Kornfeil und Weinfelden, with his entire family joined the Lutheran Church at least by 1561.[6] This is not surprising when one considers that in Lower and Upper Austria, among the nobility and officials, the Lutherans out-numbered the Roman Catholics as early as 1528. By the middle of the sixteenth century almost the entire nobility of Upper Austria had be-come Lutheran. This nobility, consisting of families of great wealth, closely inter-connected through financial interests and blood relationships, com-manded the administrative posts and exercised a strong power.

The conversion of the country population came about mostly through the activities of evangelical theologians imported as tutors to the noblemen's children. Such a tutor was installed in a vacated parish and was responsible in spiritual and lay affairs to the noble landlord. There were 233 evangelical preachers in the homes of the ninety-one lords and ninety-nine knights (among whom the Kornfeils were counted). We know the names of at least two Lutheran vicars of Würmla: Blasius Heyde who, unlike most of the others, was a native of the region, born in nearby Krems on the Danube; and Wolfgang Pöttinger, who is reported to have been a relative of the Kornfeil family.[7]

The years of this Protestant flowering in Lower Austria were, however, numbered, as they were in other Austrian lands where the new religious message had made a similarly strong appeal. The formation of a Catholic party among the nobility in 1580 strengthened the will of the Emperor Rudolf II to resist the Protestants. In Melchior Khlesl, whom he appointed Chancellor of the University of Vienna, he found a churchman able to discipline his own clergy and to initiate a vigorous campaign to regain the territory lost among the population.

The Counter-Reformation, with its bitter, ultimate goal of eradicating Protestantism in Austria, gained momentum under Frederick II who was elected Emperor on August 28, 1619, by the electoral votes of the Protestant princes of Saxony and Brandenburg. The speedy success of the Counter-

Reformation in Austria made the Protestant not only a religious heretic but an enemy of the state. Frederic II knew how to exploit his victories and to subdue the Protestant nobility. Thus he exiled thirty-one nobles who refused to render homage at the assembly at Vienna on July 13, 1620, and confiscated their estates. Yet it was at this assembly that Frederic II promised to the assembled Protestant nobility (thirty-nine lords and forty-seven knights) the right to exercise their religion – a promise which, however narrowly interpreted later, remained their sole protection and was respected even by his over-zealous son and successor, Emperor Ferdinand III (1637–1657).[8] In September 1627, Frederic II issued an edict expelling all Lutheran preachers. Many as were the gains the Protestants could register at the peace negotiations at Osnabrück and Münster at the close of the Thirty Years' War, these did not extend to the Habsburgs' hereditary lands. All Ferdinand III promised was that he would not force the Protestant noblemen in Lower Austria to emigrate; he would allow them, but not their subjects, to retain their religion if they went about it unobtrusively.[9]

Austrian Protestantism entered a new phase known as 'clandestine Protestantism' ('Geheimprotestantismus') which did not end until the reform era of Joseph II and, in particular, the Edict of Toleration of 1781, long after the Kornfeils had left their homestead.

It is within the framework of these events that we want to learn how the Kornfeils fared, in order to appreciate fully Edelmann's own record of his years with them. From the little information that is offered by Weissgrill, the industrious chronicler of the Lower Austrian nobility, we can conclude that the main Kornfeil line remained stoutly Lutheran from the time of their original conversion. They were not involved in rebellions that on occasion cost some of their neighbors loss of life and property. Hector (1575–1635), like his grandfather Johann, distinguished himself fighting for many years against the Turks in Hungary, in a war condoned by both his faith and his loyalty to the Empire. It is therefore understandable that this old fighter did not join his Protestant fellow noblemen when, in the summer of 1619, they conspired with the Siebenbürgen prince Bethlen Gabor, an ally of the Turks, against Ferdinand.[10] Hector remained on the Emperor's side and suffered imprisonment for over two years.

At the same time, we find among the ninety-six grievances listed by the Catholic Estates of the region the complaint that the Kornfeil families had appropriated the Chapel at Würmla for the observance of their own Lutheran faith. Both the grandfather and the father of Hector Wilhelm, Edelmann's new employer, continued to serve the Emperor and to remain true to their faith. The former was elevated from the estate of knight to that of lord and was dubbed with the fancy title Carrier of the Banner (Panierherr) as a permanent reminder of the family's martial glory. From 1665 to 1667 he was the last representative of the Lower Austrian Protestant estate in the Corpus Evangelicorum.[11] This body was set up to assure Protestants a fair interpretation of the Westphalian peace terms, in religious matters, but in fact proved unable to protect Austrian Protestants.

At the time Edelmann arrived, the situation of Protestantism was still precarious. Yet the way of life of the Kornfeils, that of the landed gentry ('Adeliges Landleben'), was hardly deprived or melancholy. On the other hand, it is well to remember that their final decision was a self-imposed exile, in order that they might live among those who exercised their own faith freely. We have seen that in spite of the victorious Counter-Reformation, the Kornfeils not only retained their possessions but were able through marriages and purchases to expand their landholdings. Since Würmla was a small castle with park, woods and village, it is evident that these holdings were by no means large. Economically, then, the Kornfeils undoubtedly belonged to a class of lower gentry similar to that of the Hohbergs, whose declining role Otto Brunner has defined.[12]

Edelmann's idea of aristocracy had been shaped by his family's bitter experiences with the Weissenfelses. Secure in their power, administrators of their own Protestant faith in a land where every other confession was in the minority, they appeared and acted, in spite of their financial plight, like inaccessible haughty rulers. To compare the position of even more wealthy Austrian aristocrats like the Auerspergs, whom Edelmann was also to serve, with the Weissenfelses seems to make little sense. Yet to Edelmann these were noble families from whom he was divided by an unbridgeable gap. He felt socially closer to the Austrians. The different style of life among the lower gentry was to impress him even more, though he surely needed time to find himself fully at ease in the new environment. Remembering his own trepidation at St. Pölten he wrote:

The Austrian counts were more human and therefore much more amiable.

I did not then know it, but imagined that one had to labour in fear
and trembling among them as among the immortal gods. I found that
I was not made for such servility but learned that it was unnecessary.[13]
St. Pölten with its approximately four thousand inhabitants was the center
of the region. Some of the town's finest buildings had recently been finished,
among them the institute of the 'Englischen Fräuleins', the Prandtauer
Church, and many palaces that were used in the winter by the nobility
when they found their country residences too uncomfortable.[14] As in
Bamberg and Regensburg the conspicuous presence of monks and clerics
reminded Edelmann that he was no longer in Protestant lands. He already
felt impelled into a new world when he started for Würmla, about a
two-hour coach ride from St. Pölten. The road went past the magnificent
Zinzendorf castle at Weissenburg, and Edelmann, with fresh memories of
these fine palaces, was clearly disappointed when he arrived at Würmla.

> The exterior of this residence does not present any grandeur, and surely
> there are noblemen's seats in Saxony, Thuringia and other places that
> impress one's eyes with much greater splendor: yet there reigned a
> simplicity, innocence and gracefulness in this sight that gave more joy
> than if I had been in the presence of cedars and marbles.[15]

The young tutor was received with a reverence that he had not expected;
he surely owed this reception not to his expertness as a linguist but to his
theological background, and it seems fair to guess that this qualification
had played a part in the Kornfeil choice. They were glad that a young man
with a good background in the religion to which they adhered was to share
their lives and to be responsible for their children's education. As they were
not allowed to have a pastor of their own faith living with them, their only
chance to attend Protestant religious services was on occasional visits to
Vienna, where they could attend the chapels of the Swedish and Danish
legations, or during their vacation in Ödenburg in Hungary, where Protestants were free to exercise their religion. Taking the harsh regulations
strictly, the Kornfeils were not even allowed to have a tutor who was a
trained theologian. This provision is understandable in view of the fact that
during the sixteenth century Protestant ministers had been introduced into
the region in the guise of tutors.

Edelmann liked the Kornfeil family: Count Hector Wilhelm (1686–1759),
his second wife Maria Josepha (born Countess Auersperg), the oldest

daughter Franziska Isabella (born in 1712), and Ferdinand Friedrich (born in 1719), both of the first marriage. The children of the present marriage were still infants. His schedule was not heavy: four hours were set aside for instruction on Mondays, Tuesdays, Thursdays, and Fridays, and two hours on Saturdays. Thus he had much time to roam through the countryside, and at first welcomed the opportunity to go hunting. Attracted by the sport and eager to explore the lovely woods, he learned the pleasures of the huntsman, whose alerted senses, while waiting for his quarry, are opened to the miracles of the forest. He soon began to like Austrian cooking. He was astonished to find his first meal consisting of eggs and fish, because it was Friday and the Kornfeils respected the Catholic practice of their servants, but he liked the 'Rindfleisch' and 'Sauerkraut' which were frequently served. He accompanied his employer on excursions into the countryside and to its many beautiful churches and monasteries.

It is perhaps characteristic of the Austrian temperament that, in spite of the scars of recent battles and the existing religious differences, a leisurely social intercourse continued between the few noble families who were still Lutheran, and the local Catholic clergy. Following the end of the Thirty Years' War, Catholicism in Lower Austria had reduced the number of Lutherans to a negligible minority among the aristocracy. The population had endured years of strife and bloodshed and devastation of its land concomitantly with the Turkish invasion. It was therefore more eager to turn to the solace of religion. Reawakened ardor gave rise to a new culture of piety: local pilgrimages, small sanctuaries by the roadsides, innumerable adoration pictures in Baroque chapels. Of the many pictures of Mary, the helpmeet and intercessor ('Mariahilf'), copied after Lucas Cranach, one was hanging in the church of Würmla.[16]

All this was puzzling to the young tutor, brought up as a zealous propagator of the Protestant faith. When for the first time a bearded Capuchin monk entered the room where Edelmann was studying with his tutees, he was thrown into a panic; but he easily overcame the first shock when he saw how heartily the monk was welcomed by the young count, even as he gaily teased Franziska Isabella. At the Kornfeil house Edelmann gradually became acquainted with Catholic monks and priests, who came visiting and begging, and were always well received. He returned these visits, sometimes with the Kornfeils, sometimes by himself, and thus became acquainted with representatives of a religion he had been brought up to consider the arch-enemy. Although Edelmann enjoyed 'adeliges Landleben' he was nonetheless starved for the companionship of students and teachers and for their passionate theological controversy. To satisfy his irrepressible need to dispute theological matters, he could turn only to priests and monks. With belated insight he writes:

> I concentrated on controversial theology, the so-called *Theologiam Polemicam*. I thought it wonderful how smart I was when I could impress and embarrass some local priest, often grossly ignorant, with some learned bits from the church history of which he was completely ignorant; Chemnitii *Examen Concilii Tridentinis*, Heilbrunner *Uncatholisches Papstthum*, Meyers *Kriege des Herrn*, Cyprians *Belehrung vom Ursprung und Wachsthum des Pabstthums* were the best comforters for my then truculent nature and I am still surprised that my cockiness among the papists did not get me into real trouble.[17]

It is indeed surprising that Edelmann, both tactless and careless, escaped unscarred and did not make trouble for the Kornfeils. The priests and monks were not always naive, and on many occasions Edelmann was in danger of being denounced as a 'Prädikant', the term of opprobrium for Protestant preachers. What saved him more than his religious righteousness was the 'love, courtesy and politeness' he encountered among the Catholics.[18]

Edelmann felt that nowhere did he find more gracious hospitality than among the Austrians, especially on his visits to the monasteries of the neighborhood. At Tulln, where he was a guest of the Capuchins, the kindness and simplicity of their Guardian, a venerable elder, captured Edelmann's heart. The modesty and industriousness of this monastery easily explained the wholehearted acceptance these monks had gained for themselves in the town.[19]

But while Edelmann praised the austerity of the Capuchins, he surely enjoyed the more opulent life of the Franciscans at Neulengbach. When he dined at their monastery, situated on the western slopes of the Wienerwald in the week before the Lenten fasting was to set in, the table was so well appointed that he felt it made the fast days easier to bear. The Pater Vicarius, anticipating some of Edelmann's reflections on the contrast between the life of beggars and that of the monks, pointed to a picture of the Wedding of Cana hanging in the refectory, implying that Christ, though austere, did not disdain a fine meal. Edelmann encountered similar hospitality at the Augustinian monastery of St. Andrä whose abbot, Anton von Rückenbaum, was then making the final plans for a new church building.[20] Not long before, in the summer of 1683, St. Andrä had suffered as much as any community in the neighborhood at the hands of the Turkish invaders. Peasants and their families had sought a last refuge in the tower of the old church while their village was being burned and pillaged. The church doors, however, were stormed and a gruesome massacre ensued. The flowering of monastic life and the religious piety of this region is understandable against this background of human suffering.

The income of modest St. Andrä was 30,000 gulden, and Edelmann speculated on how much greater the income of the large abbeys of St. Florian, Melk, Göttweig, and Klosterneuburg might be.[21] During these years good scholarly work was being done in both Melk and Göttweig.[22] But the 'little learning' of the average monk and country priest was disdained by Edelmann, who felt superior in matters of faith. He was also shocked to find that the monks in their explanations betrayed their own scepticism of the miracles which they expected the simple peasants to accept unquestioningly.

The need for the spiritual gifts of his own faith were hardly satisfied by the occasional visits with the Kornfeil family to attend Protestant services in Vienna. So much the more welcome were the vacations they spent with relatives at Ödenburg in Hungary. The Protestant community there had continued to be strong since the late sixteenth century, with an almost unbroken succession of Protestant clergy after 1565.[23] And in contrast to its Austrian brothers, it had suffered little persecution. By 1675 Leopold I had allowed the return of two German ministers who had been transferred to Eisenstadt for an interval of eight months. They were to serve only the town Protestants, but in fact the country population came from far and wide to attend their services.

The two Lutheran ministers serving at the time of Edelmann's visits in the summer of 1725 and 1726 were Johann Sigmund Pilgram (1682–1737) and Samuel Vilmos Serpilius (1707–1761). Pilgram had been trained at the University of Rostock, had held many posts as tutor and minister, and was appointed to Ödenburg in 1722.[24] Edelmann describes him as a bombastic, choleric preacher who delivered hour-long sermons in which the congregation was threatened with untimely death and eternal damnation. Pilgram preferred the company of men of title and wealth to that of the common man – a discrimination particularly evident to Edelmann after his experiences in Catholic Austria. He also felt that social distinctions were stronger and was appalled to see that the local aristocracy was always seated in the church, while the peasants, many of whom had walked for hours, had to stand on their weary feet.

Serpilius, the younger preacher, appealed to Edelmann with his urbane and friendly manners and informal way of preaching. During a visit at the fine school library which the book-thirsty Edelmann was anxious to see, Serpilius was hindered from showing all its treasures by the jealous and dis-interested Pilgram. Among the few books Serpilius managed to point out was a tract containing 120 differing opinions on the doctrine of the Lord's Supper. In recalling this visit, Edelmann felt that, had it not been for the presence of his not very amiable senior colleague, Serpilius would have uttered some thoughts of his own on the strange fact that so crucial a matter of faith was open to such a variety of interpretations; and Edelmann adds that 'such sophistication would have been lost on him who would then have taken Serpilius for an enthusiast or heretic'.[25]

Edelmann, like the Kornfeils, found spiritual solace in their Hungarian summers; Edelmann also appreciated the fiery Hungarian wine and the strong Turkish tobacco that his hosts were accustomed to smoke.

As much as Edelmann enjoyed his position with the Kornfeil family, his desire to find avenues that would open a pastoral career to him induced him to quit his current obligations. Count Hector had understanding for the restlessness of his tutor, who had now become a friend of the family. Although it was difficult to find a replacement, he did not try to keep Edelmann but provided him with an excellent letter of recommendation.[26] Edelmann had learned in Ödenburg of a vacancy for a tutor with Friedrich Fischer von Ehrenbach, the imperial court painter and a councillor at the court of Sachsen-Eisenach. On his occasional visits to the Swedish embassy in Vienna Edelmann had met Johann Christian Lerche (1691–1768), the preacher there.[27] In a letter dated November 1, 1727, Edelmann sought his help, presenting all the arguments that impelled him towards making a change. He states his hope better to serve God and his fellow men in Vienna and to be in a better position to help his two brothers by taking on some pastoral duties. He movingly describes the financial plight of his father, half of whose modest salary still went to help Edelmann's brothers, the older a lawyer, the younger a painter. Edelmann also implies that his future employer, a well-recognized painter, might perhaps assist his younger brother and even recommend him to a court that had shown itself favorable while he was a student in Jena.[28] Far-fetched as these speculations may appear, they nevertheless demonstrate Edelmann's near-desperate search for opportunities to become a minister. Conditions at the von Ehrenbach house turned out to be disadvantageous, financially and otherwise.[29] Lerche, apparently impressed by Edelmann, was anxious to help him and soon found a position for him as tutor in the house of the merchant Mühl in Vienna.

At Easter 1728 Edelmann began as tutor to the four daughters of the Mühls who lived 'am Hof' in the center of Vienna. Mühl belonged to the wealthy group of importers called *Niederläger*. Their international trade connections and long-standing experience in providing vital goods to the city assured them extensive economic and religious privileges. Most of these merchants were Protestants, and it has been estimated that of the eighty *Niederläger* only thirty were Catholics. In November 1653, at the height of the Counter-Reformation, Ferdinand III had to promise the Protestant merchants that their right to exercise their religion freely would not be infringed upon and that they and their heirs would not be molested.[30]

In his description of the Mühl household Edelmann has sketched the pathology and the oppressive character of excessive Pietism in a few pages – an analysis which parallels to an astonishing degree that found in Karl Philip Moritz's *Anton Reiser* (1785), an absorbing psychological novel.

Edelmann in his first impression saw Pietism as a force loosening orthodox scholarship and exercising a healthy restraint in an age of vulgar and cruel manners. In this double role, which Edelmann was not sophisticated enough to understand, it had played an important part in shaping the outlook and teachings of Edelmann's admired professor Buddeus. Different implications of Pietism made themselves powerfully felt among the Viennese worshippers, as, for example, in the Mühl home, where it had been introduced by two previous tutors. Edelmann labelled both of his predecessors 'Hallische Mucker', implying that they had been trained if not actually at the Pedagogical Institute at Halle, then at least under the impact of the ideas and practices cultivated there. The first tutor, Wendrich, had been a fellow student at Lauban. Edelmann does not challenge his sincerity; but of the other, Heinsius, he says, 'he attempted to play the comedy of Tartuffe, but was prevented from doing so by the modesty of the girls'[31] and was consequently dismissed.

Actuated by the impact of Spener's ideas, August Hermann Francke had founded at Halle an impressive complex of institutions – pedagogic and missionary – all dedicated to the implementation of Christian principles and to revitalizing piety and theology. A living faith was to be the fruit of each individual's experience of a conversion from a worldly being to one reborn in Christ. This conversion, as postulated by Francke, has since carried the label 'Hallischer Busskampf'.[32] In order to understand the religious world Edelmann found in Vienna and later on his travels, it is necessary to be acquainted with the structure of this conversion process as Francke conceived it. Indeed, much in Edelmann's own theological writings is the result of his reactions to the modes of Pietism he encountered. The first presupposition for the conversion, according to Francke, is that the biblical message of God's wrath and judgment shakes the old being out of his complacent security. This crisis is actually the struggle of repentance. Fear of judgment and hell, doubt of all previous religious security, even doubt of God and the ensuing desire to be delivered from such a lacerating condition characterize the first stage. Thus the biblical sermon has fulfilled the divine purpose and has incited in the individual an ardent desire to break with his past and to pursue anew his life in faithful obedience to God.

This act of will is the second and necessary stage of all conversion. Only then can the individual enter the third stage. As a consequence of such decision, conceived in deep prayer, God unfailingly makes his gift of faith, which assures forgiveness of sins and divine love; the heart then knows the bliss of being a child of God and the individual possessed of a living faith. But – and this is the fourth and last element of a real conversion – the new being, because of the momentous decision he has taken, must engage in an incessant self-examination of the seriousness and rigor of his life's conduct. Francke considered all natural desires sinful and only those spiritual ones worthy of a true Christian, which sprang from a heart open to God's love.[33] These supreme demands became the fountainheads for great and courageous ventures of love and charity. They also helped to create an atmosphere of inner piety and sincerity, a warm flow of religious sentiments that characterized many German homes for almost two centuries. Francke clearly opened for German Protestant theology a path where faith was to make itself visible in piety and virtuousness.

Yet these demands, becoming standard in everyday human life, could exercise a crushing tyranny which actually led to frustration and mental sickness. In *Anton Reiser* Moritz gives a classic description of such a dilemma.

> Yet Reiser remained (in spite of consolation from his minister) dissatisfied with himself; he considered it essential to his own piety and peace in God to be apprehensive of every step, every smile and expression, every word he spoke, and every thought. This self-examination met with its natural interruptions and actually could not last over an hour. As soon as Reiser became aware of his distractions, his self-dissatisfaction deepened and he finally considered it impossible to lead an orderly, pious and god-fearing life.[34]

Edelmann found his new employer in this melancholy state. He felt that Mühl was by nature a kind, honest, and cheerful man who had come under the spell of pietistic grace as expounded by Wendrich. The image of the wrathful God implanted in his mind and, at the same time, the image of the unconverted man in his utter abjection and impotence, with which he identified himself, thrust him into a state of despair. How could he know for certain that he had overcome the sinful thoughts that haunted him, when hours spent in passionate prayers did not bring comfort, although he was exhausted from sweat and tears? He was deaf to words of consolation telling of God's love for his creature, and he rejected such solace as false temptation. What way was there out of such turmoil and confusion?[35]

Mühl became for Edelmann a not atypical case of affliction from Pietism. Not only was Mühl deeply disturbed, but his whole household was in a state of constant uneasiness from which the preceptor of the children was not exempt. Edelmann writes:

> Almost everything I did was interpreted as sinful, and most of the sins were completely innocent matters to anybody, whose brain has not been damaged by holiness. For example, I talked too loud, or did not sing

enough, or dared, after five hours of diligent tutoring, to go for a walk in town or even sit in a coffee house. ...[36]

Edelmann had little freedom in Vienna. The duties at the Mühls' were heavy and his contacts outside their home were confined to members of the Protestant community around the legations, who also were under the impact of Pietism.[37] Together with Möllenhof, the newly arrived preacher to the Danish legation, Lerche initiated a prayer conventicle of the sort characteristic of and essential to pietistic religious practices. Here the faithful came together at least once a week to join in prayer and confession. To such a meeting Edelmann was once drawn by Lerche but, at least in retrospect, it did not appeal to him. Edelmann was to attend a variety of similar gatherings on other occasions, when his initial reaction recurred. This was to suspect the participants of hypocrisy, or at best of self-deception.[38] In the future he avoided the meetings, but he was careful not to offend the ministers on whom he still depended for help for his future career.

Although Lerche took the many complaints about the Mühls with a grain of salt, he arranged for Edelmann to preach at the Swedish legation. On three occasions Edelmann gave the sermons, but his performances apparently did not encourage him, nor did they impress the critical audience. At least, none of its influential aristocratic members seems to have shown any particular desire to recommend him for a position. These failures, as well as the unhappy atmosphere in the Mühl home, convinced Edelmann that he should leave Vienna, although he regretted that he had not become better acquainted with the city, which he considered 'worthy of all admiration'. He also regretted parting from his pupils who, he felt, were bright and likable girls. Even twenty years later he cites as an example of genuine and unperverted intelligence the question which Maria, then about ten years old, raised regarding passages in the books of Chronicles. The astute child, figuring the age of Ahas and Hikias, had concluded that the king was eleven years old when he sired his son, which appeared strange indeed to her.[39]

Edelmann then turned to his former employer, Count Kornfeil, who quickly found him a position in the household of his brother-in-law, Count Wolf Augustin Auersperg (1677–1750) at Purgstall, also in Lower Austria. In the fall of 1728 Edelmann arrived at Neu-Purgstall to take on his duties as tutor to Wolf Reichard Ehrenreich, thirteen years old, and his older sister, Anna Christine Carolina. They were the children of Count Wolf Augustin's first marriage to Kornfeil's sister, who had died some ten years earlier. Purgstall, a beautiful estate situated on the Erlauf river, with extensive farm and wood land, had come into the Auersperg family before 1492.[40] As recently as 1705, in accordance with the will of Count Maximilian Auersperg (1653–1705), the family had been divided into two branches, one occupying the old, the other the new castle. The Auerspergs of Purgstall, like the Kornfeils, are listed in the church records of 1580 as adherents of Lutheranism, having kept and practiced their faith despite adversities and trials. Even their own house chapel did not escape being branded as 'heretical' in 1701.[41]

A reasonable weekly total of twenty hours of teaching, the friendly atmosphere, and the lovely countryside soon restored Edelmann's spirits. Life was not much different from that at Würmla, though possibly more gay and more luxurious. As winter neared, great sleigh-rides were planned. On one occasion eight sleighs took the party over the winding road along the river and through the snow-covered fir woods to the Carthusian monastery at Gaming. Here again Edelmann met with the generous hospitality extended by the monks to their Protestant guests. Excellent entrees of fish compensated for the meat they eschewed, in accordance with their rule. The pleasures of the table, writes Edelmann, were enhanced by a violinist who played so beautifully that never again did he hear such playing – either in any imperial court or in any chapel anywhere.[42]

In recalling with scathing mockery his stay in Vienna in 1728, Edelmann has pictured himself as opposed to religious piety. This dubious recollection, hardly enhanced by the only slight success he had had as preacher at the Swedish embassy chapel, could easily give rise to a misconception of Edelmann. Actually, at that time he impressed his employers and friends as a religious person and a learned theologian. Apparently a certain authority emanated from the poor tutor, besieged by his family's financial problems, deprived of the intellectual climate he sorely desired, and still earnestly searching for a clerical appointment. It may be that various expressions of appreciation strengthened his confidence that a theological career would some day open to him. For instance, one of his successors at the Kornfeilds' sought his advice as to where to find the most convincing arguments on the Divinity of the Holy Scriptures.[43]

On another occasion Edelmann was called upon to render service as a theologian. During a dinner at Neu-Purgstall where the Auerspergs had as guests some Catholic dignitaries of the neighborhood, a letter arrived from Count Hector Kornfeil asking Edelmann's comfort for his ailing sister. The situation was embarrassing, because the Auerspergs needed at all costs to hide from their present Catholic company the fact that their tutor was a qualified minister. They called him to another room and explained to him that Maria Franziska Rosina had succumbed to a deep melancholy since her last difficult pregnancy, and that her husband, Count Stockhorner, and her brother felt that Edelmann could assist her in her painful spiritual afflictions. Edelmann immediately consented and set out for the Stock-horner residence at Heinreichs in the upper Waldviertel region, north of Krems on the Danube.[44] He remained there for a month, at the end of which time the baroness had regained her strength and had brought under control her former plaguing fears of the devil. In relating the incident Edelmann does not ascribe any success to his clerical qualifications. He had certainly not dispelled the fears of the devil by rational argument since, at that time, he himself believed in diabolic powers. At least, his cheerful company did no harm while time and nature did their healing work.

When Edelmann returned to Purgstall, he stayed for another year and a half, by which time Reichard, his pupil, was ready to study at the University of Jena.[45] Edelmann learned that the young count was to be accompanied by another mentor, while he was to remain as tutor to the children. He felt cheated and was ready to quit in anger, thinking that his patient services were not sufficiently recognized. Second thoughts, however, made him reconsider such rash behavior which might antagonize not only the Auerspergs, but also the Kornfeils – at the precise time when their plans for leaving Austria for good and taking him with them as a travel companion were just in the making.

From the letters to Lerche, it is apparent that Edelmann had become restless and was again slipping into a state of melancholy. In one letter he writes:

> If I were one of the kind who seeks the *summum bonum* in the pleasures of this life, I could not wish for any better position than my present one. Yet my horizon is wider and more noble, and therefore I do not hang

my coat according to the wind – God may do with me as he pleases, if only he does not withdraw his grace from me. I must say, I have spent this year, or half of it, in indolence.[46]
Edelmann tried to resist this atmosphere in the household of his employers, whom he considered, in questions of Christian theology, almost as ignorant as heathen. To keep his own religious fire glowing he begged Lerche to send him works by Nikolaus Hunnius (1585–1643) and Allix (1641–1717), and Robert Boyle's *De stylo scripturae sacrae*.[47] An orthodox Lutheran, Hunnius had been fiercely engaged in controversies with Roman Catholics, Calvinists, and enthusiasts, in the course of which he wrote many tracts exalting the Lutheran position on matters of creed, the Bible, and liturgy. Edelmann often confessed, during these years, his predilection for controversial literature.

It is expected of a theologian that he be interested in all questions concerning Holy Scripture, in arguments for its divine authorization and inspiration as well as in the exegeses of its component books. All matters treated by Robert Boyle, British philosopher and natural scientist (1627–1691), found a warm reception in Pietist circles. August Hermann Francke published Boyle's theological works in Latin translation at Halle.[48] To Boyle the world presents itself as a miraculous creation, and each of his scientific investigations convinces him even more of its divine nature. Enthusiastic propagator of the Christian faith, he lays the groundwork for Physico-theology, a term used by William Derham, the earliest beneficiary of the lectureships Boyle endowed. Boyle's conviction of the truth of the Scriptures is couched in language not different from that in which he praises God's creation:

> For I can scarce think any pains misspent that bring me in solid evidences of that great truth, that the Scripture is the Word of God, which is, indeed, the grand fundamental; ... And I use the Scripture ... as a matchless temple where I delight to be, to contemplate the beauty, the symmetry, and the magnificience of the structure, and to increase my awe and excite my devotion to the Deity there preached and adored.[49]

The arc from Boyle and Derham to the German Physico-theologians has been drawn by Hirsch. A rich and detailed account of these relations has recently been provided by Wolfgang Philipp in *Das Werden der Aufklärung*. Among the foremost German representatives of Physico-theology there emerges the Hamburg poet Barthold Heinrich Brockes. His works are Lerche's gift to Edelmann, whose requests for books shed light on the direction which his religious curiosity was taking. The literature defending the traditional positions also presents the arguments of those storming against it. Even for a reader imbued with an orthodox viewpoint, the effects might be eroding. The impact of a Boyle must lead to a widening of the horizon and to awareness of new impulses derived from nature itself.

In spite of the cool reception Edelmann had received as a preacher in Vienna, he had still not given up hope. When Pratje suggests that Edelmann's reason for leaving Austria was to find better remuneration, Edelmann's answer corrects him – it was not better wages but the 'desire soon to become a preacher' that made him decide to leave his kind employers, the Auerspergs. To this end he addressed letters to Hermann Neumeister (1671–1756), pastor at the Jacobskirche at Hamburg.[50]

To sell their possessions and leave their home in Lower Austria was surely not any easy decision for the Kornfeils. Edelmann was initiated into the deliberations and, as he felt himself a stout defender of the Lutheran faith, he encouraged a move which would take the Kornfeils into a world where they could exercise their religion freely. The fear that the Count's minor children would be forced to become Catholics in the event of his death, and that his widow would be exposed to hardships in Catholic Austria played a part in the decision.[51] Otto Brunner has cited some economic motives behind Wolf Helmhard von Hohberg's similar decision almost a half-century earlier; but such reasons are hard to detect in Count Kornfeil's case.[52] Later, in his own memoirs, Edelmann acknowledged that the Count had made a substantial economic sacrifice, and that he himself had contributed to a decision which led his friends to economic losses for the sake of the phantom of their faith.[53]

The exit from Austria in the summer of 1731 took Edelmann back over the same road by which he had entered this land six years before. Before embarking with the Kornfeils at Ybbs he had ample time to visit the greatest and wealthiest of the Benedictine abbeys: Melk. Though not as seasoned a traveler as Henri Bayle, who declared the spot 'one of the most beautiful in the world ... to be compared only with the terrace of Lausanne and the view from Bergamo',[54] Edelmann thoroughly enjoyed its beauty and marveled at the impressive architecture and the splendid interior decorations of the monastery. This visit to Melk may have seemed to him like a final pause, before departing, to embrace once more the Austrian world of rural charm and all-pervasive urbanity.

Perhaps it was this quality of his experiences that helped to prepare the ground for a new sensitivity and receptiveness in Edelmann. Traveling down the Danube from Regensburg on his way to Melk, he had been contemplating the poetry of Brockes, and little did he then know of it. Now, leaving by the same waterway, he carried with him the poet's works.

3. The Search for Christian Perfection
1731–1734

It is hardly extravagant to call the period from the summer of 1731 to that of 1734 the most crucial four years in Edelmann's life. It has already been suggested that the making of the radical theologian Edelmann was not as dramatic as it seemed to him in retrospect, and that his exposure to dissenting religious views lasted for a longer period than he realized. During these years, however, a change occurred in his thinking – his mind, formerly clinging zealously to its orthodox beliefs, now was open and eager for what before had been taboo. In these years, still taken up by routine jobs of tutoring and preaching, Edelmann dared to acquaint himself at first hand with the writings of Gottfried Arnold, Joachim Betke, and Johann Konrad Dippel. Under their impact he discovered his own vocation.

He was thirty-three years old when he returned from Austria to the house of his brother Heinrich Gottlob at Chemnitz in Saxony. Though a person of inner strength and one in whom confidence had been placed, Edelmann still had not found a position satisfying his own ambitions. The truth was that he still had not identified them. He no longer felt his former inclination to a career as preacher, although he again had the opportunity to try himself at pulpits in Chemnitz and Brockendorff and other nearby villages – and with some success, in contrast to his performances in Vienna. Yet in Edelmann's opinion his lack of those 'indispensable gifts' – the 'facile tongue and the gift of insolence' which Pratje ascribed to him – was so significant as to have prevented him from becoming a preacher.[1]

After a stay of two months with his brother, Edelmann took the position of tutor in the house of Johann Gottfried Werstler (b. 1684), minister to the village community of Brockendorff belonging to the Hessian church district of Freiberg. Edelmann's duties were heavy. He was responsible for the education of eight children: this meant four hours a day of tutoring for which he was to receive thirty thaler a year. Nevertheless, he was still able to accomplish some reading, note-taking, and writing. He emphasizes that he performed his duties 'faithfully ... and studied late into the night ... I hauled sleighs full of books from Freiberg and Chemnitz'.[2] The great capacity for work that emerged at this time (and which continued throughout Edelmann's later life) is an indication that he was now discovering his true creative powers. This Brockendorff position was far from satisfactory although it was to his advantage that the parish was under the oversight of Wilisch, his former beneficent rector from Altenburg, to whom he could look for future help.

A letter of January 1, 1732, to Valentin Ernst Löscher (1673–1749), then powerful church administrator at Dresden, reveals how restless, almost desperate Edelmann must have been. In this lengthy letter, worthy of the elaborate epistolary habits of the time, he expresses his desire to become minister to a party which the Saxon king was assembling for an exploration in the East and West Indies.[3] That a certain desire for adventure might have played a part in this impulsive offer is plausible. Edelmann toyed with similar ideas when, only a year later, he went to Herrnhut to visit Zinzendorf, who equipped many missionary parties. But he was genuinely ready to make a sacrifice for the religion he still embraced with passion and vigor. The zealous example of those who, like Count Kornfeil, had left their homes for the sake of their faith was before him, and he cited it in the letter to Löscher.

The example was kept the more alive as thousands of Protestants, exiled from their Salzburg homeland at the instigation of Archbishop Firmian (1727–1744), streamed through Saxony on their way to Prussia in the year 1732.[4] Their fate occupies Edelmann, and in his letters to his friend Lerche in Vienna he gives lengthy descriptions of their circumstances. In a moving account based partly on his own conversations with emigrants and partly on what he heard from others, he describes to his former employer, Count Auersperg, the hardships these Salzburg exiles had suffered at home, their sudden expulsion, and their journey through Germany. He is impressed by their thoroughly Christian attitude:

They do not curse their former oppressors, they do not express feelings of revenge, but they exemplify in their conduct truly evangelical Christians. They are well grounded in their faith and in the word of God, and when one reflects that they have no instruction from scholars of our ranks, one is greatly astonished and has to confess: this God has done and it is a miracle before our eyes.[5]

Edelmann also reports with how much open hospitality and generosity the exiles were welcomed in Saxony and that not only Protestants, but Jews and Catholics were anxious to help them.[6] The letter certainly was intended primarily to urge Count Auersperg to choose exile and leave the 'Austrian Babel'.

He imagines himself in a similar role of defender of the faith, when he boasts to Lerche of a preaching assignment in the village of Siebenlehn. The local minister, Adam Segner (1680–1741), had been preacher at Pressburg in Hungary but had to leave that post on account of his hostile attitude towards the Catholics.[7] He was then appointed preacher in Torgau, and in 1719 he had come to the parsonage in Siebenlehn. In the following years he became more and more critical of the church and was accused of Socinian and rationalist ideas. In 1732 he was suspended and after further investigation by the consistory, dismissed and forced to leave Saxony within two months.[8] Though Edelmann was at first proud of the confidence bestowed on him, he later saw things in a different light:

The church calendar prescribed that I must preach on Sexagesima Sunday the gospel message of the many acres (Is 5: 10); I adjusted my sermon to the particular situation and as I had been told that Socinians attempt to figure out all matter through reason, I heaped abuses according to my text or rather my deeply entrenched prejudices upon innocent reason, and gained from my blindfolded listeners such applause that if it had been in their power they would have appointed me their minister on the spot, and that in spite of the fact that their own minister was only under suspension.

Indeed this man certainly saw much further than I did at that time, and I repent even to this hour that I did not accept his kind invitation to his home. For this ungracious behavior I can only blame my Bible, according to which I was not supposed to sit at meat with a blasphemer (John 2: 10), which I took all Socinians to be at that time. Even then I found it hard to behave in such manner, but I had much too great reverence not obediently to convey such a holy insult, but rather denied the respect due a man who, in spite of his alleged mistaken beliefs, had shown courtesy toward me. What is one not capable of if one believes himself to be rendering to his own God a service with insults and affronts?[9]

The extent to which Edelmann's intensified religious fervor drew him to reading has been noted. It seems probable that the image of true Christian behavior was reinforced by the arguments and illustrations that he found in his reading.

Edelmann's intellectual life in this period has a double aspect: shy beginnings of intellectual criticism on dogmatic positions, and the increasing awareness of a gulf between what Orthodox believers confess and how they behave. It was his employer Werstler, the poor country priest, who prompted Edelmann to such observations. Edelmann, however, submits his own feelings towards him to frank scrutiny:

> The exposure of the weaknesses of my priest made me feel superior, whereas I was actually a hypocrite and he in truth an honest man who did not want to pretend to be anything better than he was; he was indeed a poor sinner, who wanted the respect that his office before God was supposed to carry. In other words, the good man showed himself according to his true nature without simulation, whereas I pretended to be holy.[10]

When, after a two-year stay, an opportunity arose for Edelmann to leave the Werstler home, minister and tutor separated amicably but without regrets. The minister bestowed his best wishes on Edelmann for his future at Dresden, where he had accepted a tutorship with Count Callenberg.[11] For Edelmann the change meant chiefly greater opportunities to pursue his studies and also his book purchases. He welcomed, of course, the chance to part from Werstler, of whom he had become so highly critical, and who, he also felt, had become suspicious of Edelmann's strict adherence to Orthodoxy. Edelmann never revealed in his autobiography the name of the priest of Brockendorff, the 'poor sinner'.

When one recalls Edelmann's unhappy experience with Pietists in Vienna, one cannot fail to detect a certain irony in the fact that he is now approaching their rigorous moralism, that he is sharing with them the struggle for exemplary Christian behavior. Assessing his position at that stage of his education, he writes, 'I still was more than three-quarters a Lutheran – only with the distinction that I belonged within that sect, but inclining more to the side of the Pietists and Separatists than to the Orthodox'.

He quickly adds that this inclination towards Pietism is due largely to his love for the honest Buddeus, 'whose actions and habits, to the extent I knew of them, I found much less vulnerable to criticism than those of most men who called themselves Orthodox'. While of questionable accuracy, this retrospective mathematical self-evaluation is surely conservative.

It is regrettable that Edelmann's commonplace book of excerpts from his readings during that time, which would have revealed to us just what those readings were, has not been recovered.[12] Specifically mentioned in the autobiography are Baxter's *Treatise* and the *Commentary on the First Epistle of John* by Bernhard Walther Marperger (1682–1746), who was preacher and church councillor at the Dresden court.[13] Both works greatly reinforced Edelmann's awareness of disparity between the Christian ideal and human frailty. The discussion of the reborn man in Marperger's *Commentary*, in particular, threw him 'almost into despair'.[14]

As often happens, some book of no great merit, if read at the right psychological moment, may stimulate thought and emotion. Thus Edelmann's thoughts on infant-baptism were prompted by a tract by Gottlieb Gaudliz (1694–1745): *Gründliche Untersuchung melodischer Lehr=säze unter dem Namen Christian Friedrich Taube*.[15] But towering over all these was Gottfried Arnold's *Unpartheyische Kirchen- und Ketzer-Historie Vom Anfang des Neuen Testaments biss auf das Jahr Christi 1688*, a book which had made a profound impression on Edelmann. He says:

> I borrowed the work from the otherwise very poor library of Doctor Wilisch. In this work, written with utmost frankness, I found recorded, to my great surprise, so many indecent and irresponsible acts of the clergy, which alone claims to possess the true Christian religion, that I became greatly disgusted with so-called Orthodoxy and began to lean towards the Pietists; in spite of their shortcomings, they appeared at least to aspire to a godly life whereas the Orthodox, who, for all the faith they pretended, neglected all good works and preferred to remain righteous believers but poor sinners, rather than to become right-living examples for their flock.[16]

From this first acquaintance with Arnold's monumental work, which covers the history of the Christian church and of those who rebelled against its views, Edelmann gained not only a great measure of factual knowledge but a new orientation. Arnold combined a high level of scholarship with the Pietists' concern for the implications of learning for their faith and its practice. Goethe, recalling the impression the work made on him, expressed this dual quality of Arnold precisely: 'This man is not merely a reflective historian, but at the same time a man of piety and sensibility.'[17]

In one sense, Arnold's work is not a history of the Christian church. He did not attempt to record the growth of an institution – its metamorphoses, its flowering or decay. Such a concept of the church was alien to him. What he saw was the ministry of Christ and the life of the Apostolic church in the first century, followed by a continuous process of formation of religious bodies and institutions which became ever more remote from the fountainhead. Unwilling to ascribe aberrations and errors to any particular party in the unending religious controversies, he seeks rather to acquaint his readers with all the protagonists and their preachings. As spiritual truth, or even error, is not confined to any one organizational body, those voices which have given witness to Christian truth – even those of a church, whether papal or reformed – deserve special attention. It is a radical religious truth, applied here to historiography, that Arnold suggests: 'With the introduction of sin into the world ... and the murder of Abel, was not the beginning made of a continuing process by which the strong and evil one suppressed the weaker and virtuous one?'[18] It is therefore Arnold's special concern to record lives and views and to eschew traditional evaluations. The paradox which underlies Arnold's history is that so often those who were persecuted appear as the true Christians, rather than the powerful church officials who had persecuted them.

In Arnold's presentation Edelmann encountered views and ideas altogether different from those in his readings of controversial theology. Buddeus had not been a name-caller, but the scope of Arnold's work was far beyond that of the Jena teacher's lectures. Arnold wanted to characterize his undertaking as 'unpartheiisch'. The word had appeared in the vocabulary of the sixteenth-century spiritualist historians Sebastian Franck and Valentin Weigel. According to Franck's definition it described a Christian faith free of sectarianism, in which sense Arnold uses the word. The spiritualist undertone remains essential and he takes a stand against equalization of values: 'It is impossible to write without love of good and without disdain of evil.'[19] He tries to be as meticulous in his use of his sources as the scholarship of the times enables him to be, and assembled a tremendous wealth of hitherto inaccessible material on the thoughts of mystics and nonconformists. When his contemporaries chided him for doing so, he replied that he was especially anxious that his readers judge the importance of the literature by its effect on deeds.

How much Edelmann was influenced by the style of Arnold's work may be seen from specific instances. Surely not lost on him was the significant general observation that the history had been written 'in our vernacular so that not only the academically trained but others, who ... possess considerable knowledge and experience of God, may judge it all and gain something from it'.[20] Gundolf, who does not underestimate Arnold, characterizes the *Ketzerhistorie* as a *catalogue raisonné* which 'stands between a lexicon and a tract with short comments'.[21] This is indeed true, and Arnold is far from Herder's and Gundolf's aspiration towards a genetic approach to history. Arnold was certainly not historically oriented, but his method of presentation gave strong impact to a process, already in motion, which continued for years to come.

The shape and content of this process in motion was the crucial problem for Edelmann during the first months of 1734 in Dresden. He was keenly aware that his two younger brothers had 'reached the final goal of their studies, the one as painter in Gotha, the other as "Amtsverweser" in Chemnitz', while his own theological studies had not led to any such positive result. He did not feel called to preach, nor was he 'going to force himself to preach in spite of an already tried conscience'.[22] So disturbing was the effect on him of his reading that he felt his beliefs challenged. He desperately tried to find food for reassurance in his own religion: 'I prayed, I fasted, I confessed, I went to communion, I ran to church, in short, I did everything in that first half of my Dresden stay that can be asked from a church Christian', but his needs were not answered; the sermons did not turn the audience into what Edelmann conceived to be 'real Christians'.

I sought the Christian perfection that accords with the Scriptures – a community of earthly goods, assuming that Jesus, the originator and fulfiller of our faith, would not have asked in vain of one who had from youth lived up to all the prescribed duties that, if he wants to be perfect, he must sell everything that he has and give it to the poor, and follow Him.

The search for such 'real Christians' became imperative. While Edelmann recalls this struggle in all its powerfulness, he is still able to comment: 'In fact, I was a fool to entertain these ideas. Because with such a model I could not take myself for a Christian: but as I then still believed that others had progressed further in such exercises than I, I was terribly anxious to find these people and to imitate their example.'[23]

The fame of Count Zinzendorf, who had gathered a community dedicated to Christian principles in Herrnhut in the Upper Lausitz, was now spreading. Edelmann had heard of Herrnhut when he was in Freiberg. Now at Dresden he wanted to learn more about Zinzendorf and Herrnhut in the hope of meeting 'true Christians'. That the Orthodox denounced the Count's flock as fools only encouraged Edelmann's search. He tells us that he was not even sure that Herrnhut existed and the name not a mock name,[24] a play on the word 'Hut' that has the meaning of both 'hat' and 'protection', the first amounting to nonsense, the second connoting the intended interpretation, 'in the protection of the Lord'.

If Herrnhut was a legend to be verified on the map, the name of Zinzendorf was at any rate not new to Edelmann, who had seen the family castle at Weissenburg near St. Pölten. Count Nikolaus Ludwig was a notable person in his native town of Dresden, where he had served as legal counsel from 1721 until his move to Herrnhut in 1727.[25] His older brother Count Friedrich Christian (1697–1756) was married to Countess Christiana Sofia Callenberg (1703–1775),[26] and of Count Nikolaus Ludwig's religious enterprises one spoke at the Callenberg dinner table not without mockery.[27]

As soon as he had ascertained that there was such a place as Herrnhut, Edelmann addressed himself to Count Zinzendorf, who responded quickly and invited him to visit.[28] When Edelmann admitted that he did not have money for the trip, Zinzendorf immediately sent it to him. The details for the visit were arranged by Friedrich von Watteville, Zinzendorf's close associate, who met Edelmann at Dresden. Edelmann had now made his first contact with men who, different as their religious ideas might be, sought in common for forms of expression and of living other than those offered and prescribed from the Orthodox pulpit. Acquaintance, agreement and disagreement with these and with small groups of individuals constitute from this time on an important part of Edelmann's world.

When asked to grant Edelmann a short leave, Countess Callenberg was at first reluctant as she suspected that he wanted to look for other employment. Edelmann did not want to reveal his real purpose as he was afraid that he would be teased. He assured the Countess that he had no intention of seeking another position and gladly undertook to execute a commission for her in Bantzen, the purported destination of his journey.[29]

Early in June 1734 Edelmann arrived at Herrnhut, where he stayed for only a fortnight. The account of this visit, written twenty-five years later, is filled with scorn and bitter irony. Even more damning is the pamphlet in which Edelmann published, with introduction and comments, letters which he exchanged with Zinzendorf between 1736 and 1739.[30] As late as September 1735 he had expressed the intention of returning to Herrnhut. How can this apparently sustained interest be reconciled with his subsequent negative interpretation of all he saw there. Not, surely, on the basis of a simple change of heart regarding a more permanent association, which he could not yet admit to himself or to Zinzendorf. Edelmann construed this reversal simply as the providential disappearance of a mirage which had almost entrapped him. In 'his first fervor and blindness' he was ready to accept even a missionary assignment:

At that time he [Zinzendorf] could have made of me whatever he wanted. I would have believed this to be the wish of the Savior, and so deep was my state of delusion then that he could have thrown me from one corner of the earth to the other... But when he gave me time to think and to investigate his devious purposes, he had already half lost.[31]

Zinzendorf's own explanation for Edelmann's cooling off and subsequently turning so violently against him, was also based on an over-simplification. He ascribed it largely to his refusal of a loan of 150 thaler which Edelmann had requested. In a letter of March 9, 1737, Zinzendorf wrote, 'this is the true and real crux of our controversy'.[32]

The question to be answered is not whether Edelmann's account of Herrnhut was reliable, or whether Zinzendorf was really the impostor that Edelmann later accused him of being;[33] it is rather to explain the change of Edelmann's attitude in the context of his personal predicament at that time. What we know of Edelmann thus far, and a brief but close look at Herrnhut in the summer of 1734, might help us to find the answer. Edelmann had come to Herrnhut as a passionate seeker. How much he really knew of the community is hard to determine; from his own records it appears that he knew very little. The gossip of the aristocratic Callenberg household probably made of the Count an old fool who, forgoing the advantages of his estate, preferred to associate with a mixed group of people in a kind of utopian Christian community. Edelmann might have learned that Zinzendorf was the author of *Der Dresdnische Socrates*, a series of pamphlets published anonymously between 1725 and 1726 when Zinzendorf, as legal counsel to the court, was openly defying and mocking the official censorship. Inspired by Gottfried Arnold's spirit of tolerance, he castigated the abuses and complacency of the clergy.[34]

Regardless of how much or how little he knew of Zinzendorf, Edelmann's expectations were certainly high. Zinzendorf's Herrnhut community looked back to twelve years of exciting, often hazardous, growth. In 1722 the young imperial Count had acquired the seat of Berthelsdorf in the Upper Lausitz, where he hoped he might further the reign of Christ. The ideal of the small active church community within the church ('Ecclesiolae in Ecclesia') was rooted in the concept of pietistic religiosity, propagated by Spener himself. It had appealed to Zinzendorf as early as 1716 when he and a student at Francke's Paedagogium started the 'Senfkornorden' (mustard seed order). This society united a group of aristocratic friends, among them also von Watteville. They felt 'awakened' by Francke's words and 'by the first love for Jesus, a fire that soon spreads and kindles other hearts in similar heavenly flames'; and they wanted above all to share their experience in common devotion and meditation, and to live in the fellowship of Christ.[35]

Zinzendorf, having grown up in the household of his grandmother, Henriette Katharina von Gersdorf, was imbued with pietistic religiosity; moreover he had just chosen as his wife the Countess Erdmuthe of the Reuss-Ebersdorf family, one of the aristocratic families most loyal to Francke. Theirs was to be a marriage dedicated to a fight for Christ, a 'Streiterehe'. The small church unit binding all its members in brotherly love, Zinzendorf called his 'castle'.[36] Zinzendorf was immediately challenged by a small group of Moravian Brethren. These descendants of the Hussites begged for a place to settle since their religion was tolerated neither by Protestant nor by Catholic local clergy. The ten persons who left their village of Sehlen were directed to a spot between the Hutberg and the

county *chaussée*, where they might build their houses within the Berthels-
dorfer domain but a mile from the village. The Count's desire to establish the reign of Christ, and the immigrants' dedication to their own religious persuasion, fused into an enterprise whose origins, however accidental, appeared to its participants to be providential. In 1727 Zinzendorf gave to a report describing the previous five years the proud title:
'History of the Appearance of the Reign of Christ in the Upper Lausitz'.[37]

The Zinzendorf domain with its two little centers, Berthelsdorf and
Herrnhut, was open to all who sought a philadelphian community in the
midst of the Baroque splendor and worldliness of these years. Separatists,
spiritualists like the Schwenckfelders and, of course, Moravian Brethren
found refuge in this tiny principality ruled by a count who remained Lutheran
as did Richard Rothe, his minister in the village of Berthelsdorf. Inevitably
individual and group differences arose and increased, as the dangers to
the common social framework of the community became greater. In a
sense the history of the decade from the beginnings in 1722 is also the
story of the search for a solution to this problem, the search for a formula under which all members could feel free in their own conscience,
but to which they could submit in order that the community might
survive. Not to quench religious enthusiasm while enforcing rules was a
primary concern.

A formal division between the two villages, and the order which Zinzendorf issued in May 1727 for Herrnhut, where his household had moved,
was a major step forward. The 'great awakening' which set in, this summer of 1727, the religious enthusiasm which melted the hearts of the members
of the community, suggested to Zinzendorf that he was traveling the right
road; it was to him 'the beginning of the ensuing deeds of the living and
weaving spirit of God in Herrnhut'.[38] By 'ensuing deeds' Zinzendorf meant
the missionary movement which emanated from Herrnhut in both its
enterprises: the one, to start a new nucleus after the Herrnhut model, to be
affiliated with other religious centers in Europe, particularly in Germany;
the other, the missionary enterprises, to reach overseas. Not all of Zinzendorf's attempts to associate with great personalities who were religiously
independent succeeded. Neither Johann Konrad Dippel (1673–1734) nor
Johann Friedrich Rock (1687–1749) was willing to enter into a formal
philadelphian association with him. At the pietistic court of Count Casimir

at Berleburg he first found an enthusiastic welcome; but the idea of accepting the Herrnhut discipline was soon rejected. In spite of such individual failures the Herrnhut community became the basis for a widely branching growth of colonies and missionary activities.

Herrnhut was not free of threats and attacks by the authorities. The death of the Elector August der Starke on February 11, 1733, prevented an edict of exile against Zinzendorf and his Herrnhut community. His successor, Friedrich August II, insisted on the exile of the Schwenckfelder but extended tolerance to the Count and the Moravian Brethren.[39] It is understandable that Zinzendorf was anxious to have the propriety of his Lutheran faith attested and to gain authoritative affirmation for his belief that there was nothing inconsistent between this faith and that of the Moravians. For that purpose he traveled to Tübingen to obtain a written affirmation from the University's theological faculty that he was a good Lutheran.[40] Having been examined and approved as a minister of the Lutheran church in April 1734, he also obtained from the Consistory of Stralsund admittance to the Spiritual Estate. If these moves to strengthen Herrnhut against attacks led to no orthodox narrowing, they were certainly linked to the sharpening of Zinzendorf's Christo-centricity, to utter dependence on faith as Luther understood it. In Zinzendorf's own words, 'that is the *articulus fundamentalis:* to know Jesus as he was crucified and to encompass him in one's heart'.[41]

The year 1734 was thus an important one in Herrnhut's history, and the Count dated his heightened awareness of Christ's all-encompassing part in man's life from the morning prayer hour of February 11 of this year. It is evident, even from this telescoped history of Herrnhut, that by the time Edelmann arrived a point had been reached where the tribulations of earlier years were overcome; and the enterprise, nourished from many sources, had gained under Zinzendorf's preeminent leadership its form and its firm basis for future development. The desire to enter into a dialogue with other Christians and to provide a place at Herrnhut where seekers would find a congenial philadelphian community was no less strong, the invitation to Edelmann being just one example of that spirit of outreach.

Edelmann was first met by August Gottlieb Spangenberg (1704–1792), who had joined Herrnhut when he had been expelled from Halle a year earlier.[42]

Zinzendorf was two years younger than Edelmann and, according to most contemporaries' memoirs, of a winning personality. The first encounter, as Edelmann remembered it, did not establish a real rapport between him and the Count; on the contrary:

> During our first talk something happened between us, that indicated that we were not made for each other. We examined each other from fixed positions and could not quite figure out where we stood. How he felt I cannot say, but my heart told me quite loudly that we would not harmonize. I suppressed this intimation strongly, and in a curious way set myself against my own feelings.[43]

As the mode of life at Herrnhut was set largely by Zinzendorf's style, it is not surprising that Edelmann's uneasiness toward the Count himself extended toward his world. If he expected to find his image of the early church as a community of brethren realized in a radically spiritual and economic sense, he was disappointed. Zinzendorf considered himself the servant of Christ with the role of religious leader assigned to him by the will of the community, guided by the will of God. His legal rank as imperial count he never abdicated and, with all modesty in his conduct and daily life, he remained lord of his estate. Correctly, though sarcastically, Edelmann observes:

> I saw that the head of this new Christianity was served most 'countly' and assumed he had come more to be served, than to serve others. I found indeed a courtly-appointed table at which those brethren who had to act as lackeys – though some of them had been as apostles to America and had traveled further than all the apostles of Christ, taken together, ever did – rejoiced in the honor of waiting on table.[44]

Edelmann was anxious to participate in and to understand the religious habits and peculiar worship at Herrnhut. If retrospectively all presented itself as ridiculous, this was not the immediate effect on him. The style of worship which Zinzendorf and the community at Herrnhut had developed is even today carried out by their descendants, and the sincerity and kindness implied in the simple rituals remain impressive.

The Herrnhut community of approximately seven hundred members was divided into two major units, the one comprising the Moravian Brethren, the other made up of the remaining brethren and sisters. Those units were then subdivided according to households, single males, single females, and various age groups. Within all these groupings members united according to their inclinations in 'bonds' ('Banden') for the purpose of mutual care and shared common responsibilities of the 'Streitergemeinschaft'. In the frequent gatherings for religious instruction and worship this division was reflected in the choruses. It tended also to correspond to actual worship practices. The major pattern of Herrnhut worship was an interchange of singing and preaching, the rhythm of which formed an indivisible whole. Edelmann detected some 'charm in the devotional music especially when horn and organ mixed in', but damned the Count's sermon and expounding of hymn texts that 'interrupted the agreeable sensations' the music had inspired.[45] In hymns filled with images of 'blood and wounds' Zinzendorf found the most direct representation of the *theologia crucis* that he expounded. He felt it should be accessible to everybody, in contrast to the fantasies of abstract theology.[46] He elaborated this imagery to the most minute physical descriptions of Christ's wounds and the sensations that they should stimulate in the believer. In this Zinzendorf was striving for concreteness, not unlike the physico-theological poet Brockes. His subject matter, like his theological concept was, however, centered on Christ, and while Brockes' pitfall was often triviality, Zinzendorf's error was a sentimentalization of Christ.

Upon Edelmann's insistence, Spangenberg let him participate in the celebration of the love feast on Sunday afternoon. As at other gatherings the choruses, divided according to sex, sometimes in unison with all others present, chanted hymns from the rich collection of the Moravian Brethren's Hymnbook to which Zinzendorf contributed many compositions. As a token of a common meal rolls were distributed to everyone in the hall and 'a "love-kiss" was exchanged as a seal of love, that united them all'.[47]

Zinzendorf and others often went to Berthelsdorf to attend the sermons of pastor Rothe, but did not participate in the communion service. Edelmann found Rothe 'a quite tractable fellow'. The closeness of the two men, Rothe and the Count, and the relation between the two villages, has already been discussed, as has the precarious theological situation created in Herrnhut by Zinzendorf's continued endeavors to maintain a working relation with the Lutheran church. Edelmann, who had only a limited understanding of the history and needs of Herrnhut, was appalled. 'I saw the obvious hypocrisy that the Count practiced with the Lutherans; it threw me into the greatest confusion of conscience, and I did not find a way out of this struggle.' Edelmann's judgment that Zinzendorf 'was actually much less orthodox than I was at that time and was, in spite of it, eager to deceive honest people into believing he was orthodox' misses the truth. He misrepresented Zinzendorf in order to make him suit his own needs and wishes. At the same time Edelmann eliminates all distinction between a Lutheran and an orthodox Lutheran. The crux of the matter is that Edelmann was disappointed in Zinzendorf: '... I had sought contact with him, because I believed that he would find as great disgust with Orthodoxy as I did.'[48]

In Edelmann's account of his visit to Herrnhut, his description and reflection on marriage procedures and missionary activities take their place next to those on devotional practices. Marriage was a problem likely to interest Edelmann. His flirtation with his cousin – his first love – lay eight years back, but he had not forgotten her. Not until another encounter in 1736 was there an end to his wish to ally himself with her.[49] In a world where matrimony was usually linked to status and economic security, Edelmann was a poor candidate. For a man like him, Herrnhut, where marriage was not necessarily subject to such qualifications, could have offered a powerful temptation. But it did not turn out so.

While at Herrnhut, Edelmann did not witness any selection of mates by lot, but when he returned to Dresden he heard of such procedures, which he considered as one more reason to turn against the Count: 'To be bound through lot to a woman to whom I did not feel any inclination was to me more atrocious than I am able to express, yes, such matrimony seemed to me sheer hell.'[50] The 'lot' did play an important role in the Herrnhut community. The underlying motive for drawing lots in making important decisions is generally the wish to subordinate rational consideration and individual wishes to a providential dictate.

Luther's commentary on the drawing of lots, in his exegesis of the prophet Jonah (ch. 7), may be taken as the best explanation of what such a scheme meant to Zinzendorf and the Herrnhut community:

While drawing lots, two, three or how many they are, become one, and seal a covenant over a matter, to carry it out in this or that way; as the way of the lot may fall: they do not designate a certain person but commend it to God, whom the lot shall choose, and they have beforehand agreed that who draws the lot will be the one as ordained by God. ... Christians should not consider drawing lots at random, but ought to believe that God determines the lot.[51]

The question, whether the lot was actually used in joining marriage partners, has been unequivocally answered. In his valuable study Tanner inclines to the belief that in some instances the lot was used but that Zinzendorf's enemies have grossly exaggerated the number of cases. More important than the practice of drawing lots, Tanner concludes, was the fact that frequently the community, together with the Count, decided who should be united in marriage.[52] Of an eligible marriage age, Edelmann was not altogether wrong in suspecting that pressures could be exercised on him. He was not unsusceptible to womanly graces. Thus, when describing the choruses he writes: 'So I observed more the holy posture of the men than the unnatural gestures of the weaker sex, among whom there was none that attracted me; otherwise it might well have happened that such inclinations would have bound me to the community of the New Savior.'[53]

Spangenberg, who had taken Edelmann under his wing, touched on the subject of preparation for marriage in their conversations.[54] In 1731 Zinzendorf had started systematic education for those who were ready to enter marriage. He certainly was pioneering in this area of pastoral care: 'Ehepflege', as Spangenberg called it.[55] This educational endeavor cannot be separated from the entire complex of Zinzendorf's ideas of sex and marriage. Here it must suffice to say that Zinzendorf tried to redeem the sexual function of man, so long made contemptible in Christian tradition, even in the seventeenth and the eighteenth centuries.[56] He wanted to think not only of the institution of marriage, but of its biological foundation in physical union, as having sacramental character. Zinzendorf held subtle, not unambivalent, ideas on this subject; his corporeal, image-loaded language did not always help to clarify them.[57]

We have reason to question the soundness of Spangenberg's explanation and to assume that he hardly gave Edelmann a real understanding of the marriage principles and ideas at Herrnhut. Edelmann was quick to ridicule Spangenberg's claim that the giving of physical birth carried with it 'regeneration'. Edelmann's recollections of these matters are mixed with the malicious slander that circulated widely at that time. And he seems to have been further 'confused' by the marriage problem, which inevitably also aroused in him temptation and fear.[58]

In August of 1732 the first 'Messenger', Brother Leonhard Dober, set out for St. Thomas, a Danish-owned island in the West Indies, to bring the gospel of Christ to the Negro slaves and to share their lot.[59] This journey marked the beginning of the great missionary endeavors of the Herrnhut community. 'Messengers' left Herrnhut within the following four years for North, Middle, and South America, for Greenland and South Africa, and the dedicated character of these audacious enterprises should not be forgotten.[60] While the Herrnhut community was extending itself over the oceans in those early years, the fortunes of each 'Messenger' were the paramount news at home. It became customary to read their communications as part of the religious service when many of the members were gathered, anxious to hear the news. Edelmann was present at such gatherings 'when the Count emptied bags filled with letters, from which he read passages that served the "New Savior's" cause'. It is not impossible that at that very moment Zinzendorf considered Edelmann a potential 'Messenger' to America – a proposition later transmitted through Spangenberg to Edelmann in Dresden. Edelmann ascribed this confidence to the impression made on Zinzendorf by his 'daring personality', although he considered himself 'as unqualified to act as an apostle as to be a minister'. In view of his own letter of only two years earlier offering Löscher his services as missionary with an expedition,[61] we may doubt that he was so sure of disliking the potential assignment as he later claimed to have been.

The 'Herrnhut Diarium' of June 17, 1734, relates: 'A very blessed morning-prayer-hour over the Saying "Who falls on him will be crushed". Extensive deliberation with Scharup, who, together with Seelschopp, Öttinger, Weiss and Edelmann, is about to depart; they were much moved by everything.'[62] With this entry Edelmann's own recollection of his farewell from Herrnhut accords well: 'I took my leave, half cheerful and half sad, from the Savior and His community, with the assurance that I would soon join them and share good and bad with them. As it was, I promised more than I was able to fulfill according to my most inner feelings.'[63] What stood between Edelmann and a fate that would have joined him to Herrnhut was his real vocation as writer, but of this he was not as yet fully conscious.

4. First Publications
1734–1736

Edelmann's plan of bringing out his writings in the form of a journal which would appear only irregularly was not altogether an original one. The periodical, or magazine, then a new fashion in publishing, had been welcomed in England and France, and was finding a similar reception in Germany. The first literary and philosophical journal was Thomasius' *Monatsgespräche*, which appeared in 1688, followed in 1701 by a theological periodical, *Unschuldige Nachrichten*, edited by Valentin Ernst Löscher. This new literary medium proliferated in the twenties and thirties; the poet Brockes participated in editing *Der Patriot* in Hamburg, and in 1725 Gottsched, popular philosopher, poet and translator of Bayle's dictionary, started a string of magazines with his *Vernünftigen Tadlerinnen*. The success of the literary journals is explained by the emergence of a new middle-class public avid for literature.[1] Though this public can hardly have been identical with the one that would read the theological journals, it was introduced to a large amount of moral and philosophical material in the pages of the literary journals; on the other hand, it seems apparent that the readers of the theological magazines were not confined to a professional audience. Who could feel excluded when Zinzendorf addresses his *Teutsche Socrates* 'to all those, who still love truth and see with their own eyes'?[2] Edelmann, as we shall see presently, made even more sure that no potential reader be excluded from his all-embracing love.

Although Edelmann's clear inspiration was to write 'innocent truths', he did not at first use this as the title. *Gespräche im Reiche der Wahrheit* came to mind, but, as it was identical with a publication that had just come to his attention, he dismissed it. This may have been a tract discussing Hamburg's minting regulations of 1726. What he could take for the command, however, he could also take for the title: under the name *Unschuldige Wahrheiten* he sent a sheaf of sheets, making up the first four installments, to the publisher Samuel Benjamin Walther in Leipzig.[3] *Unschuldige Wahr-heiten* – 'innocent truths' – is borrowed directly from Arnold's *Unparthey-ische Kirchen- und Ketzer-Historie.* He uses this phrase in professing to put aside 'all partiality in order that the sheer, innocent truth may shine so much the brighter before eyes thus freed from natural blindness as well as before those heretofore covered by scales accumulated by long-standing training and habit'.[4] 'Wahrheiten' – truths, and this time in the plural – appears also in the title of Zinzendorf's Socrates: *Der Teutsche Socrates, Das ist Aufrichtige Anzeige verschiedener nicht so wohl unbekannter als vielmehr in Abfall gerathener Haupt-Wahrheiten.* Thomasius, in his *Vernunft-lehre* (1691), declared truth to be 'nothing else than the congruity of cognition with the object'; he also uses 'truths' in the plural, attaching to it the same meaning.[5]

Logos, the key word of the gospel of St. John, carries much religious and mystical connotation. In its adjectival form the word is also encountered in Arndt's *Wahres Christenthum,* one of the most influential works on Pietism. Edelmann wanted to offer more than did Löscher, the Dresden Orthodox authority, in his *Nachrichten,* although this magazine was to serve him as a valuable source, and Edelmann cheerfully shared the adjec-tive 'unschuldig' with him. Although the combination of innocence and truth stems from Arnold, Löscher's title surely played a role in Edelmann's choice. If 'truths' offers an inexhaustible complexity, 'innocence' is hardly simpler. That Löscher also borrowed his 'innocence' from Arnold is likely since scarcely anyone before him had used such combinations as 'innocence' with 'things' (Dingen)[6] or with 'truths'. In the Grimm dictionary, 'innocence' is defined as 'harmless, soft, not dangerous'.[7] We sense that the poetic sweet-ness of Arnold's phrase has been turned into challenge and irony – if not in Löscher's, then certainly in Edelmann's title.

Edelmann sent the first four parts of his *Unschuldige Wahrheiten* to the publisher without an accompanying letter and without mentioning his authorship – an act of faith, entrusting his creation to fate. The signature 'Der in Christi Einfalt Wahrheit sucht'[8] does suggest the author's name but was surely unrecognizable by anybody at that time. He chose Walther, the publisher of Zinzendorf's *Socrates* and distributor of Arndt's *Wahres Christenthum,* as a person known for his interests 'in pietistic and mystic literature'.[9] The details of the journey of the manuscript and Edelmann's joy on discovering the appearance of the first pieces will be described later. Upon finding himself in print he immediately sent a fifth installment and tells us that he started to write *Unschuldige Wahrheiten* before his visit to Herrnhut. The introduction to the first part is dated September 1734. Before he left Dresden on the day of the Peter Paul Messe, 1736,[10] ten parts were completed, and the next two followed within three months after his arrival at Berleburg. Thus within two years he had written the major portion of *Unschuldige Wahrheiten*, altogether 1366 printed pages. Three more installments were written over the next several years. Later Edelmann had an index printed to the first twelve parts, rightly feeling that they formed a single unit.

During the years 1734–1736 his acquaintance with Separatists grew and he expanded his readings and studies with great intensity. Yet, at the beginning of the sixth part, he could say that he had just discovered the writings of Johann Konrad Dippel and could hardly blame any of his readers who might accuse him of plagiarizing, so readily was he able to recognize the similarity between himself and the 'much hated' Dippel, known as Christianus Democritus.[11] Edelmann was the first to acknowledge that Dippel's writings, appearing under this pseudonym, greatly influenced him. The point here is that Edelmann's initial positions and attitudes, as expressed in the first twelve parts of *Unschuldige Wahrheiten*, did not alter greatly during this period. This part of the work represents the summary of his own religious conflict with Orthodox practice and dogma, through which he had to argue and fight his way. The fight took the form of a dialogue between the two *dramatis personae* of the *Unschuldige Wahrheiten*, Philalethus and Doxophilus. Out of the dialogue slowly emerge his own radical interpretations of rebirth and baptism.

The parts of the *Unschuldige Wahrheiten* written after 1736 (parts 13 to 15) present Edelmann's mature thoughts on the nature of God, the problem of evil, the role of man in God's creation. Written while he was engaged on his major works, *Moses* and the *Göttlichkeit der Vernunft*, they reflect the stages of his intellectual growth. Before going on to any analysis of the work it seems important to reflect on the nature of Edelmann's first work compared to that of his predecessors, Arnold and Betke. Their works, which provide the immediate starting-points for the first parts of the *Unschuldige Wahrheiten*, represent the third round of spiritualist writings.

The first can be briefly characterized by the Spiritualism of the Reformation period and its major representatives, Müntzer, Franck and Schwenckfeld; the second, on the threshold of the seventeenth century, by Valentin Weigel (1533–1588), Johann Arndt (1555–1621), and Jakob Böhme (1575–1625). Any definition applying to all Spiritualists is difficult, but each of these enriched the concept. And all have in common an attitude of protest against the church or against churches which consider themselves legally ordained institutions of salvation through word and sacrament, and which make the Bible the sole source and norm for the faith and life of the Christian. To the Spiritualists the Holy Spirit revealing itself to the individual constitutes the primary source of religious life and thought.

Professor George Williams established an important typology of Spiritualism in distinguishing between revolutionary, evangelical, and rational Spiritualists. At one point he summarizes:

For all of them spirit was central in their life and thought, as the driving spirit, as the enlightening spirit, or as the rational spirit. These Spiritualists, like Christians generally, knew that the spirits had to be tested, but they were always confident that the source of their particular authority was none other than the Holy Spirit. Moreover, they felt that the Holy Spirit as the inspiration of Holy Scripture, of the prophets of old, and of the present day, and also as the cohesive power of the Christian fellowship, was superior to any historic record of the work of the Holy Spirit, be it the Bible (or any part thereof, like the New Testament) or the church (or any institution thereof, like the clergy).[12]

He talks of the Spiritualism of the Reformation Period, but both, characteristics as well as typology, apply to its later expressions.

To Edelmann Spiritualism came through Spener, Betke and Arnold. If one applies Williams' typology to these sects, these late seventeenth-century Spiritualists are closest to Evangelical Spiritualism although they evince some of the characteristics of Rational Spiritualism. To narrow down the general definition of Spiritualism it is well to quote the points of distinction. Williams writes:

Rational or speculative Spiritualism, grounded more in the *spiritus* of man than in the *Spiritus Sanctus*, emphasizes the universal aspects of Christianity ... the true church of the Rational Spiritualists is a fellowship of kindred spirits in all ages who ... have come to hold that behind the changing nomenclature of theology is a common piety and a common vision of the divine.

Evangelical Spiritualism he defines as 'a recurrent phenomenon, nurtured Biblically by the Johannine Gospel and Epistles. It is based on grace as understood in the Bible. It is not primarily an intellectual movement; it stresses piety'.[13]

These generalizations are gleaned from the works of the Spiritualists. Yet each of them has developed his own particular complex of ideas, redefining Spiritualism in the context of the experience of his time. Betke's life and ministry endured the impact of the Thirty Years' War. Spener (1635–1705) was born towards the end of the war and Arnold was born almost twenty years after the conclusion of the Peace of Westphalia. The consequences of the war were not forgotten, the wounds not healed; desire for rejuvenation was even greater than during the turmoil and chaos. While Arndt and Böhme, the interim generation of Spiritualists, were allowed, in the solitude of mystic contemplation, to reinterpret macro- and microcosm, Betke and Arnold were challenged by the judgment that God had administered to an utterly corrupt Christianity. For Betke the shepherds of the flock, the clergy, are chiefly responsible for the betrayal of true Christianity. 'Christian armies – Christian war cannot be squared with the Gospel and rule of the cross and of patience, where love of one's enemy is the command of Jesus. The religious parties fight under the guise of religion. The fruits by which they shall be known demonstrate that the religion they defend cannot be the true one, and that the war is wrong.'[14] The poet Logau expresses the same feeling of doubt:

Luthrisch, Päbstisch und Calvinisch/diese Glauben alle drey Sind/ vorhanden; doch ist Zweiffel/wo das Christenthum dann sei.[15]

Betke's *Antichristentum*, from which Edelmann quotes again and again in the first parts of the *Unschuldige Wahrheiten*, was published in 1660. The decay and corruption have not ended with the Great War and Betke finds the mores of the clergy as discouraging as before. Against this reality he proclaims his spiritualist ideal of a Christian community. Karl Holl observes: 'The war had awakened a mood of repentance among the Protestant population. ... But already during the war the serious-minded started to doubt the sincerity of these feelings.'[16] Repentance and rebirth have moved into the center of both Betke's and Arnold's philosophy and piety.

These courageous critics of established religion and the renewers of the Spiritual tradition are the godparents of the *Unschuldige Wahrheiten*. From what has been briefly sketched here, it can also be seen how substantially the origins of Pietism are connected with Spiritualism and with the men who expounded it. For the present discussion the essential conclusion is that Edelmann, although acquainted with Pietism at least since his student days at Jena, formulates his first work under the direct impact of Arnold and Betke.

Before the articles of the official Orthodox creed can be re-examined, Edelmann must first create a climate of discussion in which this is possible. As his ultimate aim is to undermine the validity of traditional positions, he has to introduce the arguments that make such a discussion possible in the first place. The climate must be one of tolerance and therefore the desirability for tolerance must be established. The first two discourses ('Unterredungen') have exactly that purpose, and it is not accidental that they end in converting one partner of the dialogue to the acceptance of the criterion of religious tolerance. The two characters carry the appropriate names Philalethus and Doxophilus, the latter, in Edelmann's own translation, a lover of not-yet-reasoned-out opinions. The choice of dialogue is explained as being popular with the reading audience and providing the right opportunity to develop the arguments.[17] The form indeed fits the dialectic process of the truth-seeker. The search for truth postulates a climate of tolerance, and thus the initial subject matter is introduced. Tolerance is argued not in a general sense but as closely related to the religious issues with which Edelmann is concerned. His argument leads into the crucial parts of the religious discussion. These opening chapters of Edelmann's first book contain much of his basic religious philosophy, including, for instance, his thoughts on the nature of revelation and the evaluation of the Bible.

Spener's and Arnold's reinterpretation of freedom of conscience mark the beginning of that struggle for religious toleration to which Edelmann commits himself. He often takes up their arguments – some thirty-five years after the publication of Spener's *Theologische Bedenken* (1701) and of Arnold's *Kirchen- und Ketzer-Historie* (1699) – and it is interesting to note what new emphasis and outlook he creates. It is also well to keep in mind that these increasingly radical arguments did not lead to any changes in the attitude of the church authorities, although they affected some secular princes. When Edelmann continued the struggle, it was not against windmills but against powerful realities, and he was willing to pay the personal price.

In 1710 the first German edition of Locke's *Letter concerning Toleration*[18] was published, to which Edelmann refers in the third part of the *Unschuldige Wahrheiten*.[19] But Locke's aim is different from Edelmann's: it is to safeguard the realm of religious faith and practice from state interference. Edelmann's primary targets are the established Church groups who claim authority in religious matters over their servants and their flock. The tolerance he seeks is for the individual Christian and for minority Church groups in a world dominated by the Roman, the Lutheran, and the Reformed Churches, for the individual Christian in order that he may be allowed to express his own ideas on religious matters. In his preface to the dialogues between Philalethus and Doxophilus Edelmann introduces two thoughts: one to justify his discussion, the other to express the role of the truth-seeker in a personal way. Religious truth is not something that belongs to a past revelation: 'What our ancestors many thousand years ago held for truth we consider to be erroneous. Remember that God, according to wisdom, saves certain truths for certain ages, and that the apostles themselves could not bear all that Christ was to reveal.' The revelation of truth becomes thus a continuous process, a process of growing enlightenment. The vista to the great concept of Lessing's education of mankind has opened. Edelmann demands that we not accept a static concept of truth, but that we 'examine everything, not in the framework of deceiving, carried-over prejudices, but ... in the light of the spirit of truth'.[20]

As to his own intention as author, Edelmann states:

My observations are taken from the Word of God according to the measure of enlightenment I have been granted. They present themselves in their innocent nakedness because fig-leaves would only shame them; they are free because they are not slavishly subjected to any human opinion; but not immodest because they do not impose themselves on anyone else.[21]

This principle remained essential for him throughout all his works; and more than a decade later it was incorporated into his great confession of faith: *Abegnöthigtes jedoch andern nicht wieder aufgenöthigtes Glaubens-*

Bekentniss (1746). The quest for truth is, then, the issue. When Doxophilus, in effect, says bluntly to Philalethus: the very fact that you are supposedly seeking truth implies that you do not consider the teachings of our Christian churches absolute truths, the reply is: 'If I look around in that society that you call Christendom and observe the variety of opinions that each party claims as unchallengeable truths, then I have to ask not with irony but with sadness: What is truth? Where is truth?'[22] Edelmann realized that one could not raise this very question among Protestants without risking punishment. The position taken by Lutherans and the Reformed was that their creed and body of theology had become untouchable, as were the doctrines of the Roman Catholic Church when they became the targets of Luther's attacks.

Doxophilus is quick to hurl the accusation of Indifferentist (one who does not distinguish between the various Protestant churches) and atheist at his partner in the conversation. But the name-calling that supposedly liquidates, or at least morally disqualifies, the adversary does not impress Philalethus. Before starting the theological discussion of the truth of dogma, he wants first to establish an image of the true disciple of Christ. For this Edelmann chooses these passages from the Gospels: Matthew 10: 38; Luke 14: 27; John 8: 31; and John 13: 4,5. From the synoptic gospels he chooses the supporting passages, Matthew 10: 38 and Luke 14: 27, that cite the bearing of the cross as the prerequisite for becoming a disciple of Jesus. The passages from John contain the promise that to continue in the word of Jesus will bring the knowledge of truth, and that the truth will make man free. The second citation from John records that Jesus washed the feet of the disciples.[23] The simple image that Edelmann intends to convey is that of the true disciple actuated by willingness to serve Jesus courageously, humbly, and in the knowledge that Jesus' message is one that does not confine but that frees. The test of true discipleship must, then, be a confrontation with reality; the true image, the answer to the question: can any of those who profess to belong to one of the established Christian churches claim to be true disciples of Jesus? The obvious disparity between reality and image challenges the claim of the established churches to discipleship.

True discipleship does not, therefore, depend on belonging to any particular Christian church but on a willingness to be guided by the spirit of truth. The various Church sects are divided on minor and major matters, and in all of them truth or partial truth may be found – but not in one to the exclusion of the other. True discipleship is not dependent on belonging to any particular church. This is the shocking message that Philalethus delivers to Doxophilus. A reference to Jesus and his disciples' relation to the various groups among the Jews of their time is meant to clarify and to strengthen the position: 'He who lives within the Christian Church as Jesus did in the Jewish community, not bound to a particular party, and follows Christ wherever he finds him is no indifferentist, much less an atheist – but a true disciple of Jesus according to his own words.'[24]

Edelmann's image of the true discipleship shines through all the discussion as does his slowly emerging image of Jesus. To his idea of Jesus Edelmann later devoted a powerful work, *Glaubens-Bekentniss*, published in 1746, but here, in *Unschuldige Wahrheiten*, the traits that form this image already become visible. The Jesus who does not join any Jewish sect which claims superiority over another has an altogether different role to play: he is the humble Jesus who came to change man's heart.

When the bars between church groups are thus let down, all claims to a monopoly of salvation are removed. Once more Doxophilus injects the accusation of 'indifferentism' and tries to recoup at least part of his position by conceding that salvation may be possible for the Christian belonging to any of the three 'Major [Christian] religions'; but by explicitly excluding such Christian sects as Anabaptists, Quakers, Socinians, etc. – and naturally Jews, Turks, and heathen – he circumscribed his concept of salvation. And what seems a concession becomes instead a new point of departure for the full unfolding of Philalethus' ideas.

A God who leaves the larger part of mankind to damnation Philalethus brands 'a tyrant, a monster of cruelty compared with whom the most gruesome monsters, Nero and Diocletian, are gentle lambs'. But this cannot be the God of whom in Paul's First Letter to Timothy it is written that He 'desires all men to be saved and to come to the knowledge of truth'.[25] What dominates Edelmann's thinking is a concept of fairness that does not allow partisan exclusiveness. He refers to the passage in Acts telling of Cornelius, the Roman centurion, and to Peter's first words on seeing this heathen, who so visibly walked in the light of God, 'Truly I perceive that

God shows no partiality but in every nation any one who fears him and does what is right is acceptable to him'.[26]

Edelmann's concept of a just or fair God and his interpretation of this message leads him to the formulation that 'God can make men blessed in whatever exterior circumstances of religion they may find themselves'. The accident of birth is thus rejected, and a universal democratic and dynamic element on the religious level is introduced. Philalethus does not refute the claim of the three main religions directly, but offers instead other criteria on which churches might base their superiority. The purpose is rather to show the relativity and the questionable significance of their claims than to establish any absolutes. As to size, the Greek church, in which he counts the Abyssinian church, could at this time claim a larger membership than the Roman Catholics, Lutherans, and Reformed together. As to age, church history clearly gives the answer. As to the teaching of truth, one may possess more than another, none commands all truth. The only supreme religion can be the one that has Christ as its true head. We return to the image of discipleship with its visible witness, which Philalethus finds lacking in the main churches. In contrast he cites the Anabaptists and the Mennonites, whose ways of daily conduct bear far more evidence of true discipleship than do those of any other Christian group.[27] It is to these groups, persecuted by the three main religions, that Philalethus would look for the image of discipleship.

It follows then that Jews, Turks, and heathen cannot be excluded from salvation. At that moment when it is understood that God is love, the prejudices perpetuated through the ages will fall away and we will see afresh – with the eyes of the spirit ('den Augen des Gemüthes'), in Arnold's imaginative expression.[28]

Edelmann's argument rests on the statement that the person who fears God and acts justly can be found outside all organized religious groups. But the faith that leads a person to such conduct can come only from Christ. He cites two passages from John: 'I am the way, the truth, and the life: no man cometh unto the Father, but by me' (14: 6) and 'no one can come unto me, except it were given unto him of my Father' (6: 65). Edelmann wants to be understood correctly. He does not claim that any religion can make man blessed, but that God can make a man a Christian within any religion. By that he means that 'God can change man's heart and enlighten his mind to recognize the abuses of his party and to renounce them according to the measure of insight God grants him'.[29]

Doxophilus finds himself at this point utterly confused: on the one hand, the Johannite passages making salvation dependent on Christ; on the other hand, salvation granted to anyone in any religion who has turned to Christ. The obvious question is, how does knowledge of Christ come to any man? As Doxophilus puts it: 'whence do the heathen you praise as blessed receive the faith? You know that Paul emphatically says, "how shall they believe in him of whom they have not heard?" ... and ... "So then faith cometh by hearing, and hearing by the word of God." (Romans 10: 14, 17)'.[30] The question, bolstered by the quotation from Romans, is intended to embarrass Philalethus (Edelmann), but it inevitably gives the interlocutor the desired opportunity to present an answer or answers that open new horizons to the reader.

Edelmann will not restrict to any written or spoken word the mode through which we hear of Christ. We know of God through his creation – as stated by Psalm 19, 'the heavens declare the glory of God'. The creator is revealed in his creation. 'Those who believe in God also believe in Christ, as He and the Father are one. Though the heathen believe in God, when Christ the true light kindles their reason so that they can recognize the Creator through his creation, they are believing according to His own expression in Him, although they are not fortified with the story of Christ.' God's power surely surpasses the limits that Doxophilus' restricted mind tries to set for him. Creation as the visible witness to God's glory is over and above the written word of the Bible. This message, rooted in Edelmann's own experience of the beauty of nature as revealed by the poet Brockes, is no sentimental or romantic awareness of nature but a mighty proclamation that from its least to its greatest wonders creation is God's. But God reveals himself not only through the word made visible, but also through the inner voice. Edelmann, without elaborating on this aspect of God's presence, assumes these two sources of man's religious education. This leaves open the question of the function of the Bible: 'Why did God let his will be recorded in the Old as well as in the New Testament?' Edelmann offers an answer that appears to him obvious and simple, close to Paul's words (Romans 2, 12), 'that men do not suppress the word that has been, partly outwardly, partly inwardly, preached to them, nor do they reject it as sheer human imagination'.[31] He formulated two more direct arguments establishing the validity of the written word: that the fulfilling of written prophecies will convince us that God really spoke to men and revealed his secrets. Finally, the Bible encourages us to seek ever more avidly the pleasures of wisdom hidden in Christ. We shall not harbor the illusion that we have mastered all theology and that nothing new is to be discovered. Edelmann's reading of the Bible was inspired by a feeling of exploring hidden truth and proclaiming the good news of the gospel.

God's mercy and the gift of salvation are offered to all men regardless of the state of the individual since 'everyone who does right is born of Him'.[32] Who will deny that 'Aristides, Seneca, Socrates have done right in a much greater measure than many among us today who are proclaimed most blessed?' If God in His mercy has made heathen obey and understand his command and law, certainly He can make Turk, Jew, and, above all, any number of the various Christian sects do so.[33]

Doxophilus is ready to accept what he himself can now declare to be 'pure and simple truth':[34] that blessedness is God's universal gift – universal and, therefore, not restricted to any particular religion. Doxophilus' and the reader's mind have been opened to the acceptance of religious tolerance. That principle has now to be applied to Edelmann's religious environment, and the consequences are squarely faced. The argument has arrived where it was intended to lead us. What must follow, then, is a direct attack on those documents of the church that make its creeds and practices the condition for the individual's salvation. With irony Edelmann registers concern for the future of 'Libri Symbolici, Decreta Consiliorum and Responsa Facultatum' in a world that will not accept them as expressions of unfailing truth. Equally precarious will become the position of those whose livelihood depends on their acceptance of these documents as instruments of grace. Or, looking at the matter in another way, priests and ministers cannot have anything but a vested interest in retaining sacred documents as the expression of the sole religious truth. In fact, their whole behavior, particularly their persistence in persecuting those who fail to conform to their idea of religious truth, is evidence of their struggle for existence. In flagrant contrast to Christ's own practice 'to tolerate even the most absurd ideas, not to expel nor exclude anyone, much less to impose prison or other physical punishment', these servants of God are set to eradicate aberration in any form. As they are too weak to make the truth acceptable by their arguments, they find ways to induce the civil authorities to serve their ends. Denouncing as rebels and breakers of the peace those who want to propagate religious tolerance and live in harmony with their fellow men, they raise the cry that the 'Christian religion is in danger'.[35]

When the established churches proclaim their dogmas as truth and the truth professed by dissenters as wild aberration to be suppressed and persecuted, then is that not

the warped language the world always spoke? Did the world not always persecute the truth as error, and proclaim lies and falsity as truth? If you survey the entire history of the church, beginning with the story of Christ to our own time, you will find truth among the very few. Christ prophesied that the fate of those who followed him would be to bear the yoke of their powerful oppressors.

Once more Doxophilus interjects a warning that libertinage often thrives under the name of godliness, and that Christian authority has an obligation to curtail it. The firm answer is,

indeed, sometimes misguided rebels do play havoc with truth, but to deny tolerance because of abuses is to throw out the baby with the bath. Church authorities are quick to denounce and then act as both accuser and judge. They take on exactly the same role as did the heathen in persecuting the early Christian and are now themselves acting the Pharisees who induced the Roman authorities to crucify Christ.[36]

Edelmann's argument for tolerance is not merely theoretical, but a forceful attack on the realities of the ecclesiastical life he knew and was ready to confront. He tries to legitimize the concept of tolerance that he seeks, by both referring to the past and painting an image of the future. The critique of the present state is predicated on an ideal image of the past. Gottfried Arnold devoted a major work to the idealization of the primitive church.[37] Ernst Benz says succinctly: 'Decay and reformation are always linked to each other dialectically and historically. Reformation means restitution and fulfillment of the forms and relations that were instituted archetypically in the primitive church ['Urgemeinde'].'[38] Benz is referring to the idea of the twelfth-century reformation of Joachim of Fiore, but the statement is intended to describe all efforts and concepts of reformation within the Christian world. The pietistic reform endeavor is no exception.

Arnold excluded the apostolic age from the scrutinizing critique that he administered to post-apostolic Christianity. In the *Unschuldige Wahrheiten* Edelmann followed Arnold, treating the apostolic community as directly 'planted by God'.[39] The unity that it presented cannot be compared to any uniformity forced upon man by one particular church, for of the three major churches Edelmann believes that 'none follows Christ – either in teaching or in practice'.[40] The claims of each of these churches as sole instruments of salvation, therefore, have to be repudiated. It was Spener who argued that if the maxim 'no salvation outside the church' has any meaning, this could apply only to a spiritual concept of a Christian community, an invisible church, but not to any of the visible institutions.[41] Edelmann follows him in his interpretation of the visible and invisible church, an essential building-block in the rising concept of freedom of conscience.

While Spener claimed superiority for his Lutheran church and praised her 'great advantage over all false sects and religions, for which reason she alone can be called the only true visible church of Christ',[42] Edelmann makes no such allowance for the 'Roman, nor the Lutheran nor the Reformed church'. All he has to say concerning their merits is negative, even ironic: '... no church should blame another church for its shortcomings and parade as the true one ... rather each should strive to gain a greater place in the realm of truth'.[43] No preconceived body of dogmas, exegeses, and learning guarantees status, but only the struggle to make truth shine brighter.

In his argument for freedom of conscience and against the dogmatism of Orthodoxy, Edelmann uses as chief witness Martin Luther. Luther *versus* the Lutheran clergy is an effective device, and Edelmann was not the first to take advantage of it. His use of quotations from Luther, however, serves a double purpose. Not only do they express thoughts that are not to be reconciled with the practices of Lutheran clergymen, but they are intended to reveal the contradiction in Luther's own life: the early *versus* the later Luther, the fighter against papal authority, whose idea of tolerance stands in contrast to that of the Luther 'who controlled entire lands'.[44]

The passages Edelmann seeks out in Luther's work are chosen to suit his arguments. He is neither interested in understanding the passages in their historical connection, nor in interpreting them in their full context. Where he thinks there is an attitude similar to the one he is championing, he seizes upon it without much regard for the particular intent of its author. In this respect Edelmann is not different from many others who quoted or misquoted with a specific purpose in mind. He selects from Luther's *Kirchenpostille* (1522) passages that ostensibly transmit a generous and irenic spirit where human differences in religious thought and practices are concerned.

There are numerous quotations from the second Epistle at Advent where Luther discussed Paul's words from Romans: 'Now the God of patience and of consolation grant you to be like-minded one toward another according to Christ Jesus.'[45] Luther's first reflection on this passage is: 'How can the weak be of the same mind as the strong? To be of the same mind means that each should leave to the other his fancy and fancy what the other fancies.' Here Edelmann ends the first quotation and interprets:

From this follows, first, that nobody should impose upon anyone else his opinion, as we do in asking an oath to be taken on the Symbolic Books and, second, that those who dispute this malpractice, as do I and others of similar inclination, are not condemned, for they do not condemn those who err, but endure them as failing in good faith and admonish them with kindness.

He conveniently changed fancy to opinion and disregarded Luther's further comments on fancy as being actually one of the worst follies that Paul was anxious to eliminate. Nevertheless, Edelmann does not distort the spirit of the text in pointing out Luther's avowed attitude of tolerance and mutual forbearing. This attitude manifests itself even more strongly in the following passage relating to confession:

You are doing right and ought to do so, this one does wrong and should not do so. This is the devil's apostle and Satan's teaching; thus act the Popes and Papists, this is not worthy of a shepherd, thus wolves are preaching. From this the split in Christian unity must follow. From this arise the judgments: You are a heretic, you are disobedient to the Church, you are not doing right; this is what the devil wanted.

Edelmann intersperses his quotations from the Lutheran text with exclamations calling attention to the parallel between the 'papists and Luther's successors'.[46]

Yet the most powerful repudiation of all claims of Orthodox wisdom is to be found in the concluding paragraphs of the *Kirchenpostille*, and Edelmann declares that, were they printed today, 'the writer would surely be denounced as a Behmenist or a Quaker'.

> O! that it would be God's wish that mine and all teachers' commentaries might perish, and every Christian take to himself the Scriptures and the pure word of God. You can gather from this babble how God's Word cannot be fathomed, how no man can adequately reach and interpret one word of God's with all his own words. It is an infinite word and wants to be comprehended with a quiet spirit as expressed in the 83rd psalm: 'I will hear what God himself says in me.' None comprehends save only such a quiet, reflecting mind. He who arrives at that state without glossaries or exegeses, does not need mine or anyone else's glossaries, for they will only be obstructions. Therefore, dear Christians, go to it and let mine and all other commentaries be merely scaffolds for the real edifice, in order that we ourselves may grasp, taste and adhere to the pure word of God. Because God lives only there in Zion, Amen.[47]

Edelmann suggests that his passage had been suppressed and refers his reader to the edition of Luther's *Kirchenpostille* printed by Michael Lotter in 1525, where he found it, and also to the one edited by Spener.

The trend of Edelmann's thought is evident in the arguments he presents. It culminates in challenging the right and wisdom of Church authorities in demanding from their clergy an oath of allegiance to a body of theological documents designated as 'Symbolic Books'. The Symbolic Books (or *Book of Concord*), declared by the Lutheran church to be its canon next to the books of the Old and New Testaments, contained the three Catholic or ecumenical symbols – the Apostle's, the Nicene, and the Athanasian creeds – and the Lutheran Confessions. The Lutheran Confessions included Luther's large and small Catechism, the Augsburg Confession of 1531, Melanchthon's *Apologia* in the Augsburg Confession of 1530, Melanchthon's essay on the power and primacy of the Pope, and the Formula of Concord.

By 1580, after a long struggle among the territorial Lutheran churches, the Formula of Concord was finally accepted as the official doctrinal collection of the Lutheran church.

Everyone aspiring to church office has to attest to his acceptance of the Lutheran faith as defined in the Symbolic Books. Elevation of such a body of documents to rules and guides ('Regel und Richtschnur') was to Arnold and Edelmann irreconcilable with their newly emerging concept of freedom of conscience. Its purpose to define the 'pure and unfalsified will of God' is doomed to failure. Granting that the men who wrote and collected the documents did so with honest intention, they were nevertheless human, with human limitations, and bound to a particular historical situation. Their interpretations cannot restrict later generations with rigid barriers which they may not transgress. If they were intended to ensure unity, in this respect they have bitterly failed. By establishing such an 'Orthodox monopoly' of religious truth, all those not willing to conform are branded as 'heterodox, fanatic, pietist *etc*.' What it took Luther's reformation to achieve – freeing the Christian from papist tyranny over man's conscience – the Orthodox Lutheran clergy have reintroduced into their church. Unity among Christians must not be uniformity of thought and belief super-imposed by ecclesiastical authorities.

> Superintendents, Consistories, and Faculties. Whenever they are ready to adhere to Jesus' teachings and to imitate him in tolerating differing opinions then will they understand that God does not distribute the measure of his wisdom according to our narrow and limited opinions, which will be recognized for what they are – impotent crutches to be abandoned. The true church has existed without such crutches in the face of the greatest persecution and the worst heresies.[48]

The image of the primitive church thus becomes the model which the present-day church should imitate.

> 'What was then practiced in regard to Christian love, will hopefully continue to be practiced by those who are ready to follow in the footsteps of the first Christians. Therefore, no person should be condemned as heretic for not accepting certain formulas, or for that reason be expelled from city and country like one afflicted with the plague.'[49]

In a later passage in the *Unschuldige Wahrheiten*, Edelmann describes the hallmark of a servant of Christ. Although his concept of a servant transcends that of an officially appointed individual, the characterization is relevant here:

> ... he who, from fear of starving with his family, conceals the truth, in order not to be deposed from office by his party, has not yet started to deny himself. However, he who does not deny himself and who yet spurns the cross of Christ, which is to be persecuted by the world, cannot call himself a follower of Christ. How can he, who is himself not ready to be His disciple, lead others to become His disciples? How can he claim that Jesus sent him?[50]

Arnold and Edelmann examine the motives of the young theologian who is forced to take the oath on the Bible as well as on the Symbolic Books. Edelmann argues that the oath as qualification for appointment to church office puts the candidate in an agonizing quandary if he has gained greater insight than that expressed in these documents. 'If he does express his real thoughts, he will be squelched or denounced as a heretic. Often worldly considerations enter. After a long study of theology and some success as a preacher while still a student, it is understandable that the young man aspires to a church position.' Rationalization helps to soothe the conscience: 'Others, God-fearing scholars, have taken the oath on the Symbolic Books before, and soon the little free will left is swept away by the power of self-love, self-esteem, and self-interest.'[51]

Arnold exposed the trap the Orthodox clergy had laid for the aspiring theologian by taking advantage of his weakness, and by trying to seduce him with the hope of advantages or to subdue him by the tacit threat of persecution.[52] Edelmann proudly claims to have avoided this trap and he now envisions a new path. He portrays his own struggle, which he believed he had won by refusing to forgo his freedom and to subject himself to the 'human yoke'.[53] At the same time there begins to emerge the image of the independent intellectual whom Edelmann represents and whose struggle with authority becomes the story of his life. Thus we have now reached the point where Doxophilus and the reader are persuaded through reason to reject the church-imposed rules and guidelines and to accept a new concept of freedom.

In his last attempt to defend the oath on the Symbolic Books, Doxophilus points out that nobody is forced to become a theologian and, further, that 'Christ also forces man to be a Christian'.[54] With this the discussion of the theological issues opens. His assertion is refuted immediately: the decision to become a minister of the church is a professional one and if the oath on the Symbolic Books, as required of the young and naive student of theology, leads him into a dilemma of conscience, the ludicrousness of the practice by the Orthodox Church is thereby exposed.

Becoming a Christian – the conversion, as Edelmann calls it – is an existential decision. Arthur Darby Nock's description of dynamic conversion is classic:

> the individual stands before a choice which means either the renunciation of his past and entry into a kingdom, which if the promises made for it are true – and that cannot be proved or disproved – is wholly other here and will be wholly other hereafter, or the refusal of this dream as chimerical. He cannot wed twice nor twice lose his soul.[55]

This is what is meant by conversion as an existential decision: the complete change and the irreversibility of the change. Both elements constitute Edelmann's understanding of what it means to be a Christian. He writes:

> In the process of conversion, of the true kind, man does not retain his free will but renders his will to his Savior from whom he receives a new will. This new will does not, like the old will, desire at times what is good and at other times what is evil, but only what his Savior wishes. Surely this new will appeared previously as a tyrant, but now, free from the dominion of evil, as he has become a servant of God he enjoys his new state. It being no longer a matter of not being allowed to be evil, but rather not wanting to be evil, he is no longer dictated to by law.[56]

That this is the work of God is emphasized by Edelmann's reference to Philippians 2: 13 'For it is God which worketh in you both to will and to do of his good pleasure.' This power of God to work change in us he then links to a conversion from an orthodox position to an enlightened one.[57] Hardly another passage can be found which is more revealing of Edelmann's state of mind. The most serious aspect of Lutheran theology, God's power, together with the dearest concept of Pietism, the act of conversion, are here marshaled to serve the new philosophy of Enlightenment. It is the peculiar situation of the theological dissenter in the early Enlightenment that in his concern for freeing Christian ideals and concepts, he is preparing the ground for new secular categories of moral and historical thinking.

Edelmann has focused this theological discussion on his interpretation of the reborn man. His dialectic mind seized on the saying in the First Epistle of John (3: 9), 'Whosoever is born of God doth not commit sin; for his seed remaineth in him: and he cannot sin, because he is born of God.' These words provided the point from which Edelmann felt he could destroy the orthodox position on the very concept of rebirth and the one closely linked to it, child baptism.

Ernesto Buonaiuti has well described the central importance of 'rebirth':

The predominant idea in New Testament literature that ... permeates all preserved utterances from the earliest beginnings of the Christian community is that of rejuvenation and metamorphosis. This idea characterizes and guides the conversion to the Gospel. ... To adhere to Christ really means to have been recreated, reborn, changed.[58]

Taking into account the truth of this broad statement, we must look closely at the concept of rebirth as it appears in post-reformation Orthodoxy and in Spiritualist writing.

Both Luther and Calvin, in their commentaries on the passage in the First Epistle of John, speak of 'regeneration' as an essential presupposition of faith.[59] This is not the place to attempt a clear-cut definition of Calvin's or Luther's concept, because it is not their definitions that are the target of Edelmann's attack, but the definition found in the *Book of Concord* and in the works of orthodox Lutheran interpreters – particularly in Marperger's *Neue gründliche und erbauliche Auslegung Der Ersten Epistel Johannis* (Nürnberg, 1710).

The 'regeneration' and the 'reborn', however, started to take on special and new significance in the writings of the Spiritualists Böhme, Spener, Arnold, and Dippel, with many of which Edelmann was familiar. But as we have no specific reference from him to a specific work it is not possible to determine who particularly shaped his concept of rebirth.

Jakob Böhme, in a small tract, *De Regeneratione*, written in 1622 and published in 1730, stresses as major conditions for the truly reborn imitation of Christ fellowship demonstrated by deed and not just words, and the spirit of harmony and love counterposed to partisanship and heresy-making. At the very beginning of his treatise Böhme analyzes Paul's understanding of the reborn in Christ 'as he who is free of whatever is damnable, and the scriptures' verdict 'that there is no man that is not a sinner'.

Böhme seeks the solution in his concept of the new man 'who has a new will and sense of obedience ... resurrected from death, who no longer seeks sin'.[60] The image of perfection is planted, a process starting with repentance and leading to regeneration. The basic elements of Edelmann's later interpretation of the reborn man can be found here, precise in language and rich in thought. While this closeness of the positions of the two on rebirth will become evident from key passages in the *Unschuldige Wahrheiten*, we should nevertheless not be deceived regarding the spiritual and temporal differences that separate Edelmann and Böhme.

Edelmann was at this time strongly attracted by the Gichtelianer (Latter-day followers of Böhme), although the mysticism that shaped much of their existence was alien to his nature. The power he was soon to discover to be guiding his life was reason and not faith, but at the time when he was writing the *Unschuldige Wahrheiten* he was not yet aware of this fact. The faith which imparted to the writings of the reformers and the spiritualists their religious depth is lacking in Edelmann. It is well for us to note this difference in order to avoid a modern confusion from a qualitative judgment. As he categorically and painstakingly sets forth his convictions on the great religious issues of repentance, regeneration, and justification, his tone is non-mystical, hardly pious. He is building his own bridge – a bridge leading to quite another shore. While Böhme's treatise almost suffices to provide the essential definitions for the concept of regeneration, the later pietistic struggle against the Orthodox position provides the background for Edelmann's argument. The trend in later Orthodoxy was an increasing emphasis on the sacraments and with it an expansion of the powers of the ministry.[61]

The Formula of Concord expressed the Orthodox position as 'the great difference between baptized and unbaptized persons', concluding from the passage in Gal. 3: 27 'that all baptized persons have put on Christ and thus are truly reborn'. The Apology, a part of the Symbolic Books, adds that 'baptism is not only necessary for children but also efficacious for salvation'.[62]

Thus Orthodoxy's faith and hope become one that expresses itself in '*notitia, assensus* and *fiducia*. Comprehension and acceptance of the articles of faith assure the Christian his salvation. The efficacy of faith as realized in a God-obedient life' is neglected. The concept of justification is, of course, central to Luther's theology; in the interpretation of the Orthodox theology it becomes, consciously or unconsciously, a tool for the aggrandizement of clerical power. Hirsch has given probably as clear and concise a definition of Luther's idea of justification as can possibly be arrived at: 'The heart of justification is that through a faith in which we embrace Christ we become just solely by the grace and merit of Christ.'[63]

The need to keep the understanding of this principle pure and the fear that salvation might be thought to be related to the merits of the individual led to the concept of satisfaction through the merits of Christ.[64] If the faith is to be defined in formalistic terms, then Luther's 'faith, a quick, active, powerful thing', becomes, in his own words, 'a sleepy idle thing in the soul'.[65] At the same time, Orthodoxy fervently guarded against any semblance of the Catholic idea of salvation by good works. Paradoxically, this led to a new connection between church and sacrament 'that gave to the ministry a position which, with certain limitations, runs parallel to the position of the clergy in the Latin and in the Greek church'.[66]

'Rebirth', then, is the cardinal new message with which Edelmann sought to shake the Orthodox edifice to its very foundations. The image of the reborn 'as he who cannot sin any more' sets an ideal goal; the absolution by which the clergy redundantly offers dispensation to the ever-failing and ever-repenting sinner, declaring him each time to be reborn, becomes a travesty. What is worse: the very ideal, having been declared by the clergy as unattainable, has been redefined according to their own debased standards. They have completely robbed rebirth of its meaning in their attempt to equate it to infant baptism. Clerical power in performing baptism and in offering dispensation of forgiveness through penance in the confessional has undercut the Christ-directed concept of rebirth; conversely, that concept reduces to naught the claims of the clergy.

Edelmann's concept quite consciously 'reverses utterly the Orthodox Lutheran system' acceptable to the sixteenth and seventeenth centuries, according to which regeneration held a fixed second place, preceded by vocation and followed by *conversio, fides, justificatio,* and, finally, *sanctificatio.*[67] The essential elements in the making of the reborn are by definition 'conversion, sanctification, [and] justification'. Hence it is logical to put them 'all before rebirth', which bears a special relation to faith, as Edelmann sees it: 'Where there is no faith, there cannot be rebirth, just as a woman cannot give birth, if no child has been conceived,' and shortly after, 'rebirth has been a creation of faith through the visible and audible word of God'.[68] With faith as the pre-condition, rebirth is a different state indeed from whatever might ensue from some routine action such as child baptism.

For an understanding of Edelmann's argument, the distinction between 'rebirth' and the 'reborn man' is significant: rebirth is a process, 'the quickening of the spirit that dwells in us'. Closely following Paul's text in the letter to the Romans (Romans 8: 10 and 13), Edelmann concludes: 'Paul talks of the life-giving event as of a thing of the future grounded on the real dwelling of the spirit in man. Rebirth, therefore, cannot be achieved before the mortal body has been made alive – in other words, not before the new man has been created.' This 'Rebirth' means perfection, however, and Edelmann reminds us that even Paul himself did not claim to such attainment; rather, he wrote: 'Brethren, I count not myself to have apprehended: but this one thing I do, forgetting those things which are behind, and reaching forth unto those things which are before. I press toward the mark for the prize of the high calling of God in Christ Jesus' (Philippians 3: 13, 14).[70]

'The inability of the reborn to sin', writes Edelmann, 'reveals to those who think themselves reborn but are nevertheless capable of sin, that they are not presently those they should be. At the same time, it says to them that they can still become what they should be, if they are willing to create their blessedness with fear and trembling.'[71] Although there is an echo of Pauline language at the end of this statement, the road to self-created blessedness cannot be found on the map of Lutheranism. As laid out by Edelmann, this road is true imitation of Christ. "Christ has given his life for the sin of man, like a physician his medicine, but not in order that the patient hold a silly belief that the health of the physician is 'transferred' to him, the patient. The truth is that the prescribed medicine has to be taken in order to effect the complete recovery from the sickness."[72]

Jakob Böhme, in the treatise on rebirth already quoted, lifted from the process of rebirth the moment that appeared to him most decisive and offered the following formulation: 'In the will the trend of the Father to Christ is to be found, but in deeds the right life is to be found ... How does it help the soul, that it knows the way to God, but does not want to walk it?'[73] If life is led in love, that is, in Christ, it will be recognizable "by its holy and blameless conduct ... therefore said Jesus 'Ye shall know them by their fruits'." The guiding image for holy and blameless conduct is Christ's ministry and the life of the apostolic community. Edelmann gives a full picture of what to him was the essential ethos of the early church:

> There could be found among the early Christians an immense zeal to accomplish cheerfully the will of God. As they knew that God himself was love, and Jesus had declared the unfailing sign of his discipleship to be their love for each other, each brother esteemed the other higher than himself, regardless of how much more or less knowledgeable one might be than another. Thus a unity of spirit obtained, although the verbal expressions of the brethren differed.
>
> There was neither excess in the taking of food or drink, neither gambling nor dancing, nor other so-called amusements and revelries. In the first place, they considered their time to be much too precious to lose any part of it, thus forgoing joyful intercourse with God ['Vergnügenden Umgang mit Gott': the language recalls a poem by Brockes]. Secondly, they esteemed the high nobility of their souls and judged as unworthy the frivolous distractions with which the world's poor children entertained themselves.

Love and simplicity are the fundamental characteristics of a life led in the imitation of Christ and he who strives to achieve it will become increasingly 'aware of life and blessedness'.[74]

If the ascetic image of imitation of Christ appears simplistic, it is well to remember that this faith is 'unto the Jews a stumblingblock, and unto the Greeks foolishness' (I Corinthians 1 : 23). The major conflict that besets the seeker on the road to rebirth Edelmann sees in the traditional and Pauline struggle with natural man: therefore, as Paul says, 'the body is dead because of sin, but the spirit is life because of righteousness. ... The spirit is called life, because he conquers death through the righteousness of Christ, who quickens and gives the strength to do so.'[75]

Edelmann's concept of man is dualistic in a Pauline sense. This creature, however sinful, can climb a steep road, abandoning the confining edifice of Orthodox Lutheran dogma. He is self-perfectible and, through Christian purification and religious philosophical education, can attain enlighten-

ment and freedom.[76] The Faustian theme, *Wer immer strebend sich bemüht,
Den können wir erlösen,* is already intoned – 'neither enlightenment nor
any other of the moments constituting rebirth takes place at once, but God
grants time to the soul to comprehend one truth after the other' – to which
Edelmann adds: 'The truth of what is said here I have experienced myself.'[77]
The God who with such caring love lets the individual grow is the same
God as Goethe's who, like the gardener, knows '... wenn das Bäumchen
grünt, Dass Blüt' und Frucht die künft'gen Jahre zieren'.[78]

5. Berleburg Years
1736–1740

With the publication of the first four parts of the *Unschuldige Wahrheiten*, Edelmann had brought himself to the attention of those eager to hear voices of dissent and criticism of the Orthodox establishment. Common interests and personal contacts linked those who had separated from the Church spiritually or formally. Certain regions and towns, in which a policy of tolerance was fostered by the masters of the domain, had since the beginning of the eighteenth century become centers around which separatists of the most varied kind gathered. Among the separatists at Frankfurt, Andreas Gross, a man of means, played an important part, both as generous host and as astute promoter of separatist literature.[1] Gross, who was obviously impressed by Edelmann's first literary performance, approached him with the proposal that he join Johann Friedrich Haug (1680–1753) at Berleburg, where a new translation of the Bible was under way.[2]

No offer could have been more welcome to Edelmann, who immediately saw himself reaping the first fruits of his bold venture as an author. And he was in dire need of new employment, since he had made up his mind that he would not under any condition accept another position as tutor. Edelmann was to start work immediately on the Bible project at Berleburg. This, like the journey to the Kornfeils' in Würmla, proved to be an exciting overture to a new phase of his life: during this period he was to produce some of his most significant writings, the remaining parts of *Unschuldige Wahrheiten* and, most important, *Moses mit Aufgedeckten Angesichte*. Edelmann left Dresden in the late spring of 1736. He made a short stop in Chemnitz with his older brother, and visited his other brother in Gotha. While there he paid a call on his relatives, the Krügelsteins, surely with the intention of seeing their eldest daughter to whom he had been greatly attracted on an earlier visit. Now, at twenty-eight, she did not charm him as she had ten years earlier:

7*

Alas I do not know if my aspiration to 'saintliness' made me insensitive to her sex, or if we both had become wiser and recognized our youthful flirtations for what they were, or if her fiancé, who seemed to me to incarnate 'magister stockfinster', made me disgusted with her; whatever the reason I was not drawn to her.

Edelmann adds, be it the truth or male ego, 'she, however, would have been glad to exchange 'Stockfinster' [whose real name was Mahn], to whom she had promised herself in order to gain assistance for her widowed mother, for me, had I given her any encouragement'.[3]

After four days in Gotha, Edelmann continued on to Frankfurt. He has left us in his autobiography a delightful description of these days: the busy scene of the entrepreneurial and humanitarian Gross household, a boat-ride by candlelight on the Main, bathing in the nude, the first encounter with a large Jewish population, and convivial conversations. Edelmann breathed the air of a free and independent patrician town-life. After a two-day journey by coach he reached his destination, Berleburg.

The rich and diversified religious life that emerged at the turn of the century in Sayn-Wittgenstein and Wetterau, with local centers at Büdingen, Wied, Berleburg, and Schwarzenau, lifted these areas out of the regular stream of events. A unique combination of social, political, and religious forces favored the influx into these regions of men and women of varied religious inclinations – Huguenots, Separatists, enthusiasts, and members of Zinzendorf's community of brethren.

Edelmann vividly testifies to his first impression of this situation at Berleburg: 'I am dreaming so to speak while awake. Here where the conscience is not under any particular religious compulsion there is full freedom to live according to one's own understanding of God.'[4] Indeed, the unique situation called for a high degree of religious toleration, which the seigniorial authorities were apparently willing to secure and support. This remarkable phenomenon belongs to the first four decades of the eighteenth century and antedates the familiar practices in Brandenburg-Preussen. Indeed the policy of Frederick II would hardly compare favorably with that of these courts of an earlier period, where the princes themselves were religiously involved and supported tolerance not because of mere political consideration or abstract philosophical reasoning.

Edelmann arrived on the scene shortly before this fruitful era of tolerance was to fade away after the death of Count Casimir Sayn-Wittgenstein-Berleburg (1687–1741). The great period of tolerance had been ushered in with the reign of Hedwig-Sophie (1669–1738); when her husband died in 1694, she took over the affairs of the principality until her oldest son Casimir came of age in 1712. The Countess Hedwig-Sophie was fully imbued with the spirit of Pietism as expressed by Spener and his disciple, Francke. Equally important in the formation of the religious attitudes of the Countess was her encounter in late 1699 with the mystic and ecstatic expressions of faith enunciated by Heinrich Horche (1652–1729), Hochmann von Hochenau (1670–1721), and Johann Heinrich Reitz (1655–1720).[5] 'Radical pietism' is the term that Emanuel Hirsch coined for their form of religious seeking, in contrast to the Pietism of Spener and Francke, which strove for inner restitution, rebirth and true Christian fellowship in word and action within the framework of the established churches. The radicals felt that the 'free miraculous work of the Holy Spirit could not be subjected to the rule, or the teaching, or the official power of an ordained church'.[6] Radical spiritualists they were, fully aware of and emphatically acknowledging their debt to Jakob Böhme, and to his English disciples the Behmenists, John Pordage (1607–1681) and Jane Leade (1624–1704). The model for the many later efforts to form 'Philadelphic communities' in the Wittgenstein areas is certainly to be found in the Philadelphian Society founded in London in 1694 by Jane Leade and Francis Lee.[7] It was this model that exercised a magnetic attraction among the religiously awakened in Wittgenstein, rather than Spener's 'collegium pietatis' – 'Ecclesiola in Ecclesia' – a gathering of believers for pious exercises in addition to the regular church services.[8]

Over the years, groups of different social composition called themselves 'Philadelphic communities', although it would be difficult to define a common organizational or theological framework. Like the rulers of Sayn-Wittgenstein-Berleburg, Heinrich Albert readily displayed his sympathy for the religious awakening and did not shy away from involvement in the religious life of his region in and around Sayn-Wittgenstein-Hohenstein.

If a rough division may be made between a first and second phase of religious life in Wittgenstein in the first four decades of the eighteenth century, it can perhaps best be done by association with the names of their major religious leaders, however disparate their qualities: for the first phase, Eva von Buttler and Hochmann von Hochenau; for the second, Carl Hektor von Marsay, Johann Friedrich Haug, and Dr. Johann Samuel Carl.

Such schematization implies neither chronological nor geographic lines of demarcation. For years Edelmann wandered on most Sundays from Berleburg to Schwarzenau to join in worship with the 'inspired ones'. A newer generation, however, was moved by new theological problems as well as by pious concerns. If the names of Böhme and Pordage shone as bright stars over the work and worship of an earlier generation, they were now overshadowed by those of Antoinette Bourignon and Madame Guyon. The fervor, even the orgiastic excesses among Eva von Buttler's clan – all meant to bring about a real transformation into a Philadelphic community, prophesied in Revelation 3: 7–13 – gave way to calmer gatherings and to long-range translation and publishing projects. If the year 1712 can be taken as the approximate year of separation, one might also put it this way. The center of gravity shifted slowly from the cabin to the castle, from Hochmann's Thoreau-like home 'Friedensburg' at Schwarzenau to Count Casimir's luxurious residence at Berleburg. The fervent desire of Philadelphic communion regardless of worldly estate had united four Berleburg countesses, all sisters of Heinrich Albert, with commoners.[9] Yet democratization had to yield to ceremonial and status-conscious court life. Casimir was brother to his brethren and sisters in their religious endeavors, but in his small land of some five thousand inhabitants he was ruler. There was no question that he was conscious of his aristocratic rank, not unlike his friend, the imperial Count Nikolaus Ludwig von Zinzendorf. A trend away from radicalism, with its implicit social consequences, and toward accepted modes of more quietistic religious behavior, was evident in both parts of Wittgenstein. Here a large number of separatists – men and women of very different religious and philosophical convictions, such as Dippel, von Marsay (1688–1753) and Dr. Carl (1676–1757) – had found a haven. Edelmann's happy satisfaction that such religious toleration existed anywhere in Germany was fully justified.

In tune with the fermenting religious life were the manifold translating and publishing ventures, the most ambitious of which was the publication of a new translation and edition of the Bible in eight folio volumes, the first to appear in 1728 and the last in 1742. The chief editor of this Bible, which became known as the Berleburger Bible, was Johann Friedrich Haug, who had been forced on February 21, 1705 to leave his native Strassburg, after the Protestant clergy succeeded in persuading the Catholic authorities to expel him. With two other ministers he was accused of entertaining conventicles in the Pietistic style, in spite of frequent warnings and admonitions.[10]

Haug, like so many of his kind, was welcomed at Berleburg and won the trust and affection of Count Casimir.[11] The Berleburger Bible represents an attempt both to retranslate the Old and the New Testament and some of the Apocryphal writings, and to provide the reader with a more appealing text as well as commentaries that would help him to a truly spiritual understanding. Thus, in the introduction, dated January 19, 1726, to the first volume the threefold task is stated: 'To render the original text literally and as simply as it was written: ... To show the way to the literal understanding of the text. In clarifying difficult passages this will be achieved by referring to other parallel illuminating passages in the Scriptures.' It is also the intent of the Holy Spirit that:

All scripture is given by inspiration of God, and is profitable for doctrine, for reproof, for correction, for instruction in righteousness: That the man of God may be perfect, thoroughly furnished unto all good works. (II Timothy 3, 16–17.) This moral and pedagogical function of the Bible will be made clear to the reader for the sake of his own spiritual improvement. The dawning of the truth that God's Spirit has already brought about in so many God-fearing souls yearning after His light, ought to take place in others, in order that they may see the door that our Philadelphic Community has opened ...

Thirdly it is to be asked of God, that we perceive and recognize the secret and spiritual meaning of the Holy Scripture, that is so to speak the spirit and life of the scripture, of which also Christ is speaking. Search the scriptures; for in them ye think ye have eternal life: and they are they which testify of me. And ye will not come to me, that ye might have life (John 5: 39–40). This life is also the spirit of the Scripture and cannot be found in our spirit, unless this our spirit is of the community of Christ.[12]

The emblematic frontispiece that first meets the eye demonstrates what is expressed in words: the grand baroque portico, to which lead seven steps, the wide open door which reveals in full view the great and high wall with the twelve gates, the twelve angels at the gate, and in the center the lamb – all as described in the 21st chapter of the Book of Revelation.

Over the doorway we read 'The Philadelphic Community' and on a banderol is inscribed the 8th verse of the 3rd chapter of Revelation: 'I have set before thee an open door, and no man can shut it: for thou hast a little strength, and hast kept my word, and hast not denied my name.' Each detail – be it pillar or palm tree, an angel holding the ten commandments and another the cross, the seven steps – has its symbolic meaning, pictorially representing passages from Psalms, Revelations, and other books of Old and New Testament.

A very small group was actually engaged in the glorious enterprise of translating the Bible; they felt themselves a 'Philadelphic community' and the manifold users of this term have already been pointed out. The chief editor was Haug, and as collaborators over the years we know only of Johann Adam Scheffer (1684-1759), princely tutor, then preacher and councillor of the Consistory at Berleburg, and Christoph Seebach (1675-1745), whose erudition and knowledge of Hebrew as well as his Socinian leanings have been noted. This might explain the fact that, according to Winckel, Haug had no more contact with Seebach after 1730. Tobias Eisler (1683-1753), who arrived at Berleburg in 1731 after having been expelled from his native Nürnberg on account of his enthusiasm, has recently been identified as another collaborator, serving until 1735 when he left for Helmstadt.[13]

An important share in the enterprise belongs to Count Casimir, whose translations of the Bible commentaries of Madame Guyon were much used in exegesis. That the work proceeded slowly is no wonder, and after the departure of Seebach and Eisler no major assistant appeared till Edelmann was recruited by Gross. Certainly assistance should not be taken in a narrow sense. The spiritually interested, the Philadelphic community at Berleburg, included more than the co-editors named. Both Haug and Count Casimir were in intimate contact with the small circle that had gathered around Carl Hektor von Marsay, son of a Huguenot family that had fled from Paris to Geneva after the father's death.

Marsay was brought up by his pious mother and by the Castell family as foster parents. As a youth he had been drawn to the writings of Thomas à Kempis. Later, while in military service he and two companions read the works of Antoinette Bourignon, which convinced them that their way of life was inconsistent with what they pretended to believe. In search of a new and ascetic way of life, they set out for Schwarzenau in the spring of 1707. On arrival, they were welcomed by Marsay's foster-mother, who was recently widowed, and by his foster-brother. The young Castell, who had been married to one of the four Wittgenstein princesses, had become a Pietist. It was in this land, where like-minded people had already found an asylum where they might pursue a life of religious dedication according to their own inclinations, that the three young men decided to settle.

The life of Marsay and his wife, Clara Elizabeth von Callenberg, once a member of Eva von Buttler's group, became one of an exemplary struggle for purity and devotion, yet filled with good works. During a sojourn in Yverdon in Switzerland in 1716, Marsay made the acquaintance of devotees of Antoinette Bourignon and of Madame Guyon. The impact of Madame Guyon's writings on him was so strong that he even undertook to travel to Blois in the hope of seeing her, even though he knew she was gravely ill. He did not find her alive, but in Paris made the acquaintance of a group who had been close to her and considered themselves her followers. All his later life Marsay was to devote himself to the translating and study of her works.[14]

Shortly after Edelmann arrived at Berleburg, Haug's wife Julianne Charlotte took him to visit the Marsay household:

[There was a group] of followers of Madame Guyon and Mademoiselle Bourignon. Among these the most distinguished was Herr von Marsay. This little group lived at the 'Haynchen', a castle that belonged to Herr von Fleischbein, located ... two miles from Berleburg. ... I found here a different kind of saint, though they too were separatists: Yet they were so enamored of the Bourignon and Guyon writings that they venerated them above the Bible. Marsay, who seemed to be blessed by the spirit of both, and all of whose writings were nourished from these two sources, was the idol of the small household. Old Herr von Fleischbein, his handmaids, his son and his daughter, with son-in-law Herr Prüschneck adored Marsay as almost superhuman and submitted blindly to his spiritual practices. These quietly led men to recover from the distraction of senses and affections ... in order to become aware of

the voice of God within them. Had this been done freely and spontane-
ously, such exercises could have only been helpful. But as the poor
people came at an appointed time each day to sit together in Marsay's
study for an hour in silence, sometimes rolling their eyes to keep themselves from falling asleep, sometimes uttering sighs, and sometimes confessing in unspoken prayer what all poor sinners do with loud voices:
that they are poor corrupt and worthless Creatures; nothing could
result from such spiritual exercise except that they remained poor
people, yet thought how wonderfully far advanced they were beyond
others.[15]

The mood and behavior at the Fleischbein household twenty years later,
as described by Moritz at the beginning of his psychological novel *Anton
Reiser*, seems exactly the same as that recorded by Edelmann. Though
Edelmann's motives in describing the pietistic microcosm were muddled, he
recognized the sterile and oppressive aspects of Pietism with an insight that
matches that of Moritz, the innovator of the psychological novel and of
empirical observations of emotional processes.[16]

In R. A. Knox's study of 'Enthusiasm', there is a damning verdict on
Madame Guyon as an authoress, and particularly on her commentaries on
the Bible, which should be noted: 'If ... we may venture to criticize her books,
what is the impression they make on the reader? An impression, I think, of
extraordinary glibness; of much unconscious imitativeness (she never quotes,
she never refers to other authors); of eccentricity rather than originality;
of very mediocre taste.'[17] Even if one agrees with Knox, the phenomenon
of the Guyon cult remains.

Marsay, Count Casimir, and Haug – they all belonged to the fellowship.
The authors of the commentaries on the Berleburg Bible texts, like Madame
Guyon herself, did not choose to give references. The translator did not
identify extensive quotations lifted from Madame Guyon's commentaries.
Like the works of Böhme, Arnold, Gells and others, they were considered a
rich spiritual reservoir from which the editors could freely draw to provide
what the reader thirsted after. Jung-Stilling, the *protegé* of Goethe and
Herder, wrote of the Berleburger Bible in his novel *Schlüssel zum Heimweh:*
'Men of different stamp gathered in Berleburg, and there originated the well-
known mystical Bible that henceforward worked like a ferment, quietly and
without much ado.'[18]

The Bible was not the only cooperative undertaking that emerged in the thirties from the religious circles at Wittgenstein. This group also spawned works by such individual authors like Marsay, Seebach, and Dippel.

The first volume of a German translation of Pierre Poiret's major work, *L'Oeconomie Divine*, appeared at Berleburg in 1735. This was a rendition of volume six of the original French edition, first published in seven volumes at Amsterdam in 1687. The plan for the edition probably emerged among Madame Guyon's admirers in the circle of Haug and Marsay. Poiret (1646–1719), who had edited her works, was considered the major promoter of her writings and had lived for many years close to the equally venerated Antoinette Bourignon.[19] Before he turned to mysticism, Poiret had been a fervent adherent of Descartes. He brought to his new religious explorations a thorough philosophical training that gave his writings their particular character. Haug seems to have assigned the translation of the first part to Edelmann soon after his arrival, since the 592-page tome was printed only a year later. The translator of the previous volume, whoever he was, had called himself an 'impartial lover of truth';[20] Edelmann hid his identity behind the self-description he had used in his *Unschuldige Wahrheiten:* 'von einem der in Christlicher Einfalt Wahrheit sucht' (one who seeks truth in Christian simplicity). Hardly any familiarity with a text can be more intimate than that of the translator. The combination of rationalistic analysis with a religion of the heart – *La théologie du cœur* was one of the treatises Poiret edited – might well have appealed to Edelmann. He translated, if not literally, then with understanding and a liveliness perhaps even more characteristic of his own style than of Poiret's. Poiret's most fundamental turn was from the Cartesian trust in reason towards feeling, whereby he anticipated Rousseau by several decades. A comparison of the critical passage in the French and in the Edelmann translation surely brings out full its import:

Cela est-il certain? Ne puis-je m'y tromper? Point de tout. J'en suis si entièrement certain qu'il ne m'est pas possible d'en douter sérieusement. Pourquoi cela?

Ist es dann also auch gewiss, dass ich da bin? Kan ich mich nicht vielleicht betrügen? Nein durchaus nicht. Ich bin dessen auf so eine überzeugende Art gewiss,

Parce que je sens et que j'aperçois très-particulièrement, que je suis.[21]

dass es mir nicht möglich ist im Ernst dran zu zweifeln. Aber warum denn nicht? Weil ich fühle und auf eine besondere Art empfinde, dass ich da bin.[22]

In 1730 the magazine, the *Geistliche Fama*, appeared under the editorship of Johann Samuel Carl, who was also Count Casimir's personal physician. In his home town of Dehringen in Franken Carl had come under the impact of the enthusiastic sermons of one J. G. Rosenbach (1679–1749). From Dehringen Dr. Carl moved his practice to Büdingen. In this tolerant principality he was associated with a group of seekers called 'the Inspired' – a contact which he continued after his move to Berleburg in about 1724.[23] Like Count Casimir, who respected him as 'a deeply pious, learned and skilled Doctor of Medicine', he was committed to the Philadelphian type of religious community life and helped to promote it in the court circle.

An account of Dr. Carl's marriage to Johanna Sophie von Bülow, lady-in-waiting, conveys a vivid impression of the religious scene. Carl and the bride, accompanied by the Count and the Countess, Rock, who was the leader of the Inspired, and other friends, gathered in a private room in Berleburg Castle. Prayers and declarations on the part of the betrothed, witnessed by those present, sealed the marriage bond. No formal action by a minister nor any prescribed ceremony took place. Count Casimir noted in his diary that 'this marriage was quite edifying to behold and followed the manner of the first Apostolic Church'.[24]

Even more remarkable than Edelmann's having been asked to help on the Poiret translation was Dr. Carl's turning over to him the editorship of the *Geistliche Fama*, which was now the admired and widely circulated magazine among the 'awakened'. Edelmann must have inspired confidence both as competent scholar and as able comrade in the common separatist cause. When Edelmann took over, the twentieth issue was almost ready for the printer, and he provided only a short introduction. Edelmann assumed responsibility for the next issue (1736). The following issue (1737) he turned over to 'Brother Küntzel', one of Haug's visitors, to whom he took a liking. To this he wrote only the introduction. Of the twenty-third issue (1737) Edelmann half-heartedly acknowledged editorship.[25]

Edelmann's deep concern with the problem of rebirth is evident in the parts of the *Unschuldige Wahrheiten* written in this period. Yet he refused collaboration on still a third project, the continuation of Reitz's *Historie der Wiedergebohrenen*, which appeared in its sixth edition in 1739. Many years later Edelmann attributed his refusal to the conviction that he could not describe as 'reborn' personalities he had not really known and for whose rebirth he could not vouch.

Edelmann's major assignment was the work on the Bible; he claims the editorship of II Timothy, Titus, and Philemon, although he disclaims responsibility for the final form in which the epistles appeared in the six volumes of the Berleburger Bible, published in 1737:

> I surely was too long-winded in my commentaries, and I could not blame my brethren had they shortened my text while keeping what was essential. On first glance, however, at the printed book I found a completely different text. Therefore, I do not want to deny that their temerity angered me and I feel compelled to reveal to my real friends that I do not consider these three epistles my own work.[26]

Nevertheless, Edelmann helped in transporting the printed volumes to the Frankfurt Easter Fair, although it had now become obvious that his relationship with Haug was deteriorating. This he made clear to his sponsor Gross in Frankfurt, in whose house he stayed.

Edelmann gives a characterization of Haug which serves to explain why the collaboration lasted for only a year:

> On the surface Haug welcomed me; I immediately recognized that he was not my man in an 'inner sense', and it soon became clear that we were not made for each other. ... He was by nature not an intractable person, though he did not possess the cheerful and open personality of Gross. Having been driven out of Strassburg on account of his Pietism, he therefore thought of himself as already being half a martyr, which made the good fellow quite conceited. He lacked fervor to match the pretense, and for this reason he resented my writings that showed all too much fervor.[27]

An adversary of Haug in Strassburg described him as 'haughty, stubborn, greatly conceited, odd and of melancholy humor'.[28] Even allowing for the bias of Edelmann's statement, it is evident that Haug was a difficult person.

After his return from Frankfurt, Edelmann felt more and more uncomfortable in the Haug home and he was also bitter because Haug had not
fulfilled the financial promises that had been made initially. In spite of
a rather heated debate over these matters, an agreement was reached when
Edelmann departed, although he received only the eighty-two guilders that
Gross had advanced, and not a penny from Haug. A lucky number Edelmann drew in the Erfurt Bible lottery brought him thirty guilders with
which to establish his own quarters, 'a fine furnished room and another
smaller one with the baker Zeppel', who also provided the heating wood
for the first half year for four guilders.[29]

After this move, Edelmann began to develop a life-style of his own,
characterized by simplicity and independence. Berleburg had been a sym-
pathetic and stimulating environment. His first year there had inaugurated
a period of great literary productivity, which continued thereafter. Although
Edelmann was not really in tune with the mystical-sentimental orientation of
Haug's Bible work, yet his experiences as translator and editor were of
immeasurable value to the development of his own thinking and literary
discipline. If, in his later works, Edelmann was able rationally to
develop religious concepts which were not devoid of feeling, it was
largely due to his intimate acquaintance with the works of Poiret and
Guyon.

In the rich religious life of the two Wittgensteins, an important and
complex role was played by the Inspired. Dr. Carl's attachment to the
movement has been mentioned. Edelmann was much drawn to these circles
during the following months, although he had made acquaintances among
them earlier. His attraction to a group committed to an evangelical spiritualism expressing itself in ecstasy at a time when his aversion to pietistic
and enthusiastic religiosity was growing is surprising. The reasons for his
interest were manifold: new personal friendships, curiosity, a predilection
for simplicity, and the somewhat cool relation to Haug, who was now
alienated from the Inspired. It was also reported to Edelmann that his
writings were favorably received among some of the Inspired – news that
of course would flatter him.[30]

Edelmann had his first encounter with the Inspired when en route from
Marburg to Berleburg 'a group of the children of the prophet, the so-called
Inspired', suddenly appeared. 'I had entertained the strangest ideas of these

people. When the coachman told me that these were the Inspired it was obvious that they did not look terrifying at all, and happily I continued towards Berleburg.'[31]

When Edelmann came to know them more intimately, his preconceived ideas changed altogether: 'I thought these people were without exception Tremblers or Quakers. But as I did not find any play-acting, my judgment became shaky; a mutual affection began to grow and I would have considered it sectarian unfriendliness if I had refused to address them lovingly as brother.' It might be added that Edelmann felt deeply hurt by Haug's never using the address common in Philadelphic circles.[32] Edelmann's association with the Inspired came at a time when the movement in its original geographic setting, the Wittgenstein lands and the Wetterau, was dying out, to be revived in the New World in Ephrata, Pennsylvania, and later in Amana, Iowa.

The history of the Inspired has been well traced by Max Goebel from a wealth of original documents.[33] After the Camisard Wars the movement was touched off by the singular prophetic sessions which took place among French exiles in England and on the Continent. Their actions were a continuation of the original outbreak of prophetic ecstasies among the Huguenots which followed the revocation of the Edict of Nantes (1685), particularly in the Dauphiné. The pattern in which the prophetic exclamation or message emerged was commonly the following: 'The prophet beat his head with his hands for some time, then fell down on his back: his stomach and throat swelled up and he remained speechless for some minutes, after which he broke out into utterances.'[34] From the very beginning the gift of prophecy proved to be contagious. Thus one can follow a direct line of those who possessed the gift from the two emigrés Allut and Marion to the brothers Pott, in Halle, and to the separatists living in the Wetterau. It was there that Eberhard Ludwig Gruber (1665–1728) and Johann Friedrich Rock (1678–1749) were drawn into the movement, took on leading roles, and worked out a discipline for a worship that would otherwise have exhausted itself in sporadic ecstatic outbursts. The form of 'Inspiration' thus became an important and influential strain in German and American religious life. Gruber, the chief architect of the discipline, began to organize the communities in Schwarzenau and Homrighausen in 1714. The first 'love feast', a communal meal that found its prototype in the practices of the

Apostolic Church, was held in December 1714 at Schwarzenau and was attended by seventeen visitors from Ysenburg.

Twenty-two years later, when Edelmann discovered it, the community of the Inspired, like any movement that starts with such fervor of awakening, had gone through many phases. By 1719, the gift of prophetic utterance had become extinct among the Inspired except for Rock, who possessed it to the end of his life. Also, the great missions of the 'instruments of the Inspired' that took Rock and others to Saxony, Württemberg, Bohemia, and Switzerland had come to an end; yet in the settlements in the United States the tradition was carried on with zest and vigor. The messengers, like the prophets of the Cevennes, were accompanied by recorders and their utterances were preserved and printed in the *Jahrbücher der Inspirierten.*[35]

Gruber himself has summarized the major thrust of the prophecies or ecstatic confessions:

> The subject matter of the utterances was how to be Christian, active in faith, repentance, prayer, and imitation of Christ; these responded to the present condition of the members, as they made their inner state known and if there was need, they provided the right medicine; often in the state of inspiration with closed eyes they would go to one or another person, indicating to them their bad or good condition of the heart, offering wise evangelical counsel for improvement, revealing damnation and blessing, prophecy and threat, much of which has come true.[36]

A passage from Johann Konrad Dippel's reflections on the Inspired, written at the request of Count Casimir in 1731, supplements this description:

> The confessions are made up almost entirely of words from the Scriptures. To deduce divine inspiration from well-intended admonitions and continuously repeated phrases from the Scriptures is a false conclusion. He whom the Holy Spirit moves directly and through whom he speaks does not have to steal his words from other prophets. He possesses in himself the same source as that from which all scriptures flow, and further I do not find that a Holy Scribe inspired by God has babbled others' words, but each has produced out of the wealth of his own vocabulary expressions for divine commands and concepts.[37]

Edelmann was in a sense still in search of the true Christian – this had taken him to Herrnhut – and the simple life and mutual concern of the Inspired attracted him to their flock. His radical idealism could find greater fulfillment with them than in the Haug–Marsay–Casimir circles. Nevertheless, the naiveté and lack of intellectual sophistication was bound to erode Edelmann's interest: 'Indeed I have to confess that never before in my life had I heard more miserable, tasteless, and feeble praying than among the enthusiastic brothers.'[38] This is probably a correct if uncharitable description. The lack of local leadership of real spiritual quality and, as a consequence, the hero-worship for Rock added to Edelmann's disenchantment, critical and suspicious of authority in matters religious as he was.

In Rock, Edelmann met a self-made uncompromising *homo religiosus*, who could look back on a life of fearless and committed Christian ministry. The saddle-maker who, with his minister and friend Gruber, had left his Württemberg home in 1707; this separatist and seeker, who found refuge in Himbach (near Büdingen) after trials and tribulations, became 'afflicted' with the 'gift' of inspiration. In the fall of 1714 Rock had emerged together with Gruber as leader of the Inspired, and certainly, after Gruber's death in 1728, as their most outstanding representative. Over the years the ecstatic bodily expressions, the convulsions and fainting had given way to more placid manners suited to the more psalmodic or poetic utterances of Rock's inspiration, prophecy, and admonitions.

A major, yet difficult task was to keep the communities of the Inspired together. The feeling of unity was an essential prerequisite for all these small Christian groups that aspired to re-enact the Apostolic community of love and harmony and, in so doing, to set examples by which a divided and quarrelsome Christianity could profit. Leadership meant keeping the community united and making it work; failure or success was a judgment on the strength and forthrightness of the commitment. The bond was of paramount importance because it provided the instrument for unity that linked the individuals together. However simplistic the individuals might appear in their beliefs and trust, it would be hard not to respect their endeavors. That individual conduct was unquestionably of foremost concern to the community is well indicated by Edelmann's slanderous remarks that, had he known of any trespass by a single member of the Inspired, 'exposure would have discredited the whole group'.[39]

8

Various factors had accounted for the estrangement between Edelmann and Zinzendorf: the underlying cause, as we have seen, was a crisis that was bound to turn Edelmann away from Herrnhut. In a similar way the rupture with the Inspired marks the beginning of a new phase in Edelmann's intellectual development. His two experiences of inspiration were strikingly similar. The call to write came to Edelmann in slumber, and in slumber Edelmann heard the initial words of the gospel of John "as if someone said to me and with a firmness that made itself felt: 'God is reason'. I must have read these words a hundred times, also in the Greek text, but never had I found the consolation and comfort that I then experienced".[40] This was the new knowledge that gave Edelmann the strength to free himself from the anti-rational Inspired; moreover, it became the measure by which all revelation and prophecy, the entire Bible, was to be tested. If the first break-through brought about the birth of the writer, then the second break-through, again so different from what the Pietist understood by it, marked the beginning of the man of the Enlightenment.

The actual trend towards the rupture with the Inspired began with a controversy between their elder, Brother Herrmann, and Edelmann over silent or audible prayer. Edelmann refused to pray aloud in the meetings, something expected of all participants; when challenged, he disputed the propriety of public prayer. Years ago Johann Konrad Dippel had been reprimanded on the same issue.[41] It was now decided to submit the question to Rock, the leader of the Inspired, who was expected soon in Wittgenstein. Challenge within the commune of the Inspired, however, was no small matter, particularly when a practice was at stake that traditionally formed an important part of their religious worship.

A newcomer, Edelmann had been associated with them for several months. In a group intent on unity, dissent by a member of Edelmann's prestige was particularly painful. It was Edelmann's temperament to push fast and relentlessly towards new positions. The zeal with which he was to proclaim the new truth as he saw it did not allow for consideration and charity. The written exchanges between Edelmann and members of the Inspired are lost. From his own account in the autobiography we may infer that he did not hide his conviction of his own superiority over their naiveté. Nor did he shy away from embarrassing Herrmann, and then Rock.

On the eve of the final encounter with Rock the second 'break-through' took place, giving Edelmann the strength he needed to free himself from the leader's authority. To Edelmann the confrontation with Rock appeared as a symbolic battle between reason, the expression of 'true light', and irrationality and fakery.[42] Rock was not an unseasoned traveler in the realm of man's mind and feelings. Although representing an entirely different religious world than the one towards which Edelmann was striving, Rock had some true insight into his adversary's intellectual condition. When addressing himself to Edelmann, therefore, it was natural that he should strike a tone of prophetic warning, because that was his own commitment and *métier*. He also sounded as if he were speaking to a much younger person; in fact, Rock was sixty and Edelmann forty, yet Edelmann was at the beginning of a new venture in his life and Rock sensed this correctly:

> Brother, you do not know through experience how great a blessing and peace is achieved by bearing all kind of mockery with a good conscience. If you could believe this and if God would consider you worthy, you would abandon your great smartness and wisdom, and you would become an Inspiration-fool with me; thus this remains hidden to you, and it serves you right. You cannot imagine what a peaceful heart I bear towards you. Therefore, I hope to fulfill your need with this letter. I do not want discipleship either from you or from others, but I am working with the Brothers in the community mainly as Jesus wills, before whom I am naked and who knows my heart and whom I serve and to whom I belong; if you cannot see me so and if my work in Him is foreign to you, then you are not capable of seeing. You only think that you are seeing, but you are blind or a weak child. Mark well: I am fond of you, therefore I act so childishly and foolishly with you. Farewell! I am your brother, who wants to please not men, but the Master, and who loves the Brothers.[43]

In these years Edelmann felt himself too much a warrior for the cause of the living God rightly to appreciate all the good he had received from the Inspired. He would not let matters rest. He had to insult Rock in the open and challenged Rock's followers to recognize that they had been misled for twenty years and that it was time to break out of the bondage. When Edelmann writes in the autobiography that some of his writings of these years had better not have been written, he probably refers to the exchange of letters with Zinzendorf and the pamphlet against Rock: *Bereitete Schläge auf der Narren-Rücken, Das ist wohlgemeinte Warnung vor denen, allen Spöttern des lebendigen Gottes, bevorstehenden Strafen. Besonders denen armen, von einem schändlichen Lügen-Geiste bisher verblendeten Inspirations-Verwandten.*

He damned Rock with such phrases as 'you miserable, pitiful creature, plagued with an anti-Christian spirit' and 'the worst rogue, thief and murderer, is not nearly as bad a person as you are. They only harm the body but you are doing harm to the soul.' More painful to the Inspired than Edelmann's verbal and written outpourings was the fact that two members of their community broke away and aligned themselves with him: Brother Jacques Langemeyer and Sister Schelldorfinn. Both were living in the baker Zeppel's house where Edelmann had found lodging. Sister Schelldorfinn was the widow of a cord and braid-maker, and Langemeyer appears to have worked for her as a journeyman braid-maker; she also provided board for Edelmann. It is easy to understand that Edelmann, who had impressed the intellectual elite of Berleburg, would quickly gain respect among more humble fellow inhabitants.

That the two members of the Inspired made the break was certainly a source of satisfaction to Edelmann. The pamphlet against Rock makes it abundantly clear that Edelmann felt it his mission to lead the Inspired out of fog and illusions. He even tried to persuade Herrmann, a local leader (with whom he had quarreled over the subject of prayer), to abandon the cause of the 'Inspired'; he sent a letter to Herrmann's brother, together with a copy of *Bereitete Schläge*, beseeching him to help to convince Herrmann of his errors and his mistaken devotion to Rock.[44]

For the intellectual development of Edelmann perhaps the greatest consequence of the encounter with the Inspired was the raising of the issue of inspiration. It became the starting-point of Edelmann's Bible criticism, on which he was soon to embark. Meanwhile, almost as if he were afraid of breaking loose from the pietistic world in which he lived, he decided to give up wearing the regular worldly cloth and he started to grow a beard. Costume and beard were to show the Inspired that he was ready to outdo them in holiness. They had objected to his fashionable dressing, while he was still theirs. The 'Mennonite frock' was intended to impress on them that he did not embrace worldliness, and the beard was meant as an outward sign of his imitation of Christ. 'The display of folly appeared then to us to be a sign of distinction, that we were willing to bear for the sake of Christ.'[45]

Edelmann's need to provide for his livelihood became more and more pressing in the late summer and fall of 1738. He was close to starvation:

> In a strange land where I was, I had scarcely a crown; my board with sister Schelldorfinn I had already given up, as I did not know how to pay her. I had to live just the same, yet I saw no prospect for relief. ... For a week I had not eaten anything but bread and water; I did not want to incur debts. I did not want to be a burden to sister Schelldorfinn and brother Langemeyer, who begged me to continue to eat with them. ... It was a time of tribulation.[46]

This rather desperate situation was linked in Edelmann's mind to the audacious step he had taken in challenging Rock. Moreover he faced the question of whether God considered him the right instrument for the dissemination of truth.

Edelmann was willing to capitulate, but a realistic assessment of his condition led him to find employment. For an independent, radical intellectual to make a living by his pen was a precarious undertaking. 'The needs of the body taught me to turn my thoughts to other matters and to explore how I could make a living in an honest manner.'[47]

Edelmann then decided to ask Brother Langemeyer to take him on as an apprentice in braid-making. The apprenticeship lasted less than a year, but it gave him a skill he was proud of and helped him over an economically difficult period. A 'separatist' and an artisan was not an unusual combination. Besides, for the members of the aristocracy and for some intellectuals, even though installed in secure positions, it was hardly possible to pursue a religiously separatist life short of martyrdom. Among the lower income groups, the artisan, working independently in his home, had the best chance to pursue his own religious inclinations. Indeed, the various separatist and dissenting religious groups recruited their members largely from this class. Their leaders likewise came from such backgrounds: the cobbler, Jakob Böhme, and the saddle-maker, Johann Rock.

The economic plight of the German principalities, after the Thirty Years' War and far into the eighteenth century, accounts largely for the willingness of some German territorial lords to extend religious toleration and economic privileges to Huguenot refugees, Mennonites, and various dissenters, among whom highly skilled artisans were predominant. One instance of this policy as directly related to the immigration of the 'Inspired' into the Wetterau may be cited. The decision of Gruber, Rock, and their friends to settle in the Büdingen area was surely influenced by the declaration of 'Privilegia und Freyheiten' issued on March 29, 1712, by Count Ernst Casimir of Ysenburg and Büdingen. After a short preamble which reviews the devastating consequences of recent warfare and states the need for repopulating and rebuilding, the first paragraph makes explicit the Count's open policy:

> We want to assure every man in our land full freedom in matters of conscience; thus none of our subjects, strangers and denizens, who profess to belong to other than the reformed religion, or who for reasons of conscience do not adhere to any formal religion, yet conduct themselves in their civic life and in their own homes towards the authorities and the citizens in an honest proper and Christian manner, will be subjected to any hardship or disturbance.[48]

Edelmann's apprenticeship, recalled in the autobiography in a hilarious account of his first clumsy attempts at braid-making, was a short-range solution. It was at best an 'honest' way, in contrast to any compromise in matters of conscience that might have provided financial support. It is important to understand that Edelmann's use of the word 'honest' does not imply a dichotomy between handiwork and the pursuit of intellectual endeavors, of writing in particular. 'Writing' was Edelmann's honest profession and his major aim was to devote his full energies to it. The long-range problem was how the writer could make a living independent of the established institutions. The term 'writer' should further be defined as the philosophical writer who presents controversial issues. The sale of the writings alone did not guarantee an income, although in later years Edelmann did benefit financially from his publications. The problem of the subsistence of the members of what Alfred Weber called the 'unattached intelligentsia' arises for Edelmann and he certainly deserves to be considered a charter member.

Edelmann's braid-making career did not last long; by the beginning of 1739 he could exchange the weaving-loom for the pen. This change in

Edelmann's fortunes is explained by the fact that there was growing interest in his writings and that those who were stirred and enriched by these writings concerned themselves with the welfare of their author. As the influential Gross at Frankfurt had been moved by the *Unschuldige Wahrheiten* and sought Edelmann out, others followed suit and there developed a whole fraternity of those reading Edelmann's works and corresponding with him. These newly won friends were scattered throughout Germany – in Darmstadt, Offenbach, Frankfurt, Strassburg, Gotha and Berlin. Their letters to Edelmann contained contributions of money to continue his studies, writings, and his publications. It is doubtful whether Edelmann could have maintained himself as an independent writer through these gifts alone, had it not been for the substantial and steady help he received from the merchant Pinell of the Cölln district of Berlin. The first letter from Pinell, and financial help, arrived at Berleburg in the early spring of 1739. Edelmann comments in the autobiography: 'Indeed, this magnanimous friend, whose modesty forbids me to call him by his real name and to whom because of his kindness I will refer as Benignus, laid the foundation of my future happiness, and I must say that God used him, more than any other of my friends, to provide for my livelihood.' [49]

Edelmann often denied accusations that he schemed to found another 'sect', and there is no evidence that his supporters created such an image. To those, however, who wanted to accuse him, this wide following, as well as the local friends who kept in daily contact with him, could well have appeared to be a new 'sect'. The title under which Edelmann's material is gathered in the archive at Neuwied, 'Johann Christian Edelmanns et Cons: Secte zu Neuwied', points to such labelling. [50]

Edelmann was naturally anxious to make the personal acquaintance of his new benefactor, and Pinell was equally curious to meet Edelmann. Pinell provided him with the necessary money for the journey, and Edelmann started for Berlin. With his cloak and beard, Edelmann felt self-conscious, and he ascribed various incidents on the road to his unusual appearance. When he arrived at Potsdam on June 6, however, the situation changed. The sentinel at the gate stopped him and said in a friendly manner: 'Oh my dear Jew, you will not be allowed to enter.' When Edelmann explained that in spite of his beard he was not a Jew, the sentinel answered in astonishment: 'Oh no, but I have to report you.' Such incidents at the gate were not unusual. In 1735 Solomon Jakob Morgenstern, setting out for Moscow, where a teaching position was awaiting him, had been stopped at the gate at Potsdam, brought before the king, and then and there recruited for the intimate Tabaks-Kollegium (Tobacco Parliament).[51]

Edelmann recorded his ensuing meeting with Friedrich Wilhelm I, and in all probability the account in the autobiography, written more than ten years later, is actually based on the one he sent to friends in Gotha in a letter of July 13, 1739.[52] Although no record other than Edelmann's own has been located, the encounter is plausible in the light of what is known of the way in which conversations and interrogations were held at the Tabaks-Kollegium. Politics, finances, religion, and general court happenings were freely and often jokingly debated at the king's informal dinner gatherings.[53] At the time Edelmann arrived the king was engaged in renewed efforts to bring back to Prussia the philosopher Christian Wolff, whom he had expelled in 1723 from his professorship in Halle and from all of Prussia. Upon reinvestigating the case, the king, finding the accusations of atheism fabricated, repented the rash action; he invited Wolff back to Halle in 1733, and in May 1739 offered him a position at Frankfurt-an-der-Oder.[54] Questions of conscience and belief were on the agenda, and thus his conversation with Edelmann is not surprising. Indeed, in its vividness and authenticity, it seems well worth relating:

"The king was sitting next to the window smoking tobacco with his generals who were seated around the table. As I remained in the doorway the king called me to approach and asked: 'Where do you come from?' The answer was: 'Berleburg.' 'Why do you let your beard grow?' My answer: 'I cannot see why a Christian should be ashamed of the appearance of his Savior.' 'Ha', said the king, 'You seem to be one of the "reborn".' 'No, your majesty, to be that I still have a great leap ahead.' The king liked the answer so well that he turned to his generals and remarked, 'He is right.' He continued, asking what my profession was, and when I answered that I had studied and had been employed by noble families as tutor he wanted me to elaborate on the circumstances. Then he asked, 'Do you attend church?' I gave the following answer: 'I have my church with me.' To which the king somewhat jokingly replied 'Oh, you are a godless man ... you are a Quaker.' Upon which I candidly replied, 'We are fools for the sake of Christ.' Upon which the king looked again towards his generals in silent astonishment and continued: 'What are you living on?' I said: 'Out of the hand of God.' At that the king countered: 'Indeed, you have been begging.' I said, 'No, your majesty, to this moment I have not been a burden to anyone, and nobody can claim that I have solicited two pence, but God still has Christians who look out for the needs of their brethren and try to help them. ...' I was also asked if I go to communion. I said: 'If I find Christians who are ready to unite in order to share with Christ his death, then I will be ready to hold communion with them, but I have not found any such yet.' He asked, 'If such communion is to be held in Church, why do I not go there?' I answered: 'I do not consider the present Communion the Lord's supper, but an anti-Christian ceremony.' At that he called me once more a godless person and wished that God would convert me. I replied that I wished that from the bottom of my heart and was again asked why I am not willing to recognize the present communion as the Lord's supper. With oblivious courage I answered: 'Your majesty, it is a midday meal and not a supper.' This reply the king did not expect and he looked at his generals in silence as if he wanted to say, it is true, but they too remained in deep silence. I then was asked where I wanted to go and I answered: 'To Berlin, with the permission of your majesty.' He said: 'No, that you will not be permitted.' I had to give the names and status of my brothers. When I tried once more to ask if his majesty would permit me to visit Berlin, he refused me again and said: 'You will be taken right away out of town to the "Black Eagle".' I remarked, 'I expected to find in your land full freedom of conscience.' At this he replied: 'Your conscience will not be hurt, but to Berlin you will not travel.' I said, 'I respect your order.' He remarked, 'If communion means nothing, then love means nothing.' I said, 'The Bible is my daily reading ... .' He did not let me finish, but wished again that God would convert me, upon which I bowed, commended the king to the grace of God, and took leave. I was immediately taken by a grenadier to the Black Eagle, where I found a fine and truly God-fearing innkeeper, who gave me my own clean room and engaged me in conversation over divine matters, although he was still a church adherent." [55]

Although Edelmann was disappointed at being so near to his benefactor without being able to see him, he later considered it providential that he had not been allowed to enter Berlin at that time. Upon his return to

Berleburg, he found a letter from Pinell, who knew that Edelmann had been turned away at Potsdam and considered it most fortunate, since the Berlin Orthodox clergy were ready to denounce him upon his arrival. Probably they had been forewarned of Edelmann's coming by the Berleburg court preacher, Victor Christoph Tuchtfeld.[56] Edelmann also reflected that Pinell might have been disappointed in him as Edelmann had not yet attained the understanding that could have helped dissolve his benefactor's religious scruples about the Bible. The studies and writings of the next years were devoted to that end.

Soon after his return from Potsdam in the spring of 1739, a skilled apothecary, 'Brother Erhart', came to Berleburg to join Edelmann in his studies and to help him with his literary enterprises. Erhart had been in contact with Pinell, who found him trustworthy. Edelmann's living quarters proved too small for two, and they moved to the house of a tailor named Balde, into the rooms once occupied by Dippel. Under the influence of Christoph Seebach the Balde family had become convinced Socinians and welcomed the controversial author.[57] Perhaps the move to the Baldes', who were Socinians, and into what had once been Dippel's quarters symbolizes well the direction Edelmann's thinking was taking. For Edelmann, who had dissolved his ties to the Haug Bible enterprise, who had left the close circle of the Inspired, and who had found the freedom to define his own way of life, a joyful and intellectually rich period opened. Of these years Edelmann wrote:

> [We] were the only ones in the entire domain who could really then claim to live as free men. Not only were we free of all imposts and taxes, but we had nobody standing behind us to drive us to work when we were inclined to go for walks. This we could do while others had to go to work, although we would work when others had gone to sleep. All was done in freedom, without any slave-holder breathing down our necks, and we therefore remained not only physically healthy, but emotionally cheerful and relaxed. We truthfully can say that this was the happiest time in our lives.[58]

6. 'Moses mit Aufgedeckten Angesichte'
1740

Never before had there appeared in the German language a book like Edelmann's *Moses*, which denies from beginning to end the entire 'Bible-faith' and with it the Christian dogmas – a book that openly confesses its adherence to the Spinozistic teachings of God and the world, and that, without any inhibition, cuts the ground from under the conventional ideas of wonder, providence, and prayer.[1] Edelmann's assault did not remain unnoticed, but brought immediate censorship and harassment to its author, in addition to a flood of rebuttals; Pratje lists twenty major works opposing or censuring Edelmann, a number which swells to two hundred when pamphlets and journals are included. In November 1740, with the help of Brother Erhart, he had rushed off to the Frankfurt printer Eichenberg in swift succession the three parts of the manuscript, *Moses mit Aufgedeckten Angesichte von zwey ungleichen Brüdern, Lichtlieb und Blindling beschauet nach Art der Unschuldigen Wahrheiten*. If the statement that this work was so radical is correct, it raises an important question. What, in 1740, was the religious situation that made the *Moses* appear to be a work so outrageous and offensive in nature? An examination of this question must be preceded by a brief consideration of Edelmann's own philosophical mood that prompted the quick outpouring of the *Moses*.

The previous chapter has described Edelmann's new understanding of the initial verse of the gospel of John, an interpretation which led him to identify God with Reason. To this overwhelming experience and new knowledge he wanted to give adequate literary expression. Witness to his groping efforts are *Die Göttlichkeit der Vernunft*, composed of the epistles dating back to September 1738 and continuing through February 1740, and of other writings not published until 1743. These did not satisfy Edelmann; in his autobiography he rather apologized for having published them at all: 'It was done in order that all this writing should not have been completely in vain.' On June 24, 1740, a shipment of books arrived from his generous Berlin friend, Pinell, containing Spinoza's *Tractatus Theologico-Politicus* – 'the book in the lot to which a strong inner inclination directed me'.[2]

To approach Spinoza was not a step to be taken lightly; he was considered the arch-enemy of the established churches and was anathematized not only by Christians but by his own Jewish community. Even the mild Buddeus, a half-century after the philosopher's death, branded Spinoza as 'the foremost atheist of our times'.[3] Edelmann, who had experienced an awakening 'from the threshold of death to life', and whom 'reason had given full freedom to speak', proudly asserts that he opened Spinoza's work 'without fear'. From Edelmann's description in his autobiography it is clear how powerfully the image of the arch-atheist and materialist had worked as a taboo to prevent the exploration of Spinoza's writings. Edelmann believed that Providence had created an opportunity for him to study Spinoza without fear. He hastens to add that he is aware of the difference between his personal situation, wherein no vested interests deter him, and that of a church official who is financially dependent on an authority that prescribes creed and dogma.[4] He was immediately fired by Spinoza's discussion of the nature and composition of the Holy Scriptures. His distinction between the Scriptures and the Word of God, and his declaration in the introduction to the *Tractatus* 'that the multitude pays homage to the Books of the Bible rather than to the Word of God' were thoughts precisely relevant to Edelmann's own search. They served to spur on the writing of the *Moses*, which he had completed by November 1740.[5] In this short period, during which he had immersed himself in the study of the *Tractatus*, he had also become acquainted with Spinoza's *Ethics* and with the writings of Matthias Knutzen (1646–1674), which he was quick to incorporate in the second part of the *Moses*.

For the first time in *Moses* a German thinker, writing in his mother tongue, openly professed his agreement with Spinoza.[6] Edelmann had no immediate followers, since his work aroused indignation against him and brought only vilification upon him. Half a century later Spinoza's name came to be mentioned openly with reverence by Goethe and Herder.[7] The story of the condemnation or silencing of the work of Edelmann and, with it, of the religious ideas and criticism of Spinoza, is part of the history of German intellectual life between 1740 and 1775, particularly in the Prussia of Frederick II.

The appearance of the *Moses* coincided with the beginning of the reign of Frederick II of Prussia (1740–1786). This is not the place to paint a comprehensive canvas of the intellectual and religious scene, which has been done before, by Karl Barth.[8] Historians agree that by the middle of the eighteenth century the forces of the humanistic movement had not only initiated a scientific revolution; they had also supplanted theological modes of thinking with secular ones, and had put society and government on a new rational and utilitarian basis. Perhaps the most painful contradiction within the newly emerging bourgeois society was becoming visible a half-century before its true birth: the contradiction between the freedom of the newborn individual, end-product of Renaissance aspirations, and the absolutism of ever more enlightened governments in ever more scientifically manipulated societies. Historians view the reign of Frederick II as the epitome of enlightened absolutism. But they stress the fact that in 1740 one could not yet foresee the crisis that the new ideological forces were to create in the realm of religion, Christendom, and the church.[9]

The first part of Edelmann's *Moses* discusses the nature of the Bible. The eighteenth-century Lutheran Church inherited from its seventeenth-century theologians a number of doctrinal assertions concerning the Holy Scriptures, foremost among these the doctrine of Verbal Inspiration. As Lutheranism accepts Scripture as the 'only rule and norm according to which all doctrines and teachers alike must be appraised and judged', the divine origin of Scriptures is an essential assumption.[10] The major seventeenth-century dogmatist, Johann Andreas Quenstedt (1617–1688), stated: 'The authority of the Holy Scriptures and the authority of God are one and the same. ... The authority of Scripture is due to a unique decree of God and to the fact that it was written by divine inspiration.' Quenstedt defines with precision the concept of Verbal Inspiration:

> The Holy Spirit inspired in the prophets and apostles not only the content and the sense contained in Scripture, or the meaning of the words, so that they might of their own pleasure clothe and furnish these thoughts with their own style and their own words; the Holy Spirit actually supplied, inspired, and dictated the very words and each and every term individually.[11]

Perhaps a certain latitude is here shown in pointing out that prophets and apostles all had their own style in transmitting the Word of God. Many of Luther's own characterizations of the style of Joel, Amos, Jeremiah, and St. Paul stressed his awareness of human participation in the writing of the Scriptures.[12] To admit participation did not, however, diminish Luther's belief in the Scriptures as the work of the Holy Spirit.

To accentuate the hardening of the Orthodox Lutheran line by seventeenth-century theologians, Paul Tillich's interpretation of Luther's position *vis-à-vis* the Bible my be cited.

> The Bible is a creation of the divine Spirit in those who have written it, but it is not a dictation. On this basis Luther was able to proceed with a half-religious, half-historical criticism of the biblical books. It makes no difference whether the five books of Moses were written by Moses or not. ... Although Lutheran Orthodoxy was unable to preserve this great prophetic aspect of Luther, one thing was accomplished by Luther's freedom; it was possible for Protestantism to do something which no other religion in the whole world has been able to do, and that is to accept the historical treatment of the biblical literature.

Tillich was well aware that the freedom he saw in Luther's position was suppressed by Orthodoxy: 'The great movement of historical criticism began around 1750. Lessing, who was the greatest personality of the [German] Enlightenment, a poet and a philosopher, was the leader in the fight against a stupid Orthodoxy which stuck to traditional terms.'[13]

However one interprets Luther, it is certain that seventeenth- and eighteenth-century Orthodox Lutherans tended to minimize the role of human cooperation in the writing of the Bible and, in their most extreme statements, tried to equate Inspiration with mere mechanical dictation by the Holy Spirit. It is not difficult to recognize such calcification of the theological position as a defense against enthusiasm in all of its variations, including its 'belief in the Spirit as the autonomous guide of every individual', and against rationalism's trust 'in rational guidance which everybody has by his autonomous reason'.[14] Edelmann wrote his *Moses* as a dialogue, a form which suited his didactic style and one in which, as the author of *Unschuldige Wahrheiten*, he was well versed. The two interlocutors he has named 'Lichtlieb' (lover of light) and 'Blindling' (blindman). It is Lichtlieb's task to enlighten Blindling who is still in the thralls of 'Stockfinster' (pitch dark), the prototype of an Orthodox pastor. Stockfinster was perhaps more than a puppet to Edelmann, since in his autobiography he called his once-beloved cousin's husband by that nickname.[15] Stockfinster's creed easily falls into the category that Tillich called a 'stupid Orthodoxy'.

The momentum with which Edelmann wrote the *Moses* gives the dialogue a powerful rhythm and drive. The *Moses* has a dual role as destroyer of traditional authoritarian myths and proclaimer of ideas of God and man to which reason leads free men. Edelmann stressed how tentative is our knowledge of matters concerning God and creation.[16] The *Moses* is not a systematic presentation of these questions on the scholastic model followed by theologians and philosophers. For Edelmann the two great opposites are the 'living God' and the 'Bible as an idol' ('Bibelgötze'). From the very beginning the theme of the *Moses* is passionately announced: the Bible, the dead letter that has become 'rule and norm', must fall, and the living God is to be worshipped. The 'unveiling' of the Bible calls for philological, historical, and moral discussions of the text in order to prove the absurdity of the doctrine of Inspiration by the Holy Ghost. 'Lichtlieb', in trying to destroy the blind faith of his friend on these matters, makes innumerable references to the 'living God'. Edelmann does not offer any neat definition of what he understands by the 'living God', but he sets out again and again to give this idea added meaning and concreteness. Thus the characteristics of the 'living God' as emphasized in the first part of the *Moses* must be kept in mind during the discussion on the nature of God and matter in the other two parts.

Unsystematic as these presentations are, Edelmann tries always to make himself clear. He follows his own advice 'that truth proves itself best through economy of words'.[17] The reader to whom he addressed himself was not a learned theologian but any person who could follow an argument well presented. Clarity does not eliminate complexity. The 'living God' is to Edelmann not an abstract power, but a force working in us as individuals. One of his many attempts to define the 'living God' seeks to make this particular idea most visible. For this purpose Edelmann introduces writings of the seventeenth-century self-avowed atheist, Matthias Knutzen, whose concept of conscience he found of great relevance. Knutzen's radical position on civil authority prompted Edelmann to turn to these issues in the last part of the *Moses*, thus adding another dimension to this work.

Although the issues are all intertwined in the conversation between Lichtlieb and Blindling, we shall turn first to Edelmann's radical Bible criticism,
and then to his discussion of the nature of God.

Edelmann bluntly declares: 'It is not true that the Holy Spirit dictated
the Bible.'[18] All the various arguments he presents to prove this have in
common the fact that they claim Reason as their measuring rod. If God is
identified with Reason, then writings which contradict Reason cannot be
considered of divine origin. Inconsistencies in the text are the obvious target
of such a critique. The Orthodox claim of authorship of the Scriptures for
Moses is another issue open to attack. Lichtlieb is anxious to enlighten
Blindling on these points, and he culminates the discussion on the authorship
of the Five Books of Moses by saying:

> The fact that in our day little or nothing of the writings of Moses has
> been preserved ... has been recognized not only by accursed heretics
> like Carlstadt, Spinoza, Collin, Whiston, and Van Dule, but also by
> honest men among the three major sects – Richard Simons among the
> Papists, Vitringa among the Reformed, and Pfaff among the Lutherans –
> to mention only a few.[19]

John Dryden's verses reflect the shock caused by the *Histoire Critique du
Vieux Testament* of Richard Simon (1638–1712), in which the author, using
the most accurate available texts and the methods of philology, concluded
that Moses was not the author of the *Pentateuch:*

> If Scripture, though derived from heavenly birth,
> Has been but carelessly preserved on earth;
> If God's own people, who of God before
> Knew what we know, and had been promised more
> In fuller terms of Heaven's assisting care,
> And who did neither time nor study spare
> To keep this Book untainted, unperplext,
> Let in gross errors to corrupt the text,
> Omitted paragraphs, embroiled the sense,
> With vain traditions stopped the gaping fence,
> Which every common hand pulled up with ease,
> What safety from such brushwood-helps as these?[20]

What had disturbed educated men in England was years later to unsettle
the blind faith of the common man – Blindling – in Germany. Edelmann

does not discuss in the *Moses* the brilliant methodology of Biblical criticism that Spinoza offered in the *Tractatus* nor the careful philological analysis of Simon. The popularization of their arguments, however, can reach Blindling. The disclaimer of Moses as the author of the *Pentateuch* deals a fatal blow to Orthodoxy's belief that each word in the Bible is a word that the Holy Spirit 'actually supplied, inspired, and dictated'. The Lichtlieb line of argument runs as follows: If the Bible word is this sacred, how could God allow His word to be corrupted or lost? How little importance God attached to the written word becomes clear from the fact that He did not even prevent the destruction of the tables of Law. Thus Lichtlieb passionately states:

I want to impress on you the way God dealt with the Laws that he had written himself as it is related in the so-called Books of Moses. Then you will easily reason from the more important to the less important. You will judge for yourself that, when the great God has so dealt with the Laws, written by himself on two different occasions, there is no trace nor speck of dust left today, he certainly did not deal more carefully with the human writings of Moses or anybody else. He was well aware of the idolatry that human beings would carry on in due course with these dead letters. If there had even been anything worthy of being preserved for posterity for the sake of its antiquity, uniqueness and sacredness, indeed it would have been the first tables, of which we read in Exodus 31, 18: 'And he gave unto Moses, when he had made an end of communing with him upon Mount Sinai, two tables of testimony, tables of stone, written with the finger of God.'

The final lesson Blindling is to learn is that 'God is not limited in communication with us to mere outward signs comprehensible to our mere physical vision ... His presence within us speaks to every conscience through thoughts of such clarity that Paul does not excuse even the heathen when they refuse to hear Him.'[21]

The disappearance of the original texts of the Books of the Bible casts doubt upon their significance. The lack of these texts makes the controversies among the theologians of the various Churches the more absurd and meaningless. Each church, claiming to have the more accurate text, tries to vindicate its own intepretation. 'The sects' – Lutheran, Reformed, and Catholic – cannot agree on a single basic text, and one accuses the other of falsification.'[22] They engage 'in bloody quarrels. And to what do verbal disputes lead? As you can see for yourself, to resentment and bitterness, instead of the peace and harmony we are called to.'[23] The direct consequence of Bible idolatry is the very opposite of God's command. Blindling, overwhelmed by Lichtlieb's arguments, gasps, 'if what you say is true, then it seems that the Bible was not inspired by God'.[24]

The problem of inspiration was at the very center of Edelmann's religious and philosophical quest. His call to write, and the dawning in him of a new understanding of the Logos sentence at the beginning of the Gospel of John, were experiences which he could identify as divine inspiration. In a more general sense the question of inspiration is one every writer lives with. The first-hand experiences that had led to Edelmann's denunciation of Rock, the leader of the Inspired, as a false prophet, were essential to him in approaching the problem. The answer Lichtlieb offers is, therefore, a significant formulation of Edelmann's ideas as they had evolved through personal experience and his study of the *Tractatus:* 'Dear Blindling, because I have shown you how tenuous the Bible texts are, do not conclude that the truths they contain are not inspired by God. Any truth is inspired by God, be it found in Ovid or in the Bible.'[25] 'Truth is ever from God, be it Aesop or Paul, Christ or Confucius who utters it. There is and remains only one spirit of truth, and we can recognize truth only through His inspiration.'[26] Blindling, deeply irritated, finds it impossible to believe that the Greek poet's fables should be put on the same level with Scriptures. Lichtlieb points out 'that the meaning of the word fable in Latin and Greek was that of Logos, a careful and intelligent saying, a tale or story by wise men'. He adds 'that the Scriptures are full of such fables, called parables, and that Jesus especially expressed his teachings in such manner'.[27] It is not because they are contained in the Bible that the messages, thoughts, or teachings found therein deserve to be called divine, 'but on account of their excellence and because they can be recognized as truth grounded in reason'.[28]

As truth does not depend on the source where it is found, the religious works of Turks and heathen cannot be excluded as sources of truth. The baffled Blindling finds it indeed hard to believe that the 'Bible is to be compared with the deceitful writings of Turks and Heathen, and that their authors should be placed on the same footing with the Prophets and

Apostles'. Lichtlieb quickly reminds him that 'truth is that which leads men to a closer knowledge of God',[29] which is the sole measure by which to judge whether writings are divinely inspired. The idea that the true religion will prove itself through deeds of love, to which Lessing gave classic poetic expression in the parable of the three rings as told by the Jew Nathan to Sultan Saladin, is implied in Lichtlieb's answer. To religious tolerance a new universal dimension has been added.

Spinoza declared 'the cardinal precept' of the Bible to be, 'to love God above all things and one's neighbor as one's self'.[30] No single group or man has an advantage over another in the pursuit of this goal. If this is the cardinal precept of the Bible then surely much that is told in the Bible in flagrant contradiction of this principle cannot be of divine inspiration. Edelmann points to three passages that show Moses demanding 'inhuman legislation, devoid of all natural charity'.[31] The passages to which Edelmann referred are the ones in which Moses admonished the military, after their victory over the Midianites, for sparing the lives of women and children (Numbers 31: 17); the second, Moses' call for utter destruction of seven nations (Deuteronomy 7: 2); and the third, the banning of all Ammonites and Moabites unto the tenth generation from the religious community of the Israelites (Deuteronomy 23: 2).

Having quoted these passages Lichtlieb concludes with the question: "Can you, dear 'Blindling', imagine that these barbaric laws were dictated by a God of whom Scripture says that He is anxious to help all men ... by the same God who through Christ has demanded that we bless our enemies?" Bible texts in direct contradiction to the supreme command of love supply the best arguments in support of Edelmann's demand that 'the Bible idol must fall, if the living God is to be known by men'. This living God is not to be found as long as he is sought 'outside' and not until it is recognized 'that our conscience, or Reason, abiding in all of us and enlightening us, is the living God'.[32]

It is well to quote from Seneca's 41st letter to Lucilius, where the Stoic prototype of this concept of God is found:

We do not need to lift up our hands towards heaven, or to beg the keeper of a temple to let us approach his idol's ear, as if in this way our prayers were more likely to be heard. God is near you, he is with you, he is within you. This is what I mean, Lucilius: a holy spirit dwells within us, one who marks our good and bad deeds, and is our guardian. As we treat this spirit, so we are treated by it. Indeed, no man can be good without the help of God.[33]

With the fall of the Bible idol dawns a new age: 'One brother shall not teach the other nor say to the other, Know the Lord. All will know Him, small and big, and the land shall be full of the knowledge of the Lord. In his inmost soul each will rejoice that the Lord, the God of truth, did let the time of fulfillment of his prophecy begin in our age.'[34] By 'the time of fulfillment' Edelmann understands the realizations of the great Biblical Peace Utopia. Yet before pursuing this vision Edelmann introduces the writings of Matthias Knutzen, whom Bruno Bauer called the 'Frisian Hercules',[35] while Pierre Bayle called him 'the miserable Knutzen', yet considered him worthy of inclusion in his *Dictionnaire Historique et Critique*.

Edelmann had rediscovered Knutzen's writings at a moment when he was intensely seeking to give to the concept of the living God a concreteness it had never before attained. Knutzen made man's conscience the sole moral agent and he denied the authority of a superimposed higher power. Edelmann did not altogether follow Knutzen and, as will be discussed presently, he made clear where he differed. The concept of conscience that Knutzen presented stirred Edelmann deeply. The prominent place given in the *Moses* to Knutzen's writings and to comments on them show their impact on Edelmann and his wish to propagate them.

Knutzen was born in Oldensworth in Holstein in 1646 – two years before the conclusion of the Thirty Years' War.[36] His parents were poor; the father, an organist like Edelmann's grandfather, died in the year his son Matthias was born. When Matthias Knutzen matriculated as a student of theology at the University of Königsberg at the age of eighteen, he too sought employment as tutor or schoolteacher, but in vain. In 1668 he continued his theological studies at the University of Copenhagen. Around 1673 the sermons he was preaching in Holstein to peasants and laborers, damning the corruption and avarice of the consistories, began to arouse the suspicion and anxiety of the local Orthodox clergy. For this reason he was forced in December 1673 to leave the vicinity.

Were it not for the events of September 1674 at Jena, we would probably know little of what Knutzen really had to say. As was often the case in these years, we owe the only record we have of radical literature to those unwitting propagators who, in order to denounce the content of radical writings, quoted them *in extenso*. Thus we have the Jena theologian and University Rector Johann Musaeus (1631–1681) to thank for a careful account of Knutzen's activities in Jena and the publication of the three writings of Knutzen now extant: the Latin pamphlet *Amicus, Amicis, Amica,* and two colloquies *Ein Gespräch zwischen einem lateinischen Gastgeber und drei ungleichen Religionsgästen* and *Gespräch zwischen einem Feldprediger namens Heinrich Brummer und einem lateinischen Münsterschreiber.* All three were included by Edelmann in the *Moses.* As his source he mentions a manuscript 'passed on to him confidentially'; since the whole text which Edelmann reproduces is almost identical with the one Musaeus printed in 1675, it seems probable that the manuscript Edelmann mentions is a copy of the latter.[37]

In brief, Matthias Knutzen and some of his friends distributed his hand-written pamphlets in the University town on Saturday and Sunday, September 5 and 6, 1674. They were found in the confessional seats and near the professors' pews in the town church. The editor and publisher of the local newspaper, *Die Avisen,* Johann Ludwig Neuenhahn (d. 1676),[38] also found a copy of the first colloquy in his room when he returned home from church on Sunday. A threatening letter was attached to the pamphlet demanding that the editor publish the colloquy, or else he might expect to be put to 'eternal sleep by means of a gunshot'. Also, the claim was made that in Jena alone there were seven hundred adherents of Knutzen's teachings among the burghers and students. This letter was signed 'Hans Friedrich von der Vernunft',[39] a saucy pseudonym reminiscent of the revolutionary spirit of the Peasants' Wars, but here used under the new sign of Reason. Musaeus felt that so impudent a challenge to clergy and authority could not be left unanswered. He was also eager to refute the claim that the town of Jena harbored seven hundred followers of an atheist – an allegation that was certainly a propaganda ruse of Knutzen. Musaeus published his refutation later in the same year. Publication of a second and enlarged edition in 1675, which included Knutzen's own letter and his two colloquies, suggests that interest in the 'Gewissener', a sect which he claimed to have established, had not subsided.

Edelmann considers it almost providential that, while God tolerated the destruction of the tables given to Moses, he allowed the writings of

Knutzen to survive and to emerge at this particular time. The first to be reprinted by Edelmann is the Latin epistle *Amicus, Amicis, Amica*, but without a German translation, such as he had usually provided for Latin texts. Edelmann concentrates his discussion of *Amicus, Amicis, Amica* on its key passage which concerned conscience. He lets the previous analysis of the inconsistencies and contradictions in the Bible speak for itself, as obviously supporting his own views. Knutzen's epistle sets out to discredit the Bible as an acceptable book of laws and the foundation of faith, because its inconsistencies and contradictions make it a tottering support; only those 'who keep reason a prisoner can find delight' in the Books of the Bible. He then turns to his own confession of faith:

> Further, we declare that there is no God, that we hold the magistrate in deep contempt and that we reject the church with all its priests. For men of conscience knowledge suffices – not that of one person, but of many (Luke 24: 39) – received in conjunction with the conscience. This conscience, which benevolent Nature has given to all men, takes the place of the Bible (Romans II, 14, 15) and of the magistrate. It stands in the place of the priest; it is our teacher who teaches us not to harm anyone, to live honestly, and to give to each his own. ... Conscience originates with us at birth, and it perishes with us in death. These are the principles we are born with, and whoever rejects these, rejects himself.

Blindling's reaction to these teachings is, as is to be expected, holy indignation and the outcry 'atheist!' Lichtlieb gently warns his outraged friend not to be completely put off by Knutzen's offensive language. He begs 'Blindling' to explore with him the real message and raises the question: 'How can he who does not act according to his conscience, believe in God, and with what right can one treat as an atheist one who lives according to his conscience?'[40]

Edelmann, as has been shown before, equates conscience with Reason and the living God. He who acknowledges conscience, therefore, also bears witness to the living God, even though in using the words of conventional language he may seem to be denying the existence of God. Edelmann tries to interpret Knutzen's position by saying that the God Knutzen justly denies is the Bible God presented by Orthodoxy who 'can never be recognized as the true God'.[41] The real atheists are, therefore, the Orthodox who proclaim their fantasy as the true God and who do not know the living God. All claims of being Christian must be deemed Christian in name only; nothing but moral conduct and the fellowship of Christ will show the true Christian. As his final comment on Knutzen's alleged atheism, Edelmann says:

> Because this man and his friends believed in a conscience and lived according to its dictate, less harm has come to the world from them than from those who with words pretend to profess God but deny Him by deeds through all their lives. ... They hang their conscience upon a nail and do nothing but live honestly, offend no one, or give each his due – the three duties that constitute true worship.[42]

Edelmann's equating of the living God, Reason, and conscience is closer to the Stoic concept than to Knutzen's radical scepticism and overt atheism. Unlike Edelmann, Knutzen refrains from a simple identification of Reason with conscience, yet he is anxious to establish a firm link between the two. In the epistle and the two colloquies where Knutzen announces his maxims of moral behavior he talks of 'reason or knowledge, not of one but of many, united in conjunction with conscience'. The principle is stated in direct refutation of any claims of Biblical revelation, and Knutzen particularly points to the passage in the second Epistle to the Corinthians when man is asked to make Reason subservient to the obedience to Christ.[43] Reason is conceived as man's capability to learn, to understand, in other words, to gain knowledge of the natural world. When, in the second colloquy, the chaplain quotes Aristotle as saying that 'it is impossible to prove all things', the cleric refuses to accept the comment as an excuse for ascribing causes to a supernatural source because no natural one has yet been found. He points out that, with all due respect to Aristotle, the Greek philosopher's knowledge of natural phenomena was limited. The 'Gewissener' accept the fact that they do not have the answers to all questions – "while you Christians know everything, we 'Gewissener' know nothing". 'Conscience', Knutzen writes in the first colloquy, 'is implanted in our bodies by the benign mother, nature; it is our Bible in this life (Romans 2: 14), our preacher, teacher and authority, with no need to exhort us to live honestly, to offend no one and to give each his due'.[44] Knutzen does not miss the opportunity to make a reference to the passage in Paul where the Christian apostle comes closest to the Stoic ideals: 'When the Gentiles, which have not the law, do by nature the things contained in the law, these, having not the law, are a law unto themselves' (Romans 2: 14). While, however, the nature the Stoic talks about and to which Paul refers 'is pervaded by a divine principle',[45] Knutzen would not accept such interpretation. Yet he, too, leaves us with a notion of a benign nature that implants conscience in us. This mythological figure of speech is to Knutzen, however, more acceptable than a reference to a divine power as the source of conscience. The implication perhaps is that in due time knowledge will substitute positive proof for myth, an end easier to achieve than the dethronement of the Bible God.

The Reason that is to work in conjunction with conscience is to Knutzen not a solipsistic phenomenon but a matter of common consent. In the second colloquy he is explicit that the 'Knowledge or Reason' must be 'not of the one who may perhaps be raving, but of the many, and not of small children but of adults'.[46] The principles, or precepts of the law: 'To live honorably; to hurt nobody; to render to everyone his due' are those announced in the beginning of the *Institutes* of Justinian. They are well characterized as ethical principles rather than positive laws.[47] Knutzen deliberately roots his ethics in the secular matrix of Roman law. Like the revolutionaries of 1789, the seventeenth-century Knutzen takes the role of a Roman tribune. The reasoning of mature human beings in harmony with their conscience and guided by the three ethical principles is all that is necessary to create a decent society. This ethos can well be identified with that of bourgeois societies. It was later challenged by the Marxian critique that was dissatisfied with the demand not to hurt anybody and asked for a change of conditions that would prevent anybody from getting hurt. Bourgeois ethos in the petty feudal Jena world was challenge enough, but Knutzen added fuel of an even more explosive nature.

In one passage the guests insinuate that their innkeeper is not a Christian but an atheist, and he confirms their suspicion by answering 'that it is true that he does not believe in God, and he further declares that the priests and secular authorities should be chased from this world because the world can live without them'.[48] Edelmann recognized these statements as the most objectionable in all of Knutzen's writings. How he tried to deal with Knutzen's atheism is apparent from the answer of Lichtlieb to the enraged Blindling, which we have discussed. Edelmann, who considers conscience equal with the living God and who is ready to justify faith by works, does not find it difficult to see in the 'Gewissener' truer Christians than those who proclaim to believe in God 'but live worse than beasts and devils'.[49] Knutzen's anarchistic demand that the secular and clerical authorities be abolished is based on two major arguments. Men who live like the 'Gewissener', who have internalized the ethical principles, do not need a secular power to police their lives. Secular authority and priests act as exploiters of 'honest and poor artisans and peasants'. Basically, Edelmann does not take up Knutzen's radical call to abolish the rule of the exploiters here and now. He is willing to concede to Knutzen that men 'who know the living God, and live according to their conscience, do not need external authority'. This sentence is, however, preceded by a strong caveat: 'In view of the present beastly state of men, authority is and remains indispensable.' Edelmann seizes the opportunity to condemn the use of force proclaimed as Natural Law. He brands as most dangerous to everyone, including civil authorities, the claim that, according to Natural Law, it is permissible to oppose force with force. If this principle prevails, 'no authority may remain in power after it is the wish of its subjects to revolt. They, for their part, do not commit any sin, but can defend their action against authority by the same reasoning as that on which authority depends. From this principle follows the *Bellum omnium contra omnes*, or constant hate and feud of all against all.'[50]

Edelmann prefaced his presentation of Knutzen's writings by stating his conviction that to deny the inspiration of the whole Bible would usher in a new age, and he concluded his discussion of the writings with an even fuller vision of such hopes. "If only all men would become 'Gewissener' the world would look different, and the new heaven and the new earth that the Bible makes us hope for will not be far off. ..." In the concluding part of the *Moses*, where Edelmann returns to the problem of secular authority, the strong impact made on him by Knutzen in these matters becomes even more apparent. Knutzen's immediate effect was to provide Edelmann with a view of a human being who has freed himself from all schackles of authority, from all tutelage over his mind, who is ready to tackle the problems of life, philosophy, and religion with his own conscience as his guide for morality. The ideal type of the 'Gewissener' that Knutzen portrayed emerges beautifully in Goethe's philosophical poem *Testament (Vermächtnis)* of February 12, 1829:

Sofort nun wende dich nach innen:
Das Zentrum findest du da drinnen,
Woran kein Edler zweifeln mag.
Wirst keine Regel da vermissen:
Denn das selbständige Gewissen
Ist Sonne deinem Sittentag.
Now on the instant turn within thee:
There is no center that will win thee,
As no high spirit will gainsay.
The rules are present for thy gaining,
For conscience, free and self-sustaining,
Illuminates thy mortal day.[51]

With his concept of conscience, Knutzen opened up for Edelmann a great new view of man. It remained for the following generation – for Kant, Schiller, and Goethe – a central concern, and it is no less ours. Edelmann, in one of his latest published works, *Die Erste Epistel St. Harenbergs* (1747), formulates his idea of conscience, again to answer those who ask the acceptance of religious precepts as prescribed by clerical authority. It is interesting to note that this demand is always backed up by similar arguments. Georg Thomas Wagner, in his attempted refutation of the *Moses*, phrased it in this way: 'One supposes that God, the Lord, would have wanted to reveal directly to everyone the truth that makes us blessed. What would have followed from that? Doubt, danger or confusion.'[52] The accusation of relativization of moral standards had already been raised by the conservative Aristophanes against Euripides, who contended: 'What is immoral, if he who commits the deed does not feel it to be such?'[53] Knutzen's definition of conscience has a built-in safeguard against such interpretation in the *sensus communis* of reasonable, mature men. Such was Edelmann's definition of 1747: 'The sentiments that I feel in my own heart are incontestably closer to me than those someone else is experiencing and they move me far more convincingly than those that someone else is subjected to; I have therefore to accept these as undoubtedly the guide of my conscience, rather than the sentiments of a person other than myself.'[54] The rationalism of Knutzen has ceded to an emphasis on feelings. Important as are the differences between Knutzen and Edelmann, it should be emphasized once more that the latter's debt to this seventeenth-century revolutionary atheist was great, and that Edelmann was eager to acknowledge it publicly.

Indebted as Edelmann was to Knutzen's idea of conscience, he was equally indebted to Spinoza's idea of God. It has been seen that Edelmann equated Reason with God. Yet this equation should not support an interpretation that puts Edelmann among the Rationalists and Deists. Kant has clearly distinguished between the Deist, who 'believes in God', and the Theist, who believes 'in a living God'.[55] Edelmann is of the party of the theist, although he fails to present a consistent concept of God. This is not to deny the significance of his struggle to shape one. The very issues that were involved in this struggle remained at the center of philosophical discussion far into the Romantic period; Fichte, Hegel, and Schelling still pondered these problems.

The Spinoza who demonstrated exemplary courage in his Bible criticism won Edelmann's overt admiration. In Spinoza's philosophy of materialistic pantheism Edelmann thought to find help in his own effort to express the relation between God and His creation. Spinoza, as a disciple of Descartes, had tried to present his philosophy as geometrical theorem. The Spinoza scholar, Harry Austin Wolfson, remarks: 'To the general reader [the] structure of Spinoza's thought is not obvious, for it is obscured by the artificial form in which the *Ethics* is written – the geometrical form.'[56]

This form and the terminology that Spinoza chose was alien to Edelmann's own habits of thinking and to his readers, who lacked philosophical education. It would be easy to discard Edelmann's own attraction to the God of Spinoza as a mistake and to claim that he never really understood Spinoza's intricate system and its unique terminology. Edelmann presented in the *Moses* a hopelessly confused idea of Creator and Creation. While he was anxious to cast his lot with Spinoza – 'rather with Spinoza and being accused of atheism, than with the Orthodox', he wrote in the *Moses*[57] – he remained deeply imbued with a Christian dualism that was the very opposite of Spinoza's *deus sive natura*. While shaping his own concept of God he made the grave error of mixing what could not be mixed: Spinozistic materialistic pantheism with a neoplatonic mysticism, gathered from many sources.

The task here is not to defend Edelmann, but to reach an understanding of his struggle in its philosophical and even its political implications.

A hundred years later Heinrich Heine, with admirable elegance and clarity, best described those aspects of Spinoza's idea of God to which Edelmann had responded most enthusiastically:

> Benedict Spinoza teaches that there is but one substance, God. This one substance is infinite and absolute. All finite substances are derived from it, are contained in it, emerge from or sink into it; they have only relative, transitory, accidental existence. Only stupidity and malice could term his doctrine 'atheism'. No one has ever expressed himself in more sublime terms regarding the Deity. Instead of saying that he denies God, we should rather say that he denies Man. All finite objects are for him only modes of infinite substance. All finite things are contained in God; the human intellect is only a ray of infinite thought; the human body only an atom of infinite extension; God is the infinite cause of souls and bodies – *natura naturans*.[58]

In his discussion in the *Moses* of the relation of the Creator to the creation Edelmann sets the idea of God the Creator against that of God the maker. The 'God the maker' image is that of the 'watchmaker who fabricates, out of some matter utterly different from himself, a watch that he leaves to itself when he is done with it'. Of such a God Edelmann disposes quickly and triumphantly when Lichtlieb announces to Blindling: 'My brother, we are more closely related to God than the watchmaker to his watch, of whom it would be absurd to claim that, having made it, he continues to be present in and to direct it. ... Were this the case, a watchmaker might well be the watch's balance or spring.' Edelmann counters this mechanical example used by the Deists with images from nature: 'We are the streams, He is the source, we are the rays, He is the sun, we are the shadows, He is the essence.'

Surely this would be strange language to Spinoza's ears, the vocabulary is derived from the *Philosophia Moysaica* of the Rosicrucian adept, the London physician Robert Fludd (1574–1637). Nevertheless Edelmann feels that he is actually following Spinoza when he has Lichtlieb state: 'All creatures are nothing, but it is He who is all, and fortunate is the creature that recognizes its own nothingness and lets God be everything.' He follows this with one of the few direct references to Spinoza: '... we are just that and no more; certain modes through which God proves that He exists; Spinoza, who preferred to express himself concisely, therefore used to say: the creatures are but *modificationes essentiae divinae.*[59] Here Edelmann adds another statement modifying his own position: 'God is the Being and Essence of all things because no creature can, for a single moment, sustain itself. In no way can He therefore be the creature itself.'[60] Behind such a statement can easily be detected the mysticism of a Madame Guyon. To relate it to Spinoza would be to force the argument. Edelmann, however, does not relent in trying to make use of Spinoza in his own way:

> I do not find any difficulty in saying that the essence of the creature – which is by no means the creature itself – is nothing less than the emanation of the essence of God. ... If, by saying that the essence of matter is an emanation of the essence of God, one claims that God is made into something material, one clearly professes one's own ignorance of the true meaning of the words Being and Essence.[61]

The acceptance of the material world as an emanation of God labels as a materialist the one who holds such views. In further support of the materialism of Edelmann, the significance of a sentence like the following should not be overlooked: 'He and matter belong together, and without matter God could never have brought about a material world.'[62] There is no reason to deny Edelmann a place among the materialists, yet his own uncertainties on the subject make such labeling less meaningful. It is important to observe that Edelmann was not afraid of being accused of materialism on account of his use of the term 'emanation'. He is well aware that all expressions used in our attempt to comprehend God are only human approximations, and he bluntly asks: 'Why should we blame each other for using sensuous concepts when talking of God?'[63]

Having emphatically rejected the deistic 'God the maker' idea, Edelmann proclaims even more passionately God the Creator: 'His existence is a steady activity, a continuous moving of matter, that manifests itself before our eyes in the continuous movement of the world, never resting by day or by night.'[64] For this, the creative force or the Spirit, Goethe found similar expression:

> *In Lebensfluten, im Tatensturm*
> *Wall ich auf und ab,*
> *Webe hin und her!*
> *Geburt und Grab,*

Ein ewiges Meer,
Ein wechselnd Weben,
Ein glühend Leben:
So schaff ich am sausenden Webstuhl der Zeit
Und wirke der Gottheit lebendiges Kleid.
As the swirling of life, the storm of action,
I rise and fall
drift here and there!
I am the womb and the tomb,
an ocean eternal,
a changing, glowing
life in ferment:
thus working on the roaring loom of time,
I weave God's living Garment.[65]

This concept of the Spirit, unceasingly creating, is far different from Spinoza's which thus inspired Heine: 'When we read Spinoza, we have the feeling that we are looking at all-powerful Nature in liveliest repose.'[66] The contemporary philosopher Ernst Bloch, making direct allusion to the Faust passage just quoted, writes as follows: 'In the depths of the Spinoza-world reigns that silence where swirling of life ['Lebensfluten'] and storm of action ['Tatensturm'] end.'[67]

Such close examination of Edelmann's language suggests that there is in him the same urge to seek after the Creator and creation in its continuing metamorphosis, that holds sway over Goethe. In this sense Edelmann and Goethe are heirs to the dynamic view of creation of Jakob Böhme rather than to the world of Spinoza seen *sub species aeternitatis*.[68]

That aspect of Spinoza's philosophy which comprehended the world *sub species aeternitatis* enabled him to present a unique identification of the Creator and creation in his own language of *natura naturans* and *natura naturata*.[69] In this geometric figure, where 'reality and perfection[70] are one', God is immanent. Edelmann, while disregarding the presuppositions that are essential to Spinoza's concept of God, senses this overwhelming immanence. Heine's comment that 'instead of saying that he [Spinoza] denies God, we should rather say he denies Man',[71] answers Edelmann's image of Man. In Man 'the most blessed and joyful Spirit will manifest itself in complete freedom, free of all fetters; it will reveal itself for what it is, whatever bliss and contentedness it possesses, how averse it is to all sadness and fear, and, finally, what man can become if he but gives the Spirit a free hand'.[72] With biting irony Edelmann says: 'When God in days to come is everything to the blessed, he will be just that only to the Spinozists, who deem it not dangerous, if God is and will be everything to them.'[73] Edelmann thus touches on Spinoza's image of liveliest repose, this state of bliss and contentedness. As Edelmann, unlike Spinoza, did not think in geometrical abstractions, he presented to himself and his readers the relation of creator and creation in a peculiar image-language that he thought preserved the Spinozistic concept of immanence: 'God as the essence of all things, as a whole (holistic entity) within His inaccessible light, and matter as its shadow, in its various movements and positions, as the creation of the world.'[74]

From this idea of essence Edelmann builds a bridge to the idea of the Logos that is important to him:

The sun forms and sustains through a light extraneous to its own shadow, a light that is, however, not foreign to the sun itself but its own, inseparably united to it. Similarly, the light radiating unceasingly from God's incomparable essence is nothing foreign, nor a thing existing separated from Him; so ineluctably is it His absolute attribute that it might be called God. Know therefore that the divine light, through which all parts of the shadow-image of God – I mean the visible world – is formed, is nothing else but divine Reason or the Logos.[75]

To further illustrate the meaning of the sun and shadow, or God and matter relation, Edelmann refers to the picture on the title-page of Robert Fludd's *Philosophia Moysaica*. Without actually attempting to analyze this complicated allegorical portrayal of creation, he points only to the two symmetrical circles in the upper part, one filled with light and the archetypical sun image in its center; the other, black with a triangle in its center, representing God. The triangle, Edelmann comments, 'is to signify that the shadow-circle is ruled by God'. He then ventures a further explanation: 'Although he [Fludd] does not say it, he intends the shadow-circle to symbolize matter and has placed it, equal in size, next to the primal light of God.'[76] The qualitative distinction between light and darkness implied in Edelmann's sentence echoes the verse of Genesis: 'And God saw the light, that it was good: and God divided the light from the darkness' (Genesis

1: 4). Associating God with light and darkness with matter corresponds to Edelmann's own deep feelings. His fellowship at Dresden with followers of the apostle of asceticism, Gichtel, who held all sexual intercourse in contempt, together with his own decision to remain unmarried, reflect his suspicion of the flesh. The Christian tradition, particularly the Pauline, of separating the world into spirit and flesh, soul and body, was too well ingrained in Edelmann to let him fully accept a world in which God and Creation are identical.

A sentence as awkward as the following reveals a great deal about Edelmann's own inconsistencies: 'Therein consists the difference between God and us – who presently are existing in His shadow, or in the darkness of matter – that He emanates the light out of Himself that casts the shadow, we, on the other hand, being stuck in matter of this dark body, can never produce a light by ourselves nor cast our own shadow.'[77] Here Edelmann distinguishes between God the source of light, God's shadow as dark matter, and man. Edelmann's concept of man follows traditional Biblical and neoplatonic teachings: 'The permission we have received [is] either to live in His light or in His shadow. What I mean [is], within or without the flesh and the material things that surround us. This power of decision which is unique to us and which we call free-will distinguishes us from and elevates us above all other works of God.'[78]

The interpretation Edelmann gives to original sin further elucidates his interpretation of man:

Listen, dear 'Blindling', what is the only sin and the reason for our present damnation? We wanted to be independent, we were not satisfied to be in and of God, but wanted to be something according to our own whims. ... The Fantasy that we would become like God, by eating from the so-called tree of knowledge, was the cause of our fall. This fantasy, however, has its origin not in unfortunate Adam, nor in a ghost called the devil masquerading under the poetic invention of a snake, and least of all is it to be attributed to God, but solely to the capacity of our will, according to which, in order to satisfy our self-love, we aspire either to the highest good or to a lesser good called evil. We ourselves were therefore satan because we did not let Him be everything in us, but we wanted to be ourselves and to act according to our own wishes without God's participation.[79]

While this evaluation of man, who by his own free-will abandons himself to corporeal existence in darkness, might easily be taken as denigrating material creation, such a reading misses Edelmann's intention: 'Matter in its various shapes and positions into which the visible things of this world are formed gives, if not a perfect, yet neither an unlikely nor unrecognizable picture of the marvelous essence of our great Creator.'[80]

Thus we see Edelmann circling around the problem of Creator and Creation. We find him still caught in his own fears of sex and body while at the same time experiencing a new joyful relation to nature, *natura naturata*. Intrigued by Spinoza, he cannot overcome a basic dualistic orientation. Surely he is oscillating between this new nature-feeling and an ideal image of a spiritual-ascetic being, while trying to de-mythologize traditional Biblical concepts as the basis for a comprehension of the relation of the Creator to his Creation. He emphasized that he did not aim for 'philosophical proofs' because such proofs demand 'accurate, clear and sufficient knowledge of all properties of a subject matter'.[81] Rather than such a Cartesian demonstration, which he considers inappropriate if not impossible, he declares that he will convey his thoughts on Creation through an image, 'because through an image we can, in our present state of mind, at least to some degree, comprehend such a procedure. Further, Scripture does not hesitate to speak in such manner to us.'[82] The image-language of Scripture was certainly more comprehensible to Edelmann's readers than were Descartes' or Spinoza's philosophical-mathematical theorems. Whether Edelmann himself realized that he was retreating into the world of myth it is difficult to say.

In choosing to express his ideas on the creation of matter by means of imagery he thought he had found the most adequate image for matter in that of the 'shadow', a term he derived from Fludd's quotations from the *Poimandres*, dialogues ascribed to the mystical figure Hermes and often called Mercurius Trismegistus.[83] Fludd's object was to apply the ideas of Greek, Hellenic and Neoplatonic philosophers to interpretation of the Genesis text and to show a congruity between their ideas on creation and the Bible. He felt particularly justified in doing so, as he claimed that Plato as well as Hermes knew the Mosaic books, and that, therefore, passages in their writings dealing with creation, Logos, and matter could be taken as direct commentaries on Genesis.[84] Following the neoplatonist

Marsilio Ficino's Latin translation of Hermetic writings and commentaries on them, Fludd quoted or paraphrased passages which interpret the first chapter of Genesis. The passage that became fascinating to Edelmann was actually a paraphrase in which Fludd compacted several sentences from Hermes and related them to the second verse of Genesis. 'The earth was without form and void, and darkness was upon the face of the deep; and the Spirit of God was moving over the face of the waters', or in the Vulgate translation, 'terra autem erat inanis et vacua et tenebrae super faciem abyssi et Spiritus Dei ferebatur super aquas'. Fludd's paraphrase of the Hermetic passages reads as follows: 'Mercurius Trismegistus illud umbram vocat horrendam quae nihil erat nec appareret, priusquam lux divina e tenebris effusit.'[85] Edelmann in turn offers a German translation and comments: 'Mercurius Trismegistus, who according to the opinion of some was Moses himself, calls that from which everything was created, the so-called first matter, *umbram horrendam*, – an astonishing shadow, ... that was nothing, nor had any shape, until the divine light shone out of darkness.' Previously in the *Moses* Edelmann had proclaimed: 'we cannot picture matter more accurately than as the shadow of God.'[86] He now followed Fludd in identifying the 'umbra horrenda' of Mercurius Trismegistus with 'first matter', though he never spelled out for his reader the line of arguments that Fludd presented. To quote the relevant passage from Fludd will clarify the process of thought that led to this identification and will also exemplify the intertwining of various philosophical and religious traditions characteristic of his writings. Fludd writes:

> The whole concurrent of the Scriptures do confirm, being that it is said, *that God created the world of matter without form* [The Wisdom of Solomon, XI, 18], *and that the heavens and the earth were first of waters, and by waters* [The Second Letter of Peter, 3, 5], *and consisting by the word of God.* And [they do further confirm] that the Original or primary womb, from whence the waters were extracted (which were the material stuff whereof all things were framed), *was this dark and deformed Abyss or Chaos,* and therefore [the water] had the beginning of their formal being, from the Father of all-informing and vivifying light and essence. But that we may directly shew unto you the egregious theft of the foresaid Philosophers from *Moses* his Principles. That Principle which *Moses* termed *darkness, the dark Abyss* or potential Principle, *Aristotle* doth

call his *Materia prima, or first matter,* which he averreth to be something in puissance or potentially only, because it is not as yet reduced into act. Again, he seemeth to term it privation, but falsely, being that no position did precede it. On the other side *Plato* calleth it *Hyle,* which is esteemed to be nothing, forasmuch as it is invisible and without form. Also he compareth it to a dark body, in respect of the soul and spirit. As for *Hermes,* he intitleth it by the name of *umbra horrenda,* or *fearful shadow.*[87]

We have already remarked that Edelmann had recourse to a myth in his attempt to explain the Creator-creation relationship. His chosen imagery of the shadow deeply reflects his own values and aspirations: ambivalence towards matter and the desire not to separate the Creator from his creation. Turning from the sublime to the ridiculous he retells, as a case in point, an anecdote once told to him in Dresden: 'A physician, on the bidding of Peter the Great of Russia, cut up a hundred people alive for the purpose of finding in their bodies the location of their souls.' Edelmann concludes the account by saying that so gruesome a search only confirms that any concept of the soul as 'coarse corporeal' is a mistaken one.[88] That Edelmann relates the anecdote at all is indicative of his own search for the stuff of which spirit and soul are made. He certainly took notice of the expression used in the *Third Hermetic Discourse,* 'spiritus tenuis intellectualis' – 'a thin intellectual spirit' – quoted by Fludd.[89] This phrase, suggesting a strange scale of more or less, grosser or thinner corporeality of spirit and soul, might also have been in Edelmann's mind when he used the words 'coarse corporeal'. In applying a mystical and mythological approach to Creation, Edelmann had wandered away from Spinoza, although he himself might not have recognized this. Bent on uniting the Creator with His creation, and unlike the Orthodox, who saw man as separated from God, he sensed in Spinoza's God *the God of oneness.*

Spinoza's philosophical method did not satisfy him and Edelmann strayed away to other teachings. He was not discriminating in his use of sources so long as he could satisfy himself that he was communicating to his readers the image of the living God, 'the all-encompassing, all-sustaining, and all-moving essence' – 'alles erfüllenden, alles belebenden und bewegenden Wesen'.[90] Here one recalls that Goethe lets Faust answer Gretchen's question as to his belief in God with the word: 'Does not the all-encompassing, the all-supporting embrace and uphold us, you, me and himself?' – 'Der Allumfasser, der Allerhalter, Fasst and erhält Er nicht Dich, mich, sich selbst?'[91] One cannot, knowing Goethe's affinity for Spinoza, miss the similarity in tone and expression.

Edelmann made no original contribution to the philosophical and psychological question of the relation of soul to body, and of spirit to matter; indeed, his presentation might even be characterized as confused and confusing. By the same token it has to be questioned whether his contemporaries were very much clearer on the subject. What distinguishes Edelmann is his willingness, his eagerness to explore any thinker's ideas without prejudice. The labels 'materialism' or 'atheism' did not prevent him from studying Knutzen or Spinoza. The use of anathematizing labels by the Orthodox clergy to prevent the search for a truer understanding of God and creation he rejected. The outcry with which the *Moses* was received by the clergy shows that they understood its message. When Edelmann wrote in his annotated copy of Pratje: 'He [Edelmann] neither approves of everything that Spinoza said nor of everything that Pythagoras taught,'[92] he did so not to absolve himself of a charge, but merely to state the fact. 'Spinozism' was a philosophy he appreciated according to his own understanding, but it was not a threat to his character. On the contrary, Edelmann was ready to say, 'I prefer to be counted among the persecuted Spinozists than with the persecutors'.[93]

When Edelmann began the *Moses* he had in mind a format similar to the one he had chosen for *Unschuldige Wahrheiten*. The publication was to appear in parts over several years, each part containing what Edelmann wished at the moment to communicate. Some parts were more closely connected than others, but the work was not to be guided by any predetermined arrangement. Edelmann had not intended to end publication of the *Moses* with the third part; circumstances prevented him from continuing publication at that time. As we know, not until 1756 did he begin writing the later parts of the *Moses;* but these were never published.[94]

Thus we can explain why the *Moses*, though in its present form it appears to be a self-contained work, was not planned to be so. The book in which its author intended to unveil the truth about the fabrication of the Bible and consequently to dethrone the Bible as an idol did not culminate in any grand finale. Edelmann turns instead to condemnation of a recently published poem in which Voltaire celebrated the accession of Frederick II to the Prussian throne. Although a connection between his discussion of the poem and his earlier treatment of Matthias Knutzen's views on civil authority can be found, such passages are by no means the climax the reader would have expected. Perhaps the very lack of a real structure of composition is one reason why Edelmann's *Moses* does not occupy the prominence in theological and philosophical literature which its merits, and the tremendous importance attributed to it by his contemporaries seemed to warrant.

Voltaire's ode *Au Roi Prusse – sur son avénement au trône*, just published in German translation,[95] struck Edelmann as a disgusting example of servility and sycophantism. What he objected to most in the poem was the glorification of an earthly ruler and Voltaire's choice of examples to indicate the new reign's promise of enlightenment and tolerance. In 1740, to praise a day when the works of Descartes, Bayle, Leibniz or Wolff could be taught freely, meant little to the propagandist of Knutzen and Spinoza. So congratulatory an attitude ignored completely contemporary German issues. If we find Edelmann's vilification of Voltaire offensive, as well we may, it should be kept in mind that our own image of Voltaire is largely shaped by his brilliant later prose works and by his courageous fight for human justice.

At the time he was finishing the *Moses*, Edelmann probably knew little of Voltaire, whose literary and historical works thus far published would hardly have interested him – for all that their literary elegance and heroic subjects were now compelling the admiration of the young Frederick. Indeed, the intimacy beginning between Voltaire and Frederick had its roots in a combination of aspirations common to the writer-philosopher and the then heir to the Prussian throne. The first letter of Frederick to Voltaire is dated August 8, 1736. That the twenty-four-year-old Frederick sensed the genius of Voltaire is testimony to the qualities of his own mind. But it is unlikely that Edelmann in Berleburg would have appreciated the Voltaire of *La Mort de César, La Henriade,* and the *Histoire de Charles XII* as did Frederick in Remusberg.

The particular sensitivity Edelmann displayed in questioning the commitment of the new regime to tolerance and in objecting to incipient hero-worship proved to be well justified. To credit Edelmann with great foresight would be rash. One might better say that his radical negation of authority made him unfailingly suspicious of such praise as Voltaire bestowed on the new king, 'Le Salomon du Nord'.

When Knutzen called for the abolition of all civil authority, Edelmann did not follow him and explained why:

> If Knutzen demands that authority be banished from the world, I have to confess frankly, not out of servile fear but because I see the real situation, which is ... that that poor man has rushed matters greatly. Authority is still necessary in view of the present beastly state of men, although a human being who knows the living God and who lives according to his conscience has no need whatsoever of such authority.[96]

If authority has to be endured for the time being, those who exercise it are not to be extolled. 'God alone deserves the attribute of Majesty. None of God's servants, even were one of them more elevated than any of the kings on earth, should command such deference.'

Wise men realize the truth that 'not to us, Lord, not to us belongs the glory, but to you; and all praise showered on rulers is flattery and blasphemy'. Incited by Voltaire's tendency to hero-worship, Edelmann sets out to deflate the royal egos. 'After all', he asks, 'what difference is there between the most serene monarch and the pitch-dark slave when night has fallen?' Towards the end of the *Moses* we find Edelmann reverting to the social criticism of the atheist and materialist Knutzen, although his own is rooted in deep religious conviction.

From the same religious convictions stems Edelmann's lack of confidence that Frederick will bring a true age of tolerance. Truth does not need royal tutelage: 'God's truth is its own shield and buckler (Psalms 91: 4) and knows how to make a place among its enemies. He who is not blind must at least have some sense of it, though he cannot see, and therefore truth needs no human support.' While writing these lines, Edelmann is aware that enthusiasm has carried him far and soberly admits 'that truth sometimes makes use of the powers of this earth to restrain bigotry'.[97] Frederick II, whose reign had just started when Edelmann was writing the *Moses*, had more than one opportunity to serve truth by means of his earthly power, as, for instance, in preventing the slaughter of Catholics by the revengeful local Protestant population after the battle of Hohenfriedberg. Frederick's tolerance had its own limitations, and on several occasions he confessed: '... my faith is lukewarm, and I tolerate the entire world, presuming that I, myself, am tolerated. I let everyone worship God as it suits him to do, and I believe that everyone has the right to take the road he prefers in getting to the unknown countries, heaven or hell.'[98] But these royal thoughts have to be understood within the realities of a government that considered the welfare of the state in preference to any private considerations and asked of its citizens 'civil obedience and loyalty'.[99] The degree of enlightenment and sophistication that Frederick claimed for himself and for some learned friends he considered a privilege strictly confined to an élite. To share it with his subjects he would have considered an act of folly, and his simple verdict was: 'The common man does not deserve to be enlightened. (Le vulgaire ne mérite pas d'être éclairé.)'[100] Frederick maintained the censorship of the press, as Lessing recalled bitterly to Nicolai in a letter of August 25, 1769: 'Do not talk of your Berliner freedom to think and to write! It comes down solely to the freedom to bring to market as much nonsense against religion as one wants.'[101]

Censorship, however, extended to religious matters, and among those administering it was the Probst Johann Peter Süssmilch (1707–1767), who later became one of Edelmann's most malicious persecutors. An amusing report by the poet Ramler to his friend Gleim well illustrates the equivocal position of Frederick and, moreover, involves Edelmann. Ramler writes in the letter of February 3, 1748:

> The king, noticing among those seeking audience, a tailor who had worked for him, but had expressed resentment that not all orders were given to him, thought he would put the said tailor in his place. The king addressed to him the question: Does he diligently read the Bible? 'No, your majesty.' To which answer the king remarked: 'That is bad!' Then he asked if he diligently read Edelmann, to which the tailor replied, wishing to appear sophisticated, 'yes'. The king said: 'That is bad', giving the man a Bible with these words: 'Read in the Prophet Daniel, Chapter VIII verse 8, where you will find your dismissal.'[102]

This discussion of the final pages of Edelmann's *Moses* has carried us into a later period. The immediate consequences for Edelmann of the publication of the work were far-reaching. If the *Unschuldige Wahrheiten* had raised fear and opposition, the *Moses* offered a far greater challenge not only to clerical, but also to secular authorities. The *Moses* made its author a public figure almost overnight. The immediate attention the book received precipitated swift efforts to suppress it. Even Count Casimir could not ignore the clamor and felt compelled to send a secretary to Edelmann's quarters to confiscate the copies that were reported to have just arrived from Marburg. The effect of the publication of the *Moses* was hardly anticipated by Edelmann, yet it brought him the response he had hoped for. Criticisms that his generous friend Pinell made concerning coarseness of expression were brushed aside in the first excitement of success.[103] The *Moses* marked the culmination of Edelmann's thinking and writing after his arrival at Berleburg; it also brought to an end this idyllic phase of his life. On June 5, 1741, the benevolent Count Casimir died. The economic conditions that had fostered a policy of religious toleration, the welcoming of new immigrants and exempting them from fiscal burdens, no longer prevailed in the 1740s. The consequence of the changes were stringent new tax regulations and hostility toward the religious dissenters. Edelmann had felt the changes occurring under the regime of Count Ludwig Ferdinand of Sayn-Wittgenstein-Berleburg, and in the fall of 1741 he made a hurried and clandestine exit from Berleburg. He left Berleburg no longer an obscure theologian, but a writer known in all of Germany.

7. Confession of Faith
1741–1749

As a refuge for religious dissenters the duchy of Neuwied on the Rhine was then well known. Yet the road conditions — long stretches flooded and rutted so that carts frequently were mired or, even worse, turned over with all their goods – were so bad that Edelmann thought it best to seek living quarters closer to Berleburg. The town of Hachenburg, seat of Count Georg Friedrich of Kirchberg and Sayn-Hachenburg (1683–1749), located about two days' walking distance from Berleburg, appealed to Edelmann as a place where he could settle peacefully. The reputation of the Count and his wife Sophie Amalie were such that Edelmann believed that he might be permitted to seek a domicile for him and his companion, Brother Erhart. He was not disappointed, and in the late fall of 1741 he installed himself and Brother Erhart comfortably in the house of the tanner Leitzschbag, to which Edelmann managed to move most of his household equipment and over one hundred books.[1] A few hours after Edelmann had left Berleburg, the fiscal officer and notary, Georg Balthasar Buchner, appeared in the apartment and was outraged to find that it had been emptied before he could collect taxes and appropriate Edelmann's possessions.[2] When within a year Brother Langemeyer and Sister Schelldorfinn decided to join them, they rented a house from the innkeeper of the Golden Lion Inn and set up a menage as they had done at Berleburg.[3]

Although Hachenburg was not a haven for dissenters, nevertheless Lutherans, Reformed Evangelicals, and Roman Catholics had their own churches and lived side by side unmolested. The great majority of the population of a little over one thousand belonged to the Reformed sect. The smaller Lutheran congregation was made up of the members of the court and its officers and servants. There were about thirty Catholic households, and a small Franciscan convent which had existed since 1637.[4] Although Edelmann had little sympathy for the order and knew of their preacher's denunciation of him, he did not turn the brethren empty-handed from his door when they came begging for alms.[5] The inhabitants of many of the neighboring villages belonged to the Catholic faith, and about an hour's walking distance from Hachenburg was the Cistercian abbey of Marienstatt, a center for pilgrimage and studies. A few Jewish families were also listed among the inhabitants of Hachenburg (three in 1729, five in 1753).[6] According to Edelmann he and Erhart found favor with the residents, who felt an affinity with the two bearded men. Perhaps his earlier experiences in Austria made it easier for him to move among the Catholic peasants and craftsmen of Hachenburg. He met with some animosity from the clergy of all three creeds, yet was able to roam freely in the area. He enjoyed the Westerwald and its relative harshness as compared to the more gentle Edertal and Sayn-Wittgenstein woods. On several occasions he visited the splendid abbey of Marienstatt with its great Gothic art treasures, in particular the impressive Ursula Altar, carved from wood and richly adorned with gold leaf.[7]

The two and a half years Edelmann spent at Hachenburg, from late fall 1741 to spring 1744, were quiet ones. The well-ordered world of a small town, with its modest and friendly court, engendered an atmosphere that was ideally suited for him, following on a period of excitement and unprecedented creativity. The publication of the *Moses* had made him a notorious figure on the German theological scene. While the clergy who were enraged did not hesitate to proclaim their condemnation of work and author from the pulpit and in print, those who were favorably impressed expressed their sentiments in more quiet ways. Individuals as well as small groups of seekers who had become acquainted with Edelmann's writings were anxious to know the author – whether for curiosity's sake or out of a wish to gain further elucidation from him.[8] Among them were some who had been deeply shaken in their traditional beliefs by Edelmann's Bible critique and by his ideas on the nature of God and Creation. There were also those – and probably they were in the majority – who were already dissenting from orthodoxy and were, as Edelmann himself had once been, avid for any writings advancing their new line of reasoning. Even before the publication of the *Moses* Edelmann recorded that 'seldom a mail-day went by on which I did not receive at least one, usually more, letters'. Now letters began to pour in on him in ever-increasing number, and by the time he left Hachenburg he estimated that he was spending eighty gulden a year on mail expenses. The mail brought him not only letters, but small and large money contributions towards his support as a free intellectual.[9]

Edelmann's information about the social and professional background of his correspondents shows that they were mostly small independent craftsmen; a few were substantial businessmen, and some medical doctors were also among his loyal supporters. With the addition of some members of the nobility, this corresponds in general to the composition of circles of religious dissenters and seekers of all varieties. A certain freedom to manage one's own precious time was necessary to allow for rumination and speculation on matters religious, and herein the independent craftsman had an advantage over boss or journeyman of a large establishment in town or country: leisure which, however, the well-off entrepreneur and the doctor also commanded. While the work-style was important for the pursuit of religious interests, these interests in turn influenced the formation of work patterns.[10] Edelmann answered his correspondents as the occasion arose, and to some of the letters he gave the more formal designation 'Sendschreiben', one of which he had printed in 1749.[11]

The sole larger work which Edelmann composed at Hachenburg, *Die Begierde nach der Vernünfftigen Lautern Milch*, belongs in this category, although it is not explicitly called a 'Sendschreiben'. It was written in response to a letter that reached him, unsigned and without trace of origin, on August 12, 1743. It turned out that the letter was written by Hulde, a linen printer at Sorau in the Niederlausitz, on behalf of himself and some friends. When he received their anonymous communication, Edelmann felt that a printed answer sent into the world would reach those for whom it was intended. *Die Begierde nach der Vernünfftigen Lautern Milch* was completed in November 1743 and was printed by Haupt in Neuwied early in 1744, shortly before Edelmann moved there.[12] The discussions of the problems of the nature of God, of sin, of rebirth, of sexual impulses do not add substantially to earlier discussions on these subjects, yet the book has an engaging quality of its own and seems to convey a rare intimacy between author and reader. One notices a marked change from a baroque vocabulary, as still used by Brockes and Zinzendorf, to the new austere and abstract language of the Enlightenment. It was addressed to people who had expressed their great admiration and friendship for Edelmann and who appeared well acquainted with his writings. Edelmann tries to respond to their wish for further clarification, confessing that he cannot provide capsule prescriptive statements which are alien to his style and would contradict his non-dogmatic treatment of religious issues.[13]

Edelmann begins his reply to the friends at Sorau by thanking them for their confidence and friendship, yet in a subtle way he refuses to accept the praise they shower on him as unwarranted for any human being. When they write that 'Dippel has overcome 1,000 followers of Sects, Edelmann however 10,000'[14] he finds their language offensive and says so. To him a personality cult is deeply suspect, as he had made clear in his comments on Voltaire's praise of Frederick II.[15] Throughout *Die Begierde* Edelmann demonstrates in a didactic and masterful manner to his correspondents their reliance on outside authorities, whether religious leaders or so-called sacred texts. In the *Moses* Edelmann had offered a full and careful discussion of conscience as the sole guide for conduct; now he wanted his friends and readers to accept this view and thus free themselves of all superimposed authorities.[16] Education toward self-reliance is Edelmann's major concern; this self-reliance is in no way divorced from trust in the one God, 'the living God', described in the *Moses* as 'the all-encompassing, all-sustaining, and all-moving essence'.[17] When asked to 'sketch in some fifty-odd pages the fundamentals of Christian teachings ... in the manner a father speaks to his children or a bridegroom to his bride'[18] Edelmann does not shy away from outspoken and even corrective answers. To speak like 'a father' to his children defines precisely the authoritarian relation Edelmann wants his friends and readers to overcome. He cannot accept an expression like 'bridegroom' as a figure of speech, but shows how absurd it is to demand such a role of him.

The request for an outline of fundamental Christian teachings prompts Edelmann to distinguish between the 'teaching of Christ' and 'Christian teachings'. For the latter as expounded in the literature of past centuries Edelmann has no use. For discussion of the Christian teachings on such matters as sin, hell, devil, rebirth, he refers the brethren to his published works. As to the 'teaching of Christ' he points out that Jesus would have outlined these teachings for us if he had wished to; 'surely nobody would have been more competent to do so than Christ himself'. The truth of the matter is that Jesus

left us with the testimony of his life, because he foresaw that the teachings would not remain undistorted by his successors. His life was committed to his struggle to de-mask the superstition and false religion of his fellow countrymen and to restore universal love among men. This testimony cannot be disputed and can be expressed in three lines rather than fifty pages. It would take much more space if one were to recount the battle of his mind with superstitions, many of them still alive in our own times.[19]

Edelmann is not ready to undertake such an enterprise in the *Begierde*, yet the question raised by the brothers may well have spurred his thinking to its crystallization in the *Glaubens-Bekentniss* of 1746. The nature of a letter allows for venting of personal feelings and opinions. Edelmann is glad that the friends are slowly freeing themselves from the afflictions of the pietistic syndrome that dictates belief in one continuous transgression and 'makes one incessantly lament, sigh and groan'.[20] Edelmann, who like many other seekers had once seen in Pietism an improvement over orthodox sterility, knew enough of the melancholic state of Pietists, their perverted self-image and inescapable hypocrisy. Ernst Bloch's programmatic characterization of liberated man: 'There sets in an upright stance, attempting to liberate itself from the old outmoded one'[21] reads like a self-characterization of Edelmann. Such 'posture allows me to see farther and thus sooner the splendor of a rising sun'. Pietism takes a wasteful depressed mood for saintliness. Faith in the living God engenders a state of joyfulness and serenity (Heiterkeit). Edelmann offers with enthusiasm all the help he can give to 'the brothers in their mighty endeavors to emerge out of the depth of old errors and to gain a serene posture'.[22]

In the 15th part of *Unschuldige Wahrheiten*, published in 1743, Edelmann had described the mood auspicious for a deeper understanding of the living God: 'a lasting liveliness of the feeling soul and an unceasing effort not to rest before one knows one's origin as clearly as one knows the objects that can be seen and touched ... What is therefore needed is not only a cheerful, but also a sober mood' ('eine anhaltende Munterkeit des Gemüths, und ein unablässiger Ernst nicht eher zu ruhen, als bis man seinen Ursprung so kenne, als man jetzt Dinge kennt, die man sehen und greiffen kan ... Es gehöret also nicht nur ein munteres sondern auch ein nüchternes Gemüth darzu.').[23] Edelmann was the first to use words like 'munter', 'heiter', 'nüchtern' to characterize the climate of feeling suitable for the contemplation of the divine. These words appeared in similar context in the poetry and philosophical prose of the German Idealists, Hölderlin, Schelling, and Hegel.

It is not surprising that the Sorauer brothers turned to Edelmann for pastoral advice on the question of marriage and sexual desires. The Christian-Pauline teachings on the spirit and the flesh, lust and sin had left its mark on the brothers as on anyone raised in the Christian tradition. In their struggle for a pure and perfect Christian life they, like Edelmann, were confronted with extreme ascetic demands. They had found help in the distinction that the Pietists made between the carnal (sensual) and the natural man, between the man who pursues his sexual desires regardless of marriage bonds and the man who practices sex only within the marriage relationship. In the *Moses* the brothers now had come across the passage in which Edelmann quotes Knutzen saying that distinctions between wife and whore are meaningless, as both are sex partners.[24] One can easily understand the brothers' wish for further elucidation if one adds the highly complicated discussion in the *Moses* on the question of spirit and flesh. Edelmann's position on the question of spirit and flesh had not altered basically since he wrote the *Moses*, three years earlier. Yet the tone of his answer suggests a subtle shift in his attitude towards sex. The move to Hachenburg had been one away from the Sayn-Wittgenstein communities of radical spiritualists. The mood of his devotion was lively and serene, not fierce and somber. When Edelmann now decided to shave his beard and to wear a conventional wig, he intended to express a further detachment from all that might reek of sects and pietism.[25]

In his answer to the brothers Edelmann retains his distinction between mortal flesh and immortal spirit. He warns, however, against branding 'the flesh as evil because as long as the spirit dwells in the flesh, the flesh can be an impediment to the spirit'. Goethe's ironic line makes the point: 'Ein Erdenrest zu tragen peinlich.' From the distinction between flesh and spirit, in which values are inherent, emerge two types of human beings: the one seeks sensuous pleasures, the other 'more noble, lasting, less animalistic pleasures'.[26] Edelmann identified with the latter. He saw as the purpose of education a providential process, the emergence of an enlightened spiritual being. To use Freud's vocabulary, what he actually sensed and celebrated was the power of sublimation. The first type – the sensuous, pleasure-seeking man – is not to be condemned; his impulses are natural, and to characterize them as perverse or sinful is wrong. Edelmann follows Knutzen in rejecting matrimony as an institution necessary to sanctify sexual intercourse. This does not imply that Edelmann objected to marriage: he just meant that sexual intercourse was not evil.

Edelmann is well aware of the radical nature of his comments on sex and sin. The brothers had found in Edelmann's writing much that they felt to be true, even in contradiction to the accepted values of the churches: 'Much that has so far been considered in matters of belief and life-style, heresy, obscenity, and sin has to be recognized as truth.' Edelmann's message has been understood and he must lead his readers to the realization that they had been living in a world of perverted values and 'that therefore the world had to be turned upside down again'.[27]

Early in the spring of 1744 Edelmann was informed that the dwelling in which he and his friends were so comfortably installed had been sold, and he was therefore forced to look for new quarters. When no suitable housing could be found in Hachenburg, Edelmann decided to seek permission to make his home at Neuwied, as there seemed 'no more advantageous place in the whole neighborhood'.[28] Count Johann Friedrich Alexander zu Neuwied (1706–1791) had met Edelmann at Hachenburg, the court of his wife Carolina's parents, and on one occasion after listening to Edelmann disputing had asked for a copy of the *Moses*.

When Edelmann approached the Count for permission to seek domicile in Neuwied, Alexander granted it but warned against incensing the clergy. In response Edelmann pointed to his peaceful record at Berleburg and Hachenburg and said, in reference to his writings, that while challenging refutations, they aimed to strengthen the faith. Further, he asserted that such freedom could not be denied to him or any other scholar. Edelmann recalls the Count's answer: 'That is all very well if quarrels and bitterness do not result from it, even though accidentally.' Edelmann closes the account: 'To that I answered that I would not give such an opportunity to the reverend clergy if they leave me unmolested. Indeed I should have kept my promise if they had not forced me to show them a confession of faith, a demand for which they paid dearly and one they still regret ever having made.'[29]

Neuwied could look back on an even longer period of religious tolerance than that in the Sayn-Wittgenstein principalities. The policy that fostered the influx of Catholics, Lutherans, and Reformed alike and provided that such a settlement could be economically feasible can be traced back to a pioneering ordinance, the *Privilegia* of 1663.[30] This document reflects the conscious design of Count Friedrich III (1618–1698) to elevate Neuwied to a town of economic consequence. Friedrich's successors continued and strengthened the policy of toleration in matters of conscience. When Edelmann entered the town, Catholics, Lutherans, Reformed, Mennonites, followers of Zinzendorf and Rock, and Jews lived peacefully together within its boundaries.

Edelmann found pleasant quarters in the house of Christian Kinzing (1706–1804), 'a whiz in mechanical construction, and particularly in clock and organ-making'. Kinzing belonged to the Mennonite community, to which the privilege 'of freedom of conscience and teaching in their homes' had been extended since 1680.[31] At Hachenburg the mere presence of Edelmann had been reason for great uneasiness on the part of the local clergy of all confessions. They preached to their congregations against Edelmann's heretical writings, of which the Hachenburgers would probably never have heard otherwise. At Neuwied his arrival triggered a similar reaction among the churchmen, who began to call attention to the author of the atheistic books offensive to their faith. To Edelmann the furor of the clergy was not surprising. However peaceful his behavior was, he could not escape the attacks.

It was part of the pattern of this era of controversial theology and religious zeal continuously to give and to demand professions of true faith. Little more than a year after Edelmann's arrival in Neuwied, the Consistory persuaded Count Alexander to demand from him a confession of faith. In several interrogations by members of the Consistory Edelmann tried to avoid giving such testimony in writings, pointing out that his published works demonstrated 'what he does or does not believe'. The reply, however, was that 'the writings were too extensive and not everybody could be expected to read them'.[32] On September 14, 1745, Edelmann submitted the requested document with the understanding that neither he nor the authorities would make it public. However, it was not long before a distorted text was in circulation. Edelmann, in protest, published the original manuscript, but in a much enlarged and augmented version; in its printed form it had grown to a book of 376 pages. Thus it is to the insistence of the Consistory that we owe one of Edelmann's finest major works, *Abgenöthigtes Jedoch Andern nicht wieder aufgenöthigtes Glaubens-Bekentniss*, printed by Haupt in Neuwied in 1746.

From documents in the ducal archives at Neuwied it is clear that an interesting episode, of which Edelmann certainly did not have the slightest inkling, was taking place behind the scenes.[33] It centers around the wish of Count Alexander to have the *Glaubens-Bekentniss* printed and the opposition as stated by the councillors of the Consistory. One councillor urges 'that he who is full of absurd opinions be expelled, and thus be prevented from sowing the malignant weed in the land'. This opinion is footnoted by the Count: 'If the weed festers in the wild meadow instead of in our garden, the odor is not kept from reaching us, but the printing will perish. In so far as Edelmann is wrong, it will be possible to refute him, even if his obstinacy cannot be overcome; yet other measures like expulsion and persecution are like unkind name-calling,'[34] – obviously unworthy actions. Count Alexander's brief remarks express splendidly the thinking which guided the religious policy of an enlightened ruler. He is convinced that human error has to be countered with superior arguments, not with persecution. The Count, favoring religious freedom, combines a policy of toleration with the commercial interest: that of the local printing trade.

In the course of all these negotiations it is not surprising that the text was not kept secret.[35] Count Alexander was unsuccessful in finding an author who could effectively refute Edelmann's *Glaubens-Bekentniss*. Among the *Acta* is a manuscript containing only a few major points, with refutations, of the *Glaubens-Bekentniss*, under the title, 'Idée generale de la confession de foi', to camouflage it as a translation from the French. It was sent to Haupt for an estimate of the cost of reprinting. The pamphlet was never printed by Haupt, but rather by Johan Friedrich Fleischer in Frankfurt-am-Main in 1747, as an anonymous publication carrying the title: *Kurzer Inhalt, desjenigen Glaubens-Bekentnüsses, welches unlängst, Hr. J. Chr. Edelmann zu Neuwied am Rhein, hat heraus gegeben. Aus dem Französischen, welches zu Neuwied heraus gekommen ist ins Teutsche über-*

setzt, und mit einigen nöthigen Anmerckungen, herausgegeben. The flimsiness of the argumentation doubtless prompted the anonymous editor to add a few footnotes. In these he even defends Edelmann against obvious distortions of his ideas – distortions to be excused because of the language difficulties of the 'French' author. It is unlikely that this pamphlet was finally printed at the wish of Count Alexander, since it appeared in Frankfurt rather than in Neuwied. It is not without irony that Haupt, to whom the anti-Edelmann pamphlet was entrusted, had printed works by Edelmann since 1741, and was also the printer of the *Glaubens-Bekentniss.*

Edelmann was correct in pointing out to the Consistory that he had made his beliefs known in his previous writings; yet in the *Glaubens-Bekentniss* he found some of the most precise and impressive formulation for his thoughts. At the center of the *Glaubens-Bekentniss* is Edelmann's struggle for an understanding of the personality of Jesus. The Jesus-image that emerges has much in common with that of seventeenth-century English radicals and of Spinoza. Here Edelmann set out to demolish the entire order of salvation – the belief in the Bible's account of paradise, the fall, damnation and salvation – which had been imposed by the Christian churches 'through cunning and violence under the cloak of revealed religion'.[36] The church's teachings of a wrathful God whom humans can insult is contradicted by all that natural reason tells us about the Creator and his creation. This contention of Edelmann 'that God was never separated from his creatures'[37] negates the orthodox teaching of the economy of salvation and leads to the re-evaluation of Jesus' role in the history of mankind. Edelmann's attacks are directed against the doctrine of the devil, the fall, and Jesus' death as an instrument of redemption.

If one proclaims that Jesus has promised to man forgiveness and the taking away of their sins, because he himself suffered the sacrifice of redemption for them, then one makes of Jesus a liar. It is evident in the eyes of the world that neither has he freed man from sin nor united him with God. On the contrary we have never before had more poor sinners and a more angry God (according to the clergy) than since the Gospel was proclaimed and the so-called sacrifice of redemption was preached.[38]

For Edelmann Jesus is 'a true human being as are we – one who has all our natural properties without exception'.[39] The characterization of Jesus as a 'human being who more than any other was endowed by God with extraordinary gifts and virtues' opens the way to Edelmann's own image of Jesus.

All that Jesus wanted to demonstrate was that God's judgment is exercised through men on this earth; He alters their estate, in such wise that He can make out of a beggar a king and out of a king a beggar. By so doing He wished to nurture among men mutual love and charity, and to eliminate all cruelty and inhumanity; in a word, he wanted to make us happy both now and in the future.[40]

Edelmann sees Jesus as the messenger of the gospel of love. But he is not only the messenger; he is also the true philosopher 'who does not teach truth with words alone, but also exemplifies it by his actions'. The image of Socrates, Saint of the Enlightenment, in whose name Zinzendorf had proclaimed truth – *Sokratische Wahrheiten* – merges for Edelmann with that of Jesus. The gospel of love that Jesus brought makes demands that are new in the ethical evolution of mankind. Edelmann asked pointedly in the *Moses:* 'Have you ever heard of anybody who gives his cloak when asked for his coat, who turns the other cheek when smitten on one, and who teaches that nobody will gain life who is not ready to lose it for the sake of truth?'[41] To ascribe to Jesus the role of a founder of religion appears to Edelmann to set him in direct opposition to his teachings: 'Because the chief characteristic of every religion is, as unfortunate daily experience shows, to hate adherents of religions other than one's own and to consider them damned and depraved individuals.' There is an even stronger expression in another passage: 'The more religion appears in the world ... the less love is apparent among men.'[42] If such condemnation seems not altogether justified today, it is well to recall how much Edelmann, Reimarus, and Lessing have contributed to the development of an ecumenic consciousness, and how much prejudice and hate still remain to be overcome.

Just as Edelmann sees Jesus' role as savior in a new light, he also reinterprets his messianic role. He construes the Old Testament as dealing with the expectation of a worldly king to free the Jews from Roman rule and make them the masters of the world. He declares this concept to be a fairy tale invented by Ezra as a political ruse. Edelmann also finds it impossible to identify Jesus with the Messiah who will restore peace on earth as prophesied by Isaiah. Such identification contradicts reality, and Edelmann

11*

considers it absurd to ask the Jews to accept the idea. He feels that this very demand has created 'a bar to all possible conversion of the poor Jews' and has closed their access to Jesus.[43]

Edelmann likewise raises the question of the contradiction between ideal and reality in the Christian concept of the messianic role of Jesus with the following question: 'What reasonable explanation have the Christians to offer, why Jesus, after having conquered sin, death, devil and hell, has not kept his word? ... Why does the devil, whom he allegedly overcame seventeen hundred years ago, still rules the entire world?' Edelmann denies that Jesus is the Messiah because the contradictions between Messiah and reality make such identification meaningless. He also questions the entire method that seeks in the Old Testament the arguments for the legitimacy of Jesus' messianic role. He declares: 'It is stretching far beyond imagination to interpret sayings in the Old Testament as presaging Jesus; ... every application and interpretation is arbitrary and is dependent on the vivid imagination of the commentator or on his prejudices, as we experience daily.' While Edelmann denies Jesus the messianic function as conceived in the Old Testament and anchored in Christian doctrine, he concludes: 'It suffices that I believe and confess that I consider Jesus a true *Magus*, that is, a wise man of God, who recognizes the inner forces of nature and knows how to use them.'[44]

Edelmann also rejects the concept of Jesus as the fulfiller of the law and, squarely confronting the saying of Jesus in Matthew 5: 17, he concludes:

One has to say that Jesus acted contrary to his own sayings when he eliminated the commands of oath-taking and of irreconcilable revenge, or else one has to admit that law and prophet meant something entirely different to him from what we understand by them today. To him all it meant was that we fulfill the natural obligations that love dictates to us as the members of one body.[45]

Edelmann's eyes are focused on a Jesus who breaks the barriers that national and religious prejudices had erected.

Jesus was not afraid to associate with sinners and publicans; he admitted the Samaritan; he subordinated the sabbath law to the deeds of love, and showed the adulteress the way to change, at the same time unmasking hypocrisy and self-righteousness. Anyone who is not ready to see in this a new direction is either 'blind or frivolous', because Jesus is not only its herald but also 'the example, who with his deeds and words contradicts the laws of the Jews, that are proclaimed divine'.[46]

Edelmann implies an evolution of the moral sentiments of mankind when he describes the human sacrifices of the Druids and the superstition of the Jews. The study of heathen religions has made him aware of the common structure of underlying myths. His analysis of the story of the birth of Jesus starts with a comparison of God-birth theologies in Hellenic and Egyptian tradition. It is actually the same method that Strauss considered a decisive turning-point in Biblical interpretation, assigning its origins to J. G. Eichhorn and Georg Lorenz Bauer.[47]

Eager as Edelmann is to express his concept of Jesus and to make us understand the 'quiet Jesus' who gave his life for 'outspoken testimony against superstition',[48] he rejects any idolatry founded on Jesus. In the final analysis Edelmann's Jesus is the supreme example of divine manifestation in man, from which no one is excluded. As he had written in his *Moses*, 'If I know that Jesus is that in me which was in the person of Jesus of Nazareth, what do all fantasies matter.'[49]

8. Refuge in Berlin
1749–1767

Edelmann's autobiography, which has been a splendid guide thus far, ends abruptly with the description of his settling at Neuwied in the spring of 1744. He had divided the work into three parts, giving November 9, 1749, as the date he began to write the 'account of his life'. The first part, finished in Berlin on December 5, 1750, ends with his leaving Dresden in the early spring of 1736. He later added another date, perhaps that of a final revision: Hamburg, May 15, 1759. The second part of the autobiography, begun on January 3, 1752, was concluded in Berlin on December 22, 1752.[1] Although the final part, beginning with his arrival at Hachenburg in the late fall of 1741, is not dated, Edelmann tells us that he is writing about these events in the spring of 1753 and that he should be excused if he does not remember the precise date of his move from Berleburg. Actually, he did err in giving 1742 as the year of the death of Count Casimir, and thereby pushed events that belong to the winter of 1741 one year ahead. This part of the autobiography, which comprises only forty-eight printed pages, ends with 'Ich' as the first word of a new sentence. It is idle to speculate on what prevented Edelmann from continuing it.

The *Acta* at the Neuwied archives, together with Edelmann's own account, make it possible to piece together the story of the publication of the *Glaubens-Bekentniss*. From the moment the autobiography ends, it is no longer possible to follow Edelmann's movements closely. Documents – his own writings, as well as those directed against him, the copy of Pratje's bio-bibliographical work with Edelmann's annotations – enable us to form some idea of his life from the time of the publication of the *Glaubens-Bekentniss* in 1746 to his death in 1767. It must be noted that Edelmann published no work after 1749, and of his unpublished manuscripts none is dated after 1759. The severe enforcement of censors' injunctions against his writings after 1749 and the imperial order that led to the burning of his works in Frankfurt on May 9, 1750,[2] account to some extent for the absence of publications. If Edelmann had been intent on further publishing, he could certainly have found ways and means to do so, in spite of the censorship. For a full understanding of his public silence one may recall a passage in *Die Begierde nach der vernünfftigen lautern Milch*. In 1744, in response to a criticism that many who are called 'Mysticus' are pouring out much printed trash, Edelmann writes:

... not everyone who is called a 'Mysticus', or who thinks he is one, is really one. A true 'Mysticus' is truly a secretive man, who does not ring the big bell wherever he walks. He is content with the bliss that God in secret has given him to enjoy and does not divulge much of it. When it pleases the Lord to make a 'Mysticus' of me one day, I will no longer have to plead with the authorities of my German fatherland to prevent me from writing; I will be silent and will let others speak in my place. For the present I speak as the Lord bids me, and I wait until the time of silence approaches.[3]

In fact Edelmann's great period of intense productivity as a writer had lasted twelve years, from 1735 to 1747, and his statement may be seen as a self-fulfilling prophecy.

After the publication of his *Glaubens-Bekentniss* Edelmann anticipated further harassment by the local clergy. In order to avoid any public disturbance that might occur, thereby turning the benevolent Count Alexander against him, Edelmann decided to leave Neuwied early in 1747, though he did not yet seek a permanent abode. He visited friends in the north of Germany in the duchy of Braunschweig and in Hamburg, where he was one of the thousand who paid their last respects to the poet Heinrich Brockes on the occasion of his funeral on January 23, 1747. Edelmann had been greatly moved by Brockes' poems and felt a deep affection for the man, although contact between them had been established on only one occasion when he addressed a poem to Brockes and received a kind acknowledgment.[4]

In the early fall of 1747 Edelmann decided to visit Berlin, perhaps with the intention of seeking a permanent residence. He was sure to find a warm welcome from his loyal friend Pinell. On an earlier occasion, when Edelmann had tried to reach Berlin to make the acquaintance of Pinell, he had been turned away at the gates. Now, in the Berlin of Frederick II, where as Lessing wrote one might 'bring to market as much nonsense against religion as one wants',[5] there should be a place for Edelmann. An anecdote circulated at the time reports Frederick II's answer when questioned as to Edelmann's taking residence in Berlin: 'One should not find it strange that Edelmann be allowed to live freely in Berlin; since permission is given to so many fools to reside in my country, why not make it a place for a reasonable man?'[6]

For more than two months Edelmann lived quietly and undisturbed;[7] then once again a local clergyman, the 'Probst' and pastor at the Peterskirche in Cölln, roused the congregation against the iconoclast in Sunday sermons and followed up these verbal attacks with a printed pamphlet. Johann Peter Süssmilch (1707–1767) 'was base enough, from the pulpit and in a pamphlet heaven, to implore congregation and authorities once again to chase into misery this enemy of all religion, who had found a refuge among his friends in Berlin'.[8] The title of Süssmilch's pamphlet left little to the imagination: *Die Unvernunft und Bosheit des berüchtigten Edelmanns durch seine schändliche Vorstellung des Obrigkeitlichen Amts aus seinem Moses dargethan und zu aller Menschen Warnung vor Augen gelegt.* From the *Moses, Dritter Anblick,* Süssmilch reprinted pages 149 to 165 with a running commentary and added a brief introduction and conclusion. His justification for the pamphlet was that: 'This misfortune has befallen us, that this miserable man has found his way into our midst and has succeeded in finding a number of friends and followers.' Yet it was seven years after the publication of the *Moses* when Süssmilch was moved to this attack. The pages he chose do not pertain to any of the central religious themes of the work. They deal rather with the relation of the philosopher to secular authority and of the independent thinker to his lordly protector. The selection was aimed to expose Edelmann before Frederick II, and to prove that Edelmann was the type of a man 'who could not be tolerated by civil society and by the Christian Church'.[9]

Pinell's home where Edelmann stayed was in the Brüderstrasse in Cölln, close to the Peterskirche. Thus it was almost under the eyes of the pastor that Edelmann's visitors – among them perhaps some members of the Peterskirche congregation – walked in and out. It is difficult to ascertain how much attention Edelmann received in Berlin. An anonymous report which appeared a year after his arrival there spoke of large crowds gathering to see the 'Antichrist', but this would seem to have been more sensation or fantasy than fact. Edelmann himself said that he had lived quietly in another quarter prior to moving to Pinell's house, where his 'good luck provided him with the provost Süssmilch as his neighbor'.[10] Süssmilch was a stalwart of the church and a member of the board of censors. He was not however one of the many clergymen ever ready to engage in theological controversy. He could rightly state: 'Very much against my inclination I have to engage in matters I would otherwise have avoided. Quarreling I have always considered unsavory.' Indeed, among the writings of the pastor the pamphlet against Edelmann is exceptional, since Süssmilch's literary contributions were not in the field of theology. His major work was a pioneering study in the newly emerging science of population statistics: *Die göttliche Ordnung in den Veränderungen des mensch-lichen Geschlechts, aus der Geburt, dem Tode und der Fortpflanzung desselben erwiesen* (1741). It has been recognized as a precursor of Malthus' work, and its impact on Herder's *Älteste Urkunde des Menschengeschlechts* (1744) was acknowledged by the author, who wrote that 'not the least of his virtues was exact conformity to truth'.[11] Herder also took Süssmilch's *Versuch eines Beweises dass die erste Sprache ihren Ursprung nicht vom Menschen, sondern allein vom Schöpfer erhalten habe* (Berlin 1766) as the basis for his own essay, *Abhandlung über den Ursprung der Sprache* (1770). These, together with Süssmilch's other scholarly achievements, demonstrate that the pastor of the Peterskirche was more than an undistinguished little priest.

Edelmann's rather frivolous comments in the *Moses* on Christian Wolff, who had contributed a laudatory introduction to Süssmilch's *Göttliche Ordnung*, had surely angered the pastor. Wolff was a favorite of Frederick II, as was Voltaire, and it seemed easy to denigrate Edelmann to the Prussian king. That a man of such great learning debased himself to such vicious attack is deplorable. Edelmann could not let Süssmilch's accusations rest unanswered, and he countered with a twenty-seven page epistle which could easily have been reduced to half its length had not such large type been employed. Tongue in cheek, he called the epistle *Schuldigstes Danck-sagungs-Schreiben an den Herrn Probst Süssmilch vor Dessen, Ihm un-bewusst erzeigte Dienste*. His strategy was to appear conciliatory and urbane and to embarrass the Probst. Süssmilch had 'presented him, to his innocent congregation and the entire worthy citizenry, as a monster, despised by God and man'. Was that the charity to be expected from a Christian minister? Edelmann is eager to express his gratitude to the Probst 'for showing him even the smallest of his infirmities through the strongest magnifying glasses'. Contrary to Süssmilch's contention that he is incorrigible, he declares himself ready to learn and to amend his faults. He frankly acknowledges that in previous writings he had used abusive language. As one explanation for using harsh words, he points to his and the pastor's upbringing in the Lutheran church, where crude and insulting language was all too common. Edelmann composed the epistle in the house of his friend Pinell, who had been the first to reprimand him for the use of vulgar language in the *Moses*. At that time Edelmann had resented his friend's just criticism,[12] but he knew better now and in publicly apologizing asked his friend's pardon.

The most delicate task Edelmann faced was to make a convincing show of his respect for the royal office, without simultaneously giving the impression of being a sycophant. In the *Glaubens-Bekentniss* and in *Das Evangelium St. Harenbergs* (1747) Edelmann wrote in different terms of secular authority than he had some six years earlier in the *Moses*. Experience had taught him that he could find sympathy and protection among secular princes, while clergymen were ready to persecute him. In the brief account of his life in *Das Evangelium St. Harenbergs,* he expressed his gratitude to and affection for Count Casimir of Berleburg, Count Georg of Hachenburg, and Duke Alexander of Neuwied. In the same book, talking of the intolerance of the clergy, Edelmann expressed the wish 'that not only his majesty the wise King of Prussia, but other Gods of this earth, might be inclined to follow the poet's admonition to protect the philosophers from the priests'.[13] How different from the contempt for Voltaire expressed by Edelmann on account of this very same tribute to the new king. The passage, however, served Edelmann well as an alibi, and he could point out that he had made amends for any previous insult to Frederick before Süssmilch undertook to denounce him. Quite disarmingly he stated: 'Out of false perspective I viewed in my *Moses* the kings and mighty ones of this earth as very small in comparison to the infinite majesty of our great Creator.'[14] We might wonder if the distance between God and temporal powers really diminished between 1740 and 1747. Edelmann had indeed suffered from ecclesiastical authorities and he had reason to be grateful to secular rulers. He also was ready to accommodate himself to the Berlin of Frederick II, where he wanted to settle. To do so he needed the king's indulgence.

It appears that Edelmann's purpose in the epistle had been accomplished: 'The answer has improved Edelmann's reputation considerably and the Probst is confused and undecided what to say now.'[15] For the moment Edelmann preferred to leave Berlin and let the storm subside which he, or rather the pastor, had stirred up.

Of Edelmann's travels from the time he left Berlin in the winter of 1747 to his return two years later, our information is sparse. He stayed from time to time with friends in the Hamburg and Bremen area, and accomplished some writing. Letters to the book dealer Georg Christoph Kreyssig (1697–1758) at Dresden give us some idea of his circumstances at that time and reflect his changing mood. In a letter of March 28, 1749, he writes lightheartedly: 'The sole complaint I have, in my otherwise quite agreeable and cheerful solitude, is that I am deprived of my library. In order to avoid any suspicion, the books are dispersed to all the four winds and are lying *in obscuro* in Berlin, in Altona, in Neuwied, and in Frankfurt am Main and the Lord alone knows how they can be gathered again.'[16] Edelmann refers to a notice of July 28, 1749, in the *Neue Hamburgische Gelehrte Zeitungen* announcing and commenting on his supposed death, and continues:

… as the dead are sometimes in quite good spirits I make use of a piano that has been put in my grave. If it is not too much trouble I would like to ask you to provide me with the two arias for piano *Scherzo talor sul prato* and *Non hà piu pace l'Amor zeloso* from the opera *Fabricii*. The accoustics in my grave will not be too resounding, but the scores will serve as welcome entertainment in my isolation.

Thus Edelmann wished again to play from Adolf Hasses' (1699–1783) Italian opera *Cajo Fabrizio* which he himself had tried to translate into German verse when a tutor in Dresden in 1735.[17]

Different in mood was Edelmann's letter of May 25th, written when another move was imminent:

What disturbs me most is that in view of these continuous interruptions I am unable to undertake anything for which the concentration of all the mind's faculty is required. I am forced to write while on flight, without the help of my useful 'Bibliothecchen'. The best of all worlds is a strange abode: Deceit and falsehood are favored with full sails and favorable winds, while truth and honesty have to fight incessantly, even to the point of exhaustion, with storm and waves.[18]

However difficult and unsettled his life, Edelmann managed to write *Die Andere Epistel St. Harenbergs an Johann Christian Edelmann ihrem vornehmsten Inhalt nach von demselben beantwortet ...* 1748; a manuscript *Sendschreiben an seine Freunde den Vorzug eines Freygeistes vor einem armen Sünder zeigend,* dated March 1, 1749; a second *Sendschreiben,* the manuscript of which has been lost;[19] and a *Sendschreiben an Seine-Freunde. Darinnen Er seine Gedancken von der Unsterblichkeit der Seelen eröfnet,* dated November 3, 1749. Edelmann did not want the authorities to know where he was staying while writing. He put only the letter 'M' next to the dates of completion of his writings, thus revealing to the initiated his abodes. The meaning has not surely been identified since, but probably stood for a location in the neighborhood of Hamburg.[20]

In his answer to the thirty chapters of Johann Christoph Harenberg *Die Grettete Religion. Zweyter Theil* (1748), Edelmann did not go beyond what he had already written. Harenberg's conventional and orthodox treatment of the questions raised in the *Glaubens-Bekentniss* did not force Edelmann to serious re-examination of his positions nor did they inspire him to seek new arguments in support of what he considered correct. His most important passages deal with Hachenberg's attacks against Pantheism but do not add substantially to what he had written on these problems in the *Moses.* His appreciation of Spinoza has not diminished and, although he certainly has not become a Pantheist, he does not hesitate to defend Pantheism against Orthodox outrage.[21]

We do not know what prompted the three *Sendschreiben.* The first, the last of Edelmann's writings to be printed in his lifetime, contains some spirited passages on his favorite subjects. Once more accentuating the ideas of God, the freethinker, and the orthodox he writes: '... I wish no more than to be shown the undeniable traces of the omnipresent ... Being, for which I have as much reverence as any mortal is capable of. But I cannot show appreciation for a book in which God reveals to me nothing more than how perverted and erroneous humans can think of Him and His marvelous works.' Edelmann emphasizes that the Old and New Testament ideas of the relation between Creator and creation are modeled after our human understanding of ruler and subject. The Bible teachings of man endowed with a will free to insult his Creator, Edelmann considers to be offensive to 'a sane mind'.[22] His attack is specifically directed against the anthropomorphic concepts of God that dominate the Bible. In the *Glaubens-Bekentniss*, the teaching of Adam's sin and offense is rejected and with it the entire orthodox economy of salvation overturned. The idea that the creature cannot insult its Creator also served as a starting point for Hermann Samuel Reimarus' critique of the Christian theory of the economy of salvation. He had been led to this position by Johann Konrad Dippel's declaration that God could not be offended by human sin.[23]

A central place in the *Sendschreiben* is occupied by Edelmann's report of the falsified account of confession. A letter published in the *Bibliothèque Raisonnée des Ouvrages des Savans* (1748) by Vernede, pastor of the Walloon church of Maastricht, made a great stir and its content was reported in several German journals. Vernede relates that he was called to a 'Mr. de la Serre, ci-devant Lieutenant de la Compagnie Franche de Mr. le Chevalier de Vial' who was condemned to hanging for espionage and wanted to confess his sins. Vernede subjoins a written declaration which he claims to be La Serre's acknowledgment of the authorship of blasphemous writings, the published *Examen de la religion dont on cherche l'éclairissement de bonne foi*, and of two manuscripts. La Serre, repentant sinner, asks that those who have copies of the book or the manuscripts burn them – 'de vouloir bien le bruler'.[24]

Edelmann was acquainted with the *Examen de la religion*, or *Petit Burnet*, as the book was often referred to. He had also received from friends in Rotterdam a manuscript *Seconde Partie de l'Examen de la Religion, ou Caractere d'un Philosophe, ouvrage posthume de Mr. Varenne, alias St. Evremond*. His friends were convinced that the author of both book and manuscript was Jean-Baptiste de la Varenne (1689–1745). Of such opinion also was Georg Friedrich Meier (1718–1777), the author of *Rettung der Ehre der Vernunft wider die Freigeister* (1747), an attempt to refute the *Examen de la Religion*, and also of *Vertheidigung der Christlichen Religion wider Herrn Johann Christian Edelmann* (1749). La Varenne was known in the world of letters as the editor of a literary and philosophical magazine, *Le Glaneur historique;* in private, he had worked for eight to ten years examining his own conscience, which found its expression in the *Petit Burnet*.

La Varenne's ideas on the question of the Bible, the divinity of Jesus, and on reason were close to Edelmann's and were likewise formed under the impact of Spinoza's work. Vernede's attempt to discredit such works, with which Edelmann could identify, enraged him and he, like his Rotterdam friends, saw nothing but a sinister clerical plot in the letter and document. He did not hesitate to declare the document a hoax.[25]

Edelmann concluded this first *Sendschreiben* with a triumphant description of the free thinker as one to be preferred to a poor sinner:

My idea of the free thinker is that of a person who according to his given faculties strives incessantly to be free of all error and prejudice that impede reason and of all excessive passions that interfere with his present state of content and happiness. His endeavor is in all seriousness to seek truth and virtue and to serve human society in which he lives according to his best abilities.[26]

The manuscript of the *Sendschreiben: 2tes Sendschreiben an seine Freunde, die Geschichte des Varenne und La Serre verfolgend 1749,* has been lost, but the title indicates that Edelmann continued to occupy himself with La Varenne.

The title of the third *Sendschreiben: Gedancken von der Unsterblichkeit der Seelen* suggests rather than defines its theme. Edelmann starts out to demonstrate the inadequacy of the philosophers' definitions of concepts like soul, matter, immortality:

Most, I should say all, existing descriptions of the soul do not convince. In some the soul is considered materialistic, yet one does not yet know what matter is. Then again the soul is supposed to exist entirely without matter, yet one cannot say what is the other component of which it exists. Some also describe the soul as 'spirit' yet one is incapable of saying what kind of a thing a spirit is.

This uncertainty sends even the 'great and wise Holberg' in confusion back to the revelations of the Bible.[27] This observation leads Edelmann to a critique of the ideas on immortality of the Old and New Testament. He exposes contradictions, and attacks, as he had in previous writings, the concept of a hereafter linked to paradise and hell. From this he moves on to a critique of the concept of man as a machine. The *Sendschreiben* was written a year and a half after La Mettrie's *L'homme machine* (1748), but Edelmann makes no mention of it nor of La Mettrie's earlier *Histoire naturelle de l'âme* (1745). In no way does he enter on a discussion of La Mettrie's ideas, but directs his attack against a simplistic lifeless robot model.[28] It is to the credit of Frederick II that he, among the few who recognized La Mettrie's importance, extended generous hospitality to that persecuted philosopher and scientist.

Edelmann attempts to formulate his own idea of immortality connecting it with the survival of a 'something'. To this 'something' he tries to give an empirical basis. He concludes his discussion of the idea of a creation of nothing as follows: 'There can be no stronger argument against such a meaningless concept than to assert that we all presently see and feel, that not a *nothing* but a great and manifold *something* exists.' Edelmann leaps from the existence of the something to the indestructibility of this something:

> If *nothing* was since eternity a *nothing* and will remain, without any objection being raised, for all eternity a *nothing*, then by virtue of the opposite a *something*, that is unquestionably more noble than a *nothing*, must have been *something* since eternity and will remain in eternity *something*. The reason for this sequence lies partly in the general sentiment, partly in the nature of the matter, according to which the human mind is hitherto incapable of comprehending the destruction of *something* into *nothing*, as it is of the change of *nothing* into *something*.[29]

Thus Edelmann connects traditional elements of the Anselmian proof of the existence of God with the search for empirical and common-sense explications.

It is intriguing to watch Edelmann's attempts to offer proofs for some form of immortality. He does not want to construct a sytem. His judgment on systems is severe: 'Most, if not all systems', he writes, 'are nothing but thought-edifices of men, who cannot derive their ideas from real conditions, but who try to construct the composition and properties of a thing according to their own ideas and concepts. They then condemn as false and incorrect everything, be it as true as true can be, that does not agree with their ideas.'[30]

Edelmann was, as the *Moses* shows, ambivalent towards materialism. In the third *Sendschreiben* we see him honestly struggling with problems that were and still are providing the subject for philosophical discussions.

The confiscation of the *Moses* at Berleburg and of the *Glaubens-Bekentniss* at Hamburg (January 27, 1747)[31] were actions by local authorities who had come under pressure from churchmen. The investigation undertaken by the 'Bücherkommission im Reich' was of a different magnitude and finally led to the burning of Edelmann's writings in public in Frankfurt-am-Main on May 9, 1750. The bureaucratic machinery of the 'Bücherkommission', dating back to the latter part of the sixteenth century, did not move easily or swiftly, nor did it initiate an auto-da-fé too often. Between about 1700 and 1760 the commission occasionally ordered that books be burned.

The extreme measure is indicative of the authorities' fear of the spreading influence of Edelmann's works. The history of the 'Bücherkommission' has not been written and the knowledge of how the commission worked over the years is scant, but the story of the censoring and burning of Edelmann's books is one of the few actions taken by the commission that is fairly well documented.

The commission was originally instituted by Emperor Rudolph II in Frankfurt because it was the center of the German book trade and the site of the book fair. From its beginning the imperial commission worked in close conjunction with the diocese of Mainz and the ministry of preachers of the city of Frankfurt. The commission was small, made up of two or three members – a chief-officer from the imperial fiscal court of Vienna and an Actuarius, a glorified errand boy. The third person was at least for a time a member of the Mainz diocesan administration.[32] While the major task of the commission was at first to protect the Catholic interests in a trading center that was Lutheran-oriented, by the late seventeenth and eighteenth century it was charged with censoring religious literature that expounded views contrary to the official teaching of the Lutheran, Calvinist and Catholic church.[33]

From documentary evidence it appears that an investigation of Edelmann's writings had started at the time of the fall fair of 1748. Printers and booksellers were, according to their own later testimony, aware that Edelmann's works were likely to be banned.[34] How the investigation was initiated, and who actually had asked to suppress Edelmann's writings and to proceed against those who printed and distributed them, is not evident from the documents. They record only the interrogations of the printers, beginning in April 1749, the measures taken against them, and the orders for the public book-burning. In these documents Edelmann is referred to as the 'notorious Edelmann' and his writings are labeled 'highly offensive and condemned'.[35] The interrogated printers and booksellers confess having either printed or sold Edelmann's *Moses, Glaubens-Bekentniss* and *Die Erste Epistel St. Harenbergs*. J. B. Haupt of Neuwied does not hesitate to name the books which he had printed, as this was done before he knew that action by the commission might be initiated against them. When he learned 'that an investigation was pending at the Easter fair of 1749 he returned a new manuscript to the author', referring to it as *Die 2te Epistel St. Harenbergs*.[36] In a letter of June 6, 1750, from Berlin we know how much Edelmann regretted that this work was never printed: 'When my books were burnt at Frankfurt I wished nothing more than that the *2te Epistel St. Harenbergs* could have burnt with them, the manuscript is lying *in obscuro* and could not have been released on account of the vigilance of the *Corsaren*.'[37] It appears from the interrogation of the 'Bücherkommission' that five hundred copies was the size of the average initial printing, whereas of the *Moses* another five hundred were printed later, and of the *Glaubens-Bekentniss* another three hundred copies.[38]

By April 1750 the chief officer, Johann Conrad von Birckenstock, had received opinions on Edelmann's books from both the vicariate of the archdiocese of Mainz and the ministry of preachers of Frankfurt.[39] The commission then issued an order asking the city council to prepare a public burning of all the confiscated copies of Edelmann's *Moses, Glaubens-Bekentniss,* and *Die Erste Epistel St. Harenbergs*. That order is acknowledged in the record of the mayor of Frankfurt on April 30, 1750.[40] The mayor noted that information was needed as to how such book-burning had been accomplished in the past, another indication that such a measure was not on the city's daily agenda. Of the same date is the Senate proclamation, read on the occasion of the conflagration, which outlined the procedure: 'The burning of the offensive and godless Edelmann writings in front of the city hall is to serve others as a deterrent and example.' On the appointed date eight drummers and seventy men formed a circle around the square pile of birchwood to which were consigned the one thousand confiscated volumes, tightly wrapped in three big bundles. The presence of the two mayors and three notaries as witnesses added solemnity and weight to the occasion. Even with two torches and several straw wreaths saturated with tar, the fire ignited but slowly, and then took an hour and a half to perform its duty.[41] Such an auto-da-fé was later witnessed by the fifteen-year-old Goethe, who in *Dichtung und Wahrheit* commented on its propaganda value: 'If the author was seeking publicity, he could have not made better provision.'[42] At the conclusion of the burning, the mayor had the report read and put *ad acta*, May 14, 1750.[43]

Edelmann's statement in the *Begierde* that a time will come when he will impose silence on himself emerges as a self-fulfilling prophecy. Pratje attributed the suspension of Edelmann's publishing activities to imperial censorship, which elicited from Edelmann the comment that: 'this interdiction Edelmann did use to show to his enemies that he is capable of being silent after he had spoken.' The clear implication is that the interdict was not the cause for his silence, but the chosen opportunity. At the same time Edelmann clears up a story, reported by Pratje and perpetuated, that the Prussian king offered Edelmann asylum in Berlin in return for a promise from Edelmann not to publish. Edelmann repudiates Pratje:

> It is completely erroneous that Edelmann was promised personal security when he finally moved to Berlin but had in return to promise not to spread his teachings further and to abstain from writing books. Nobody ever asked him why he wanted to live in Berlin and why he was going to stay. The censoring of his books occurred long before his second arrival became known in Berlin.[44]

Edelmann continued to write, although he did not publish. The first years in Berlin proved to be a highly productive period, although the literary work of these years, the autobiography, differed in *genre* from his previous works. The immediate impetus to the writing of the autobiography was provided by an anonymous pamphlet *Des berichtigten Johann Christian Edelmanns, Leben und Schriften* (Frankfurt 1750), which gives a rough biographical account of Edelmann's life and describes his writings. The title makes the author's intention clear: to show how the 'notorious Edelmann ... studied theology in Jena, then abandoned it to ridicule the Christian religion, the Holy Scriptures and the clergy.'[45] Edelmann, who rarely took up his pen to answer an opponent, was always quick to correct false or inaccurate statements about his life. This pamphlet, which seems of little significance, actually provided him with the structure for the autobiography.

He uses passages from the pamphlet in their chronological order to introduce the discussion of the various phases of his life. Although such an approach could prove tedious, the lively presentation makes the reader oblivious to the method. Here is a splendid record of Edelmann's own intellectual growth, closely interwoven with the development of theological thought of the period. It is a work rich in its description of social and economic conditions – in short, one of our finest sources for details on local history, the *mores* of the time, and aspects of social history. The librarian of the Hamburg Stadtbibliothek brought the manuscript to the attention of Carl Rudolph Wilhelm Klose. He recognized its significance and undertook to edit it, yet felt compelled to apologize for making public the work of Edelmann the heretic. Such apology seemed still to be called for in 1848, even though almost a hundred years had elapsed since Edelmann wrote the autobiography and Germany was facing a 'revolution'.

Edelmann's contemporaries were not aware that he was writing an autobiography; so far as they knew he remained silent. He also wrote additions to the *Moses*, and recorded observations on his reading, but none of these pages adds substantially to what he had already said. In a letter to Pratje, dated August 6, 1754, Edelmann drew an image of himself as a resident of Berlin, lodging in the respectable home of Frau Präsidentin von Osten, at the Wilhelmsplatz, associating freely with persons from all social classes. He refutes an allegation that he had to fear the anger of the Jewish community on account of his *Moses:* 'I thank God that I have nothing to fear from Jews or Christians, although the latter could be a greater threat than the former ... I do not live in seclusion as someone tried to make you believe, nor do I keep pistols or other murderous weapons in my rooms because of my fear of Jews, some of whom I count among my good friends.'[46]

This description of a proud man, at ease with himself and the world around him, contrasts strongly with Moses Mendelssohn's reference to Edelmann in a letter to Lessing, dated November 19, 1755:

I have encountered new faces ... I do not want to say anything good or evil about these people. I exclude Edelmann, of whom I do want to say a few words, because he astonished me so much. What a wooden man! I bet the man has as much lead in his head as he has iron in his shoes. You know him, don't you, dear Lessing? Did you not find him as clumsy as I did? I wish he were a real light-foot. Such a person I did expect when I was told that Edelmann would appear. It may well be that persecution, misfortune, and hardship have so beaten him down that all *Lebensgeister* have deserted him.[47]

It is difficult to reconcile Edelmann's self-image with Mendelssohn's account of him. Was it just that the young philosopher's expectations that the author of the *Moses* had to be a wild-eyed radical were disappointed, or were Edelmann's spirits really dimmed by the winter of 1755? There is evidence that Edelmann continued writing until 1759, recording his readings in the *Collectaneenbuch*, which Büsching described.[48] But concerning the last seven years of his life there is complete void. Had there been some physical decline over a longer period of years? The account of his death neither confirms nor excludes such speculation. The *Berliner Nachrichten von Staats- und Gelehrten Sachen*, dated February 24, 1767 reported:

On the 15th of this month Johann Christian Edelmann, well known through his writings to the learned world, died, in his 69th year. His life was marked by polemics that his ideas evoked among clergymen and philosophers, and therefore his death deserves to be noticed. His death was caused by a stroke that he had while sitting in his chair in the evening close to nine o'clock; it removed him, quietly and unexpectedly, from the scene. The instruction he left, that he should be buried in the presence of a few good friends in the cemetery at the *Halleschen Thore*, seems to indicate that he met his fate not altogether unwarned nor unprepared.[49]

Conclusion

Paul Tillich has stated that the great movement of historical Bible criticism began around 1750.[1] He also argued that it was the philosopher and poet Lessing who took the leadership in the fight against Orthodoxy. In linking Lessing's contribution specifically to historical Bible criticism Tillich refers to the fact that, between 1774 and 1778, Lessing published fragments from a manuscript of Hermann Samuel Reimarus (1694–1768), whose children had entrusted it to Lessing.[2] Lessing disguised the real authorship by claiming that the writings were found in the Wolfenbüttel library and that the writer was unknown, thereby keeping his promise to Reimarus' children who feared for the reputation of their father. Many of the radical ideas concerning the Bible, the teachings of salvation, and the person of Jesus are similar to those that Edelmann had published some thirty years earlier. Of Reimarus, whose dates of birth and death almost coincide with Edelmann's, his great admirer David Friedrich Strauss (1808–1874) wrote that he 'was not frank with his contemporaries; he preferred to transmit his thoughts to posterity only through unpublished manuscripts'. In his brilliant sketch of previous research in the introduction to his own *Das Leben Jesu*, Strauss gave Reimarus credit for introducing to a German audience the 'Deistic attacks on the Bible and on its divine authority'. In his *Christliche Glaubenslehre* Strauss remarks on his later discovery of Edelmann:

> The writings of this frail and restless personality from the midst of the last century have been called to my attention by the pamphlet of W. Elster, dean of the gymnasium at Clausthal: *Erinnerung an Johann Christian Edelmann*. Its purpose is to discredit me as the Edelmann redivivus. I am indebted to that publication for an interesting acquaintance – not perhaps with the dean, but with this alleged precursor, who has been abused much more than he has been studied.[3]

In 1906 Albert Schweitzer, following Strauss, programmatically called his history of the research on the life of Jesus *Von Reimarus bis Wrede. Eine*

Geschichte der Leben Jesu Forschung. This book, which was to become the classic in its field, thus firmly established the reputation of Reimarus as the first who applied historical methods to the study of the Biblical tradition.[4] The question that a study of Edelmann raises is why his contribution, whatever its magnitude, was not acknowledged by the men of the German Enlightenment in the 1760's. It has been suggested that the silencing of the work of Edelmann is to be understood in the context of German intellectual life between 1740 and 1770. An examination of the question why Edelmann was ignored should shed some light on the more hidden seamy side of the scene and underscore the difficulties which the intellectuals suffered. Differences as well as similarities between Reimarus and Edelmann have to be considered.

A comparison between the writings of Edelmann and the *Apologie oder Schutzschrift für die vernünftigen Verehrer Gottes* of Reimarus discloses some striking similarities. Reimarus, like Edelmann, rejected the Bible as a source of a supernatural revelation. The Bible like any other written work is open to the scrutiny of reason: "... when the words are added 'God has appeared to me, God has said or ordained' does that turn lies into truth, and make of the worst ungodly actions deeds pleasing to God?" asked Reimarus.[5]

Reimarus rejects the entire Christian economy of salvation, as did Edelmann, declaring the doctrine of the estrangement of man from God, the story of the fall, to be a fabrication unworthy of the benign Creator. A manuscript of a *Sendschreiben* by Reimarus, written before 1723, shows his acquaintance with Johann Konrad Dippel's *Summarische und aufrichtige Glaubens-Bekäntniss (1700)* in which the author claimed that God could not be insulted by man and that therefore the death of Jesus cannot be considered atonement for any such invented insult. Reimarus, in a preliminary plan to the *Apologie,* made direct reference to Dippel's work and to an attempt by Friedrich Wagner to refute it in *Der sich selbst verurtheilende Demokrit.*[6] Reimarus in the second part of the *Apologie* reiterates Dippel's position that man's failing cannot insult God nor can Christ's death be accepted as a sacrifice of atonement. Edelmann acknowledged his indebtedness to Dippel in *Die Begierde.* One may conclude that Dippel provided both Edelmann and Reimarus with the basic thesis from which they developed their attack on the Orthodox concept of the economy of salvation.[7]

Reimarus, like Edelmann, argues vigorously for the autonomy of reason over blind faith and against the Orthodox demand 'that obedience to faith makes a captive of reason'.[8] He condemned intolerance and the persecution of those who express different views on matters of religion and faith. In grim terms he paints a picture of the tactics of the Orthodox clergy:

> Thus they rally to the suppression of reasonable religion a whole army of themselves, and the civil authorities, as defenders of faith, are asked to interdict the circulation of writings by free-thinking authors in the bookstore; the booksellers are threatened with severe punishment in cases of transgression, and the books are burned by the executioner; worse fate may be in store for the authors, who will be chased from their office, put in jail, and left to their misery.[9]

Actually this is an accurate description of how Edelmann was persecuted by the Orthodox clergy and how those who printed and distributed his book were taken to task and punished.

Concerning the power of Christianity to improve man's moral behavior, Reimarus arrives at the same conclusion Edelmann reached, and the words he finds recall the *Glaubens-Bekentniss*. Reimarus expressed the dilemma thus: 'If we look today upon the influence and the moral benefits the Christian religion has exercised to improve the human heart, then we must acknowledge that from the history of these 1700 years and from the experience of today there is no indication that Christianity has increased man's reverence for God, morality, virtue and conduct, or that it has made man more devout, just, loving and moderate.'[10]

Edelmann and Reimarus both subscribed basically to Spinoza's concept of Jesus. Edelmann emphasized in Jesus' message the transvaluation of values, its radical aspects. Reimarus is more cautious in his evaluation of Jesus, but he too proclaims: 'See what pure and sublime holy morality Jesus is preaching. He seeks to shut off the source of evil, the sordid desires of the heart and to imbue it instead with love of self and neighbor.'[11]

Just as Edelmann and Reimarus took similar positions on major points, they also use the same examples and arguments in many instances in their Bible criticism; even a cursory inspection of their sources demonstrates their knowledge and use of the same works, though Reimarus shows little interest in documentation. Edelmann's scholarship was not small, though he was not as erudite as Reimarus, who was professor of Hebrew and oriental languages, and lecturer in philosophy, mathematics and natural sciences at the Akademische Gymnasium at Hamburg. Edelmann knew French, but it is unlikely that he knew English. His acquaintance with the English Deist writers shows itself mainly in references to works that have appeared in German translation or to reviews and summaries he found in German journals. Reimarus was fluent in English, a language most educated Hamburgers were familiar with.

Edelmann put into print ideas that some forty years later Lessing discovered in a manuscript of unacknowledged authorship; why then did Lessing not propagandize Edelmann as the one who introduced radical Bible criticism in Germany? The answer is linked to the historical situation of the period, above all to the differences between Edelmann's and Reimarus' work. Albert Schweitzer wrote in praise of those parts of Reimarus' work that Lessing had made public: 'Of the grandeur of the work not enough can be said. This work is not only one of the great events in the history of criticism, it is also a masterpiece of world literature.'[12] Indeed the almost serene tone of Reimarus' work, lightened on occasion by wit and irony, must have appealed to Lessing tremendously. This was a systematic investigation of both New and Old Testament from the vantage point of the Enlightenment, and was written in splendid German style. When it came to Lessing's attention, he must have wanted to share it with his contemporaries. None of Edelmann's major works could lay claim to such distinction as one readily concedes to Reimarus' *Apologie*. Edelmann never intended to offer his readers a systematic and thorough critique of all the Books of the Bible. His style had evolved slowly from baroque opulence to more sober rational diction. He often coined a felicitous phrase, gave forceful expression to what he wanted to convey, and linked his arguments skillfully together; in short he was a fine philosophical writer. His style suited his purpose: to instruct and persuade his readers of what he thought to be true. He wanted to combat their prejudices and to open their minds to receive a message of reason and freedom. That his enthusiasm often shows in his writings is not necessarily a fault, as even Lessing could be carried away when envisioning the advent of truly enlightened mankind. Edelmann addressed himself to a lower-class audience. His ambition to reach people certainly went beyond any circumscribed group, but he wanted to be sure of being understood by those who were lacking in education though not in willingness to listen and learn.

Reimarus definitely did not want his *Apologie* to be published at the time when he wrote it, nor did he anticipate its publication in the near future. He did not intend to become, like seventeenth-century English radicals, a 'publisher of truth'. 'The manuscript', he wrote, 'may remain secret, available only to a few understanding friends. With my consent it will not appear in print, until times become more enlightened.'[13]

'Dippel and Edelmann', Strauss remarked, 'were free thinkers and enthusiasts and therefore they found it easier to put up with the insecure existence that their frankness demanded as its price.'[14] That is too cavalierly said. Dippel suffered imprisonment, and Edelmann certainly preferred to live and work peacefully to being forced to seek new quarters frequently.

Yet Strauss had put the finger on the sensitive spot. At the beginning of the *Glaubens-Bekentniss* Edelmann has drawn the portrait of the ideal teacher: 'His life is a free one and consists more in doing than in mere talk, he loves truth in everyone, bears the errors of others with patience, although he exposes them with candor and without hesitation ... hates all violence and persecution, and proves by deeds and not by pompous oratory that he is a true lover of the frank and impartial Jesus.'[15] Reimarus' life was not free, he was attached to a highly reputable gymnasium, and his values were deeply embedded in the commercial bourgeois society. These values are given high visibility in many passages of the *Apologie*. One example may suffice:

Never has he [Jesus] made it a general rule for all Christians to give away all their goods. Such generosity dries quickly at the source. Who gives of what he can spare has a long time to give. He who just disburses his goods and makes himself a beggar, is callous towards wife and children and becomes a burden to human society. I want to go a step further: community of goods, a 'Saviour's' cash box in private hands, deprives the state of taxes from well-to-do citizens, makes for a state within a state, and is a dangerous thing, not to be tolerated anywhere.[16]

Reimarus paid for his silence. In a moving sentence in the *Apologie* he gave expression to this feeling – a luxury he did not otherwise permit himself: 'The preachers should be well aware that it is no small suffering an honest man inflicts on his soul if all his life through he has to feign and pretend.' Reimarus projects the consequence if the honest citizen were to reveal his true thoughts: 'Friendship, kindness, confidence, sociability, his very economic existence would be denied him; he would be avoided as a wicked and despicable malefactor.' The beloved family head and honored Hamburg citizen could not envision such ostracism as his lot. The real motive for sequestering his writings in his desk was, he confessed, his 'own peace of mind'.[17] In this manner the great scholar and writer had to unburden himself of what he found to be true; otherwise the frustrations would have become unbearable.

Lessing did not publish the *Fragments* without encountering opposition from the clergy. As a consequence he became embroiled in a controversy with the Hamburg pastor Goeze, which in turn brought him into conflict with the Braunschweig authorities. Under the threat of losing the privilege of publishing his own journal, *Für Geschichte und Literatur*, free of censorship, Lessing was forced to surrender the Reimarus manuscript to them.[18]

Let us return to the question: Why did Lessing, who was familiar with Edelmann's work, not give him due credit as a radical critic of orthodoxy and a champion of reason? The answer is partly implied in the qualitative differences between the works of Edelmann and Reimarus. The political hazards facing a champion of natural religion in German states and towns, including the Prussia of Frederick II, were not greatly diminished between the 1740s and the 1770s, as evidenced by the story of Lessing's publication of the *Fragments*.

Edelmann's case is further complicated, first by his frank acknowledgment of Spinoza's contribution to Bible criticism; secondly, by his attempt to redefine Spinoza's interpretation of the relation of God to his Creation. Rightly or wrongly, the stigma of materialism was pinned on Edelmann. To be a Spinozist or materialist was still the worst charge that could be levied against an intellectual.

In 1785, Friedrich Heinrich Jacobi reported a conversation with his friend Lessing dating back to July 1780. Jacobi reported Lessing's comment on Goethe's *Prometheus:* 'The view from which the poem arose, is my own ... The orthodox views of divinity are not for me, I can not bear them anymore: Hen Kai Pan [one and all]: I do not know anything else ...'

This unexpected remark was queried by Jacobi: 'Then you are in accord with Spinoza', to which Lessing replied: 'If I were to identify myself with anyone, I should not recognize anyone else.' When Lessing visited Jacobi the next morning, he reaffirmed his declaration for Spinoza: 'There is no other philosophy than Spinoza's.' Jacobi's report was immediately challenged by another of Lessing's friends, Moses Mendelssohn, who felt that these apocryphal sayings would endanger Lessing's reputation. He exclaimed in indignation: 'the editor of the *Fragments*, the author of *Nathan*, the great and admirable defender of theism and the religion of reason, a Spinozist, atheist and blasphemer!'[19] In the preface to the second edition of the *Critique of Pure Reason* (1787) Immanuel Kant wrote that speculative reason would find a better reception when recommended as a tool in combating the potential dangers 'of materialism, fatalism, atheism, libertine disbelief, enthusiasm and superstition'.[20] Within a decade Bible criticism and natural religion had become acceptable, yet Spinozism had not. Even in the minds of intellectuals like Mendelssohn it was associated with atheism and materialism. Herder's and Goethe's admiration for and true understanding of Spinoza's work were the exceptions. The 'public silence' – 'öffentliches Schweigen' – of Lessing on his Spinozism, to use Lukacs' expression, is indeed the forced silence of a man who certainly cannot be accused of cowardice and hypocrisy.[21] The fact is that in 1780 it was still hazardous to write or to say what Edelmann had dared to say in 1740.

With the advent of pre-1848 radicalism, Edelmann re-emerges. Excerpts from the *Glaubens-Bekentniss* appear in pamphlet form in Leipzig and Bern. Bruno Bauer poses, in his *Entdeckten Christentum* as 'Edelmann redivivus'.[22] The young Friedrich Engels, in a satirical poem, *Die frech bedräute, jedoch wunderbar befreite Bibel*, calls him the 'roaring Edelmann' and places him in the illustrious company of Voltaire, Danton and Hegel.[23]

Notes

1. NOTES TO 'CHILDHOOD AND EDUCATION — 1698–1724'

1. Rudolf Kötzschke and Hellmut Kretzschmar, *Sächsische Geschichte* (Frankfurt am Main, 1965), p. 263.
2. Arno Werner, *Städtische und fürstliche Musikpflege in Weissenfels bis zum Ende des 18. Jahrhunderts* (Leipzig, 1911), pp. 43–44.
3. Wilhelm Dilthey, *Gesammelte Schriften* (12 vols., Stuttgart, 1957–1960), Vol. III, p. 79.
4. *Die Musik in Geschichte und Gegenwart* (14 vols., Kassel, 1949–1968), Vol. V, p. 1230.
5. Fritz Hamann, 'Die Greiffenberger Orgelbauer Familie Edelmann', *Schlesisches Blatt für evangelische Kirchenmusik,* (March 1933), pp. 150–162.
6. Werner, *Städtische Musikpflege*, p. 72.
7. Hellmut Kretzschmar, 'Zur Geschichte der Sachsischen Sekundogenitur Fürstentümer', *Sachsen und Anhalt,* 7 (1925), p. 331 n
8. Johann Christian Edelmann, *Selbstbiographie. Geschrieben 1752* (Berlin, 1859), p. 6.
9. Loc. 11778, Staatsarchiv Dresden.
10. 'Schlosskirche Tauf Buch Register', MS., Evangelische Gemeinde, Weissenfels, no. 1: 1682–1700, 59.
11. *ES,* p. 6.
12. Friedrich Gerhardt, *Geschichte der Stadt Weissenfels a. S. mit neuen Beiträgen zur Geschichte des Herzogtums Sachsen–Weissenfels* (Weissenfels a. S., 1907), 229.
13. *ES,* p. 7.
14. Friedrich Schmidt, *Geschichte der Stadt Sangerhausen* (2 vols., Sangerhausen, 1906), Vol. II, p. 37.
15. Leonhard Hutter, *Compendium Locorum Theologicorum* (Berlin, 1961), p. 5.
16. *Ibid.,* pp. 13, 14.
17. *ES,* p. 9.
18. *Ibid.,* p. 65.
19. Schmidt, *Sangerhausen,* Vol. II, pp. 17–18.
20. *ES,* p. 12.
21. *Ibid.,* p. 20.
22. *Ibid.*
23. Cf. *infra,* p. 199.
24. Christian Heinrich Lorenz, *Geschichte des Gymnasii und der Schulen zu Altenbut* (Altenburg, 1789), p. 160.
25. *Ibid.,* p. 355.

26. Woldemar Boehne, *Die pädagogischen Bestrebungen Ernst des Frommen von Gotha* (Gotha, 1888), p. 222.

27. Friedrich Paulsen, *Geschichte des gelehrten Unterrichts auf den deutschen Schulen und Universitäten,* 3rd ed. (Leipzig, 1919), p. 580.

28. Lorenz, *Geschichte der Schulen zu Altenburg,* pp. 241–245.

29. *ES,* p. 23.

30. Christian Friedrich Wilisch, *A. D. A. M. Martinum Lutherum Restauratorem Rei Scholasticae sollertissimum orationibus saecularibus* (Altenburg, 1717).

31. Christian Friedrich Wilisch, *Wilischii Liebstadiensis Oratio Saecularis de amore et meritis Principum Saxonicorum in catechismum Martini Lutheri* (Altenburg, 1717).

32. *ES,* p. 22.

33. *Ibid.,* p. 23.

34. Lorenz, *Geschichte der Schulen zu Altenburg,* p. 321.

35. Cf. Introduction.

36. Gerhardt, *Weissenfels,* p. 242.

37. *Ibid.,* p. 244.

38. *ES,* p. 27.

39. *Ibid.,* p. 31, and Gustav Heinrich Heydenreich, *Kirchen– und Schulchronik der Stadt und Ephorie Weissenfels seit 1539* (Weissenfels, 1840), p. 173.

40. Johann Heinrich Pratje, *Historische Nachrichten von Joh. Chr. Edelmanns, eines berüchtigten Religionsspötters, Leben, Schriften, und Lehrbegrif, wie auch von den Schriften, die für und wider ihn geschrieben worden,* 2nd ed. (Hamburg, 1755).

41. The entry in the matricle reads: 'Joh. Chris. Edelmann: Weissenfeld. Misn., 4. Mai 1720.' And for his brother: 'Hch. Gottlob Edelmann, Leucopetr. Misn., 12. Nov. 1720.' 'Misn.' is the abbreviation for Misnicus, i. e. Merseburg, the margravate to which Weissenfels belonged in the tenth century. Reinhold Jauernig, *Die Matrikel der Universitaet Jena* (Weimar, 1902), Vol. II, p. 228.

42. Karl Heussi, *Geschichte der Theologischen Fakultät zu Jena* (Weimar, 1954), p. 152.

43. *ES,* pp. 43, 35.

44. *Geschichte der Universität Jena, 1548–1958* (2 vols., Jena, 1958–1962), Vol. I, pp. 192, 197, 201.

45. Georg Mentz, 'Eine Visitation der Universität Jena vom Jahre 1696', *Festschrift Alexander Cartellieri zum 60. Geburtstag* (Weimar, 1927), p. 79.

46. Heussi, *Jena,* p. 151.

47. Arnold F. Stolzenburg, *Die Theologie des Jo. Franc. Buddeus und des Chr. Matth. Pfaff* (Berlin, 1926), p. 249.

48. Johann Franz Buddeus, *Supplementum epistolarum Martini Lutheri, continens epistolas CCLX* (Halle, 1703), p. I.

49. Johann Franz Buddeus, *Catechetische Theologie aus dessen hinterlassenen Handschrift, nebst Herrn Johann Georg Walchs, Einleitung in die catechetische Historie, ausgearbeitet und herausgegeben von M. Johann Friedrich Frisch...,* Erster und zweyter Theil (Jena, 1752).

50. Johann Arndt, *Des ... Herrn Johann Arndt ... Sämtliche Geistreiche Bücher vom Wahren Christenthum* (Leipzig, 1715), p. 9.

51. Johann Franz Buddeus, *Historische und theologische Einleitung in die vornehmsten Religionsstreitigkeiten, aus Hrn. Johann Francisci Buddei Collegio herausgegeben, auch mit Anmerkungen erläutert und vielen Zusatzen vermehret von Joh. Georg Walchen* (Jena, 1724), p. 89. The first Latin edition was published in 1716, the first German edition in 1717.

52. *Ibid.*, p. xviii.

53. *Ibid.*, p. xiii.

54. Emil Clemens Scherer, *Geschichte und Kirchengeschichte an den deutschen Universitäten* (Freiburg, 1927), p. 230.

55. Christian Matthäus Pfaff, *Institutiones Historiae Ecclesiasticae* (Tübingen, 1721), p. ix.

56. *ES*, p. 32; Pfaff, *Institutiones*, p. ix.

57. Cf. Buddeus, *Einleitung in die Religionsstreitigkeiten*, Ch. 6.

58. Johann Franz Buddeus, *Theses theologicae de atheismo et superstitione variis observationibus, illustratae ... suas quoque observationes et dissertationem contra atheos adjecit Hadrianus Buurt* (Trajecti ad Rhenum, 1737), p. 138.

59. *ES*, p. 35.

60. *Ibid.*, p. 43. Cf. Christian Wolff, *Vernünftige Gedanken von Gott der Welt und der Seele des Menschen* (Halle, 1720), pp. 289, 487.

61. Wilhelm Schrader, *Geschichte der Friedrichs-Universität zu Halle* (2 vols., Berlin, 1894), Vol. I, pp. 216, 231 n. 33.

62. Max Wundt, *Die deutsche Schulphilosophie im Zeitalter der Aufklärung* (Tübingen, 1945), pp. 243, 238; Johann Franz Buddeus, *Bedencken über die Wolffianische Philosophie, nebst einer historischen Einleitung zur gegenwärtigen Controversie, zum Druck übergeben von Jo. Gustabo Idirpio* (2 vols., Freiburg, 1724), Vol. II, pp. 8, 16, 14.

63. Cf. Wundt's discussion of Wolff, *Deutsche Schulphilosophie*, p. 243.

64. *ES*, p. 43.

65. *Ibid.*, p. 39.

66. *Geschichte der Universität Jena*, Vol. I, p. 171.

67. Richard Keil, *Geschichte des Jenaischen Studentenlebens von der Gründung der Universität bis zu der Gegenwart* (Leipzig, 1858), p. 158.

68. *ES*, p. 38.

69. Edmund Kelter, *Jenaer Studentenleben zur Zeit des Renommisten von Zachariae* (Hamburg, 1908), p. 13.

70. Keil, *Geschichte des Studentenlebens*, pp. 199–200.

71. *ES*, pp. 41–42.

72. Keil, *Geschichte des Studentenlebens*, p. 16.

73. *ES*, p. 42.

74. *Ibid.*, pp. 44, 13; Kelter, *Jenaer Studentenleben*, p. 39.

75. *Geschichte der Universität Jena 1548–1958*, Vol. I, p. 101.

76. Friedrich Christian Laukhard, *Magister F. Ch. Laukhards Leben und Schicksale* (2 vols. Stuttgart, 1930), Vol. I, p. 197.

77. Pratje, *Historische Nachrichten Edelmanns*, p. 6; *ES*, pp. 33, 42.

78. *Ibid.*, p. 34.

79. *Ibid.*, p. 45.

80. *Ibid.*, p. 46.

81. Cf. *Geschichte der Universität Jena 1548–1958*, Vol. I, pp. 311, 108.

82. *ES*, p. 49.

83. *Ibid.* p. 53.

2. Notes to 'Tutor in Austria — 1724–1731'

1. *ES*, p. 54.

2. Alfred Stange, *Malerei der Donauschule* (Munich, 1964), p. 53.

3. *ES*, p. 63.

4. *Die Donau von Passau bis Wien*, ed. Josef H. Biller (Passau, 1963), p. 237.

5. *ES*, p. 66.

6. Franz Karl Wissgrill, *Schauplatz des landsässigen Nieder–Österreichischen Adels von Herren- und Ritter-Stande, von dem XI Jahrhundert an, bis auf jetzige Zeiten* (5 vols., Vienna, 1794–1804), Vol. V, pp. 258–260.

7. Grete Mecenseffy, *Geschichte des Protestantismus in Österreich* (Graz, 1956), p. 85; Bernhard Raupach, *Erläutertes Evangelisches Österreich* (2 vols., Hamburg, 1738), Vol. II, p. 243; Anton Kerschbaumer, *Geschichte des Bisthums St. Pölten* (2 vols., Vienna, 1875), Vol. I, p. 334.

8. Mecenseffy, *Protestantismus*, p. 156.

9. Franz Martin Mayer, *Geschichte und Kulturleben Österreichs*, ed. H. Pirchegger, 5th ed. (5 Vols., Vienna, 1960), Vol. II, p. 91.

10. Mecenseffy, *Protestantismus*, p. 155.

11. Wissgrill, *Schauplatz*, Vol. V, p. 26.

12. Otto Brunner, *Adeliges Landleben und Europäischer Geist; Leben und Werk Wolf Helmhards von Hohberg 1612–1688* (Salzburg, 1949), p. 49.

13. *ES*, p. 65.

14. Karl Gutkas, *St. Pölten, 800 Jahre Stadt* (St. Pölten, 1959), pp. 15–16.

15. *ES*, pp. 68–69.

16. Gustav Gugitz, *Österreichs Gnadenstätten in Kult und Brauch:* 'Niederösterreich und Burgenland' (2 vols., Vienna, 1955–1958), Vol. II, p. 221.

17. *ES*, p. 71.

18. *Ibid.*, p. 75.

19. Anton Kerschbaumer, *Geschichte der Stadt Tuln* (Vienna, 1874), p. 282.

20. Edelmann's memory of the name is inaccurate als he calls it 'Neues Lembach', cf. Ernest Tomek, *Kirchengeschichte Österreichs* (3 vols., Innsbruck, 1935–59), Vol. III,

p. 404; *ES*, p. 77; *St. Andrä*, zusammengestellt aus den Chroniken von R. U. H. Zurhofer, mimeographed, n. d.

21. *ES*, p. 77.

22. Cf. Tomek, *Kirchengeschichte*, pp. 156–159.

23. Wissgrill, *Schauplatz*, Vol. V, p. 262; Victor Hornyanszky, *Beiträge zur Geschichte Evangelischer Gemeinden in Ungarn*, 2nd ed. (Pest, 1867), p. 157.

24. Jozsef Szinnyei, *Magyar Írók* (14 vols., Budapest, 1891–1914), Vol. X, 1159; *Ibid.*, Vol. XII, p. 954; Hornyanszky, *Beiträge*, p. 158.

25. *ES*, p. 86.

26. *Ibid.*, p. 89. Date of the letter of recommendation is March 18, 1728.

27. Christian Gottlieb Jöcher, *Allgemeines Gelehrten-lexicon* (Leipzig, 1810), Vol. III, p. 1667.

28. Georg Theodor Strobel, *Miscellaneen literarischen Inhalts*, Zweite Sammlung (Nürnberg, 1779), p. 184.

29. *ES*, pp. 87–88.

30. Wilhelm Kühnert, 'Johann Christian Edelmann, ein Beitrag zur Geschichte des Österreichischen Protestantismus in der ersten Hälfte des 18. Jahrhunderts', *Jahrbuch der Gesellschaft für die Geschichte des Protestantismus in Österreich*, Vol. 67 (1951), pp. 25–35; Karl von Otto, 'Evangelischer Gottesdienst in Wien vor der Toleranzzeit', *Ibid.*, Vol. 7 (1886), p. 121; Karl Weiss, *Geschichte der Stadt Wien*, 2nd ed. (2 vols., Vienna, 1881), Vol. II, p. 437.

31. *ES*, p. 90; Jöcher, *Allgemeines Gelehrten-lexicon*, Vol. III, p. 1667.

32. *ES*, p. 90.

33. Emanuel Hirsch, *Gesichte der neuern evangelischen Theologie*, 4th ed. (5 vols., Gütersloh, 1968), Vol. II, p. 157.

34. Karl Philip Moritz, *Anton Reiser; ein psychologischer Roman* (Frankfurt a. M., 1959), p. 131.

35. *ES*, p. 93.

36. *Ibid.*, p. 90.

37. Otto, 'Evangelischer Gottesdienst', p. 122.

38. *ES*, p. 94.

39. *Ibid.*, p. 97; Edelmann, *Moses*, pt. II, pp. 24–25.

40. Wissgrill, *Schauplatz*, Vol. I, pp. 277, 263.

41. Raupach, *Erläutertes Österreich*, pt. II, p. 240; Kerschbaumer, *St. Pölten*, Vol. I, p. 458.

42. *ES*, p. 106.

43. Strobel, *Miscellaneen*, p. 186.

44. Wissgrill, *Schauplatz*, Vol. V, p. 278; *ES*, pp. 109–110.

45. Wissgrill, *Schauplatz*, Vol. I, p. 278.

46. Strobel, *Miscellaneen*, p. 188.

47. *Ibid.*, pp. 186, 187.

48. Wolfgang Philipp, *Das Werden der Aufklärung in theologischer Sicht* (Göttingen, 1957), p. 26.

49. Robert Boyle, *The Works of the Honourable Robert Boyle* (6 vols., London, 1744—1772), Vol. II, 107.
50. Pratje, *Historische Nachrichten Edelmanns*, p. 20, where the quoted remark is a hand-written interpolation; Jöcher, *Allgemeines Gelehrten-lexicon,* Vol. V, p. 583.
51. *ES,* p. 108; Georg Loesche, *Geschichte des Protestantismus im vormaligen und im neuen Österreich,* 3rd ed. (Vienna, 1930), p. 122.
52. Brunner, *Helmhard von Hohberg,* p. 50.
53. An account of the financial side of the transaction is given by Kühnert, 'Edelmann', pp. 32–33.
54. Stendhal, *Correspondance,* ed. Henri Martineau (3 vols., Paris, 1962–1968), Vol. I, p. 528.

3. Notes to 'The Search for Christian Perfection — 1731–1734'

1. Pratje, *Historische Nachrichten Edelmanns,* p. 23.
2. Christian Gotthold Wilisch, *Kirchen–Historie der Stadt Freyberg und der in dasige Super-Indentur eingepfarrten Städte und Dörffer* (Leipzig, 1737), p. 261; *ES,* pp. 129–130.
3. *Ibid.,* pp. 128–130.
4. Mecenseffy, *Protestantismus,* pp. 196–197.
5. Strobel, *Miscellaneen,* p. 202.
6. *Ibid.,* p. 195.
7. *Ibid.,* p. 193; C. E. Schmidt, *Geschichte der evangelischen Kirchengemeinde zu Pressburg* (2 vols., Pressburg, 1906), Vol. II, p. 70.
8. Wilisch, *Kirchen-Historie,* p. 556.
9. *ES,* pp. 132–133.
10. *Ibid.,* p. 124.
11. Pratje, *Historische Nachrichten Edelmanns,* p. 22; *ES,* p. 135 – reference is probably made to August Heinrich Gottlob, chancellor to the electoral Saxon court, died 1766. *Neues allgemeines Deutsches Adels-Lexicon,* ed. E. H. Kneschke (Leipzig, 1858–64), Vol. II, p. 197.
12. Cf. Introduction.
13. Jöcher, *Allgemeines Gelehrten-lexicon,* Vol. III, pp. 197–198.
14. Bernhard Walther Marperger, *Neue gründliche und erbauliche Auslegung des Ersten Epistel Johannis* (Nürnberg, 1710), p. 805 *ff.*; *ES,* p. 124.
15. Jöcher, *Allgemeines Gelehrten-lexicon,* Vol. II, p. 885.
16. *ES,* p. 131.
17. Johann Wolfgang von Goethe, *Gedenkausgabe der Werke, Briefe und Gespräche,* ed. Ernst Beutler (24 vols., Zürich, 1953–1966), Vol. X, p. 385.
18. Gottfried Arnold, *Unparteyische Kirchen- und Ketzer-Historie, von Anfang des Neuen Testaments biss auf das Jahr Christi 1688* (2 vols., Frankfurt, 1699), Vol. I, p. 4.
19. *Ibid.,* Vorrede, p. VI.

20. *Ibid.*, Vorrede, p. VIII.
21. Friedrich Gundolf, *Anfänge deutscher Geschichtschreibung* (Amsterdam, 1938), p. 151.
22. Strobel, *Miscellaneen,* p. 192.
23. *ES,* pp. 139–140.
24. *Ibid.,* p. 141.
25. Erich Beyreuther, *Zinzendorf und die sich allhier beisammen finden* (Marburg an der Lahn, 1959), p. 13.
26. *Ludwig und Karl Grafen und Herren von Zinzendorf ...,* ed. Gaston Pettenegg (Vienna, 1879), p. 32.
27. *ES,* p. 142.
28. This first exchange of letters is not recorded in the Archives at Herrnhut and my account follows the *Selbstbiographie.* The fairly close dating of Edelmann's visits at Herrnhut has been possible thanks to information provided by Richard Träger, archivist at Herrnhut. For these and other references quoted later I am most grateful to him.
29. *ES,* p. 142.
30. August Gottlieb Spangenberg, *Leben des Herrn Nicholaus Ludwig Grafen von Zinzendorf und Pottendorf* (3 vols., Barby, 1773–1775), Vol. II, 882; Edelmann, *Christus und Belial* (1741), in *Sämtliche Schriften,* ed. Walter Grossmann (vols. I–IV, VII/1, IX, X, XI, Stuttgart-Bad Cannstatt, 1969–   ), Vol. XI, pp. 31–272.
31. *ES,* p. 155.
32. Edelmann, *Christus und Belial,* in *Sämtliche Schriften,* Vol. XI, p. 45.
33. *Ibid.,* p. 44.
34. Beyreuther, *Zinzendorf,* pp. 35, 46–47.
35. *Ibid.,* p. 92; Paul Gruenberg, *Philipp Jakob Spener* (3 vols., Göttingen, 1905), Vol. II, p. 176; Beyreuther, *Der junge Zinzendorf* (Marburg an der Lahn, 1957), p. 117, quoting Francke's sermon of Christmas 1715, 'Von der ersten Liebe'; *Ibid.,* p. 118.
36. Sigurd Nielsen, *Intoleranz und Toleranz bei Zinzendorf* (2 vols., Hamburg, 1952–1960), Vol. I, p. 13.
37. Beyreuther, *Zinzendorf,* p. 92.
38. *Ibid.,* p. 200.
39. *Ibid.,* p. 286.
40. Spangenberg, *Ludwig von Zinzendorf,* Vol. II, p. 786.
41. Nicholas Ludwig von Zinzendorf, *Discurs über die Augsburgische Konfession* (1748), pp. 63, 46.
42. Beyreuther, *Zinzendorf und die Christenheit, 1732–1760* (Marburg an der Lahn, 1961), pp. 63, 46.
43. *ES,* p. 143.
44. *Ibid.,* p. 144.
45. Nicholas Ludwig von Zinzendorf, *Ergänzungs Bände zu den Hauptschriften,* facs. ed. (5 vols., Hildesheim, 1965–1972), Vol. VII, p. 60; Spangenberg, *Ludwig von Zinzendorf,* Vol. II, p. 820, Vol. I, p. 432; *ES,* p. 150.

46. Wilhelm Bettermann, *Theologie und Sprache bei Zinzendorf* (Gotha, 1935), p. 66.
47. *ES*, p. 146.
48. *Ibid.*, pp. 145, 153.
49. *Ibid.*, p. 117.
50. *Ibid*, p. 167.
51. Beyreuther, *Studien zur Theologie Zinzendorfs* (Neukirchen-Vluyn, 1962), p. 113.
52. Fritz Tanner, *Die Ehe im Pietismus* (Zurich, 1952), p. 156.
53. *ES*, p. 149.
54. *Ibid.*, p. 147.
55. Spangenberg, *Ludwig von Zinzendorf*, Vol. I, p. 672.
56. Tanner, *Die Ehe*, p. 131.
57. Beyreuther, *Studien*, p. 42.
58. *ES*, pp. 147, 153.
59. Spangenberg, *Ludwig von Zinzendorf*, Vol. I, p. 705.
60. Beyreuther, *Zinzendorf und die Christenheit*, p. 18.
61. *ES*, pp. 149, 154.
62. Transcript by Archivist Träger.
63. *ES*, p. 155.

4. Notes to 'First Publications — 1734–1736'

1. Eric A. Blackall, *The Emergence of German as a Literary Language, 1700–1775* (Cambridge, 1959), pp. 51, 88.
2. Nicholas Ludwig von Zinzendorf, *Hauptschriften* (6 vols., Hildesheim, 1962–1972, reprint of 1732–1760 ed.), Vol. I, pp. XII, XXXIII.
3. Christlieb von Clausberg, *Gespraeche in dem Reiche der Wahrheit, zwischen einem Dänen, Lüneburger, und einigen Hamburgern, die von dieser stadt im Jahr 1726 einge-führten Münz-Neurungen ... betreffend, etc.* (1735).
4. *ES*, p. 160; Arnold, *Unparteyische Kirchen-Historie*, Vorrede, p. 28.
5. For 'Wahrheit' see Jakob und Wilhelm Grimm, *Deutsches Wörterbuch* (Leipzig, 1854–1954).
6. Arnold, *Unparteyische Kirchen-Historie*, p. 24.
7. Grimm, *Deutsches Wörterbuch*, Vol. XI, III. Abteilung, 1355.
8. He who seeks truth in the sincerity of Christ.
9. Albrecht Kirchhoff, 'Lesefrüchte aus den Acten des städtischen Archivs zu Leipzig', *Boersenverein der deutschen Buchhändler, Historische Kommission. Archiv für Geschichte des deutschen Buchhandels*, Vol. 15 (1892), p. 295; Kirchhoff, 'Die Acten über die Buchhändler Gesellschaft von 1696', *Ibid.*, Vol. 14 (1891), p. 140.
10. *ES*, pp. 163, 214.
11. *UW, II*, pp. 423–424.
12. *Spiritual and Anabaptist Writers*, ed. George Williams (Philadelphia, 1957), pp. 31–32.

13. *Ibid.,* pp. 33–34.
14. Margarete Bornemann, *Der mystische Spiritualist Joachim Betke und seine Theologie,* diss. (Berlin, 1959), p. 134.
15. *Das Zeitalter des Barock: Texte und Zeugnisse,* ed. Albrecht Schöne, (Munich, 1963), p. 894.
16. Karl Holl, *Gesammelte Aufsätze zur Kirchengeschichte* (3 vols., Tübingen, 1927–1928), Vol. III, 324.
17. *UW, XIII,* p. 300 ('Doxophilus das ist ein Liebhaber unergründeter Meinungen'), and *UW, I,* Vorrede, 6.
18. John Locke, *Reasonableness of Christianity (Vernünftigkeit des biblischen Christentums),* trans. C. Winckler (Giessen, 1914), p. XVI.
19. *UW, I,* p. 141.
20. *Ibid.,* Vorrede, p. 4.
21. *Ibid.,* p. 5.
22. *Ibid.,* p. 8.
23. *Ibid.,* p. 9.
24. *Ibid.,* p. 11.
25. I Timothy 2: 4.
26. Acts 10: 34, 35.
27. *UW,* pp. 17–19.
28. Gottfried Arnold, *Das Geheimniss der Göttlichen Sophia oder Weisheit, beschrieben und besungen von Gottfried Arnold* (Leipzig, 1700), p. 36; *UW,* p. 20.
29. *Ibid.,* pp. 22–24.
30. *Ibid.,* p. 35.
31. *Ibid.,* pp. 29, 4, 41.
32. Cf. Romans 2:14, 15. 'For when the Gentiles, which have not the law do by nature the things contained in the law, these having not the law, are a law unto themselves. Which shew the work of the law written in their hearts, their conscience also bearing witness ... .'
33. *UW,* pp. 48, 55.
34. *Ibid.,* p. 48.
35. *Ibid.,* pp. 50, 54.
36. *Ibid.,* pp. 53–55.
37. Gottfried Arnold, *Die erste Liebe Der Gemeinen Jesu Christi Das ist Wahre Abbildung Der Ersten Christen nach Ihrem Lebendigen Glauben und Heiligen Leben ...* (Frankfurt, 1669).
38. Ernst Benz, *Ecclesia Spiritualis* (Stuttgart, 1934), p. 27.
39. *UW,* p. 116. Refers to I Cor. 3:6.
40. *UW,* p. 77.
41. Ernst Walter Zeeden, *Martin Luther und die Reformation im Urteil des deutschen Luthertums.* (2 vols., Freiburg, 1952), Vol. II, p. 204.
42. *Ibid.,* p. 202; Hirsch, *Geschichte der neuern evangelischen Theologie,* Vol. II, p. 96.
43. *UW,* pp. 68–69.

44. *Ibid.,* p. 110.
45. Romans 15:5.
46. *UW,* pp. 107–108.
47. *Ibid.,* pp. 83–84.
48. *Ibid.,* pp. 103–104, 112.
49. *Ibid.,* p. 116. A. F. Walls writes in 1962: 'The apostles are the norm of doctrine and fellowship in the New Testament' and makes special reference to Acts 2:42 (J. D. Douglas, *The New Bible Dictionary* (Grand Rapids, 1962), p. 49).
50. *UW,* p. 350.
51. *Ibid.,* p. 97.
52. Arnold, *Unparteyische Kirchen-Historie,* Vol. II, p. 670.
53. *UW,* p. 97.
54. *Ibid.,* p. 98.
55. Arthur Darby Nock, *Conversion* (Oxford, 1933), p. 5.
56. *UW,* p. 99.
57. *Ibid.,* pp. 179–180.
58. Ernesto Buonaiuti, 'Wiedergeburt Unsterblichkeit und Auferstehung im Urchristentum', *Eranos-Jahrbuch,* Vol. 7 (1939), p. 295.
59. Albert Lindenmeyer, 'Regeneration', *Kirchliche Zeitfragen,* Vol. 5 (1943), p. 45.
60. Jakob Böhme, 'Christophia, oder der Weg zu Christo', *Sämtliche Schriften* (11 vols., Stuttgart, 1957), Vol. IV, pp. 111–112.
61. Cf. Werner Elert, *The Structure of Lutheranism,* tr. Walter A. Hansen, Vol. I (St. Louis, 1962), p. 293.
62. J. T. Müller, *Die symbolischen Bücher der evangelisch–lutherischen Kirche, deutsch und lateinisch* (Gütersloh, 1876), p. 604; Elert, *Structure of Lutheranism,* p. 292.
63. Hirsch, *Geschichte der neuern evangelischen Theologie,* Vol. II, pp. 139–141.
64. An interesting discussion of Jakob Böhme's critique of the concept of satisfaction (Genugtuung Christi) is to be found in Heinrich Bornkamm, *Luther und Böhme* (Bonn, 1925), p. 264.
65. Paul Gennerich, *Die Lehre von der Wiedergeburt* (Leipzig, 1907), p. 223.
66. Elert, *Structure of Lutheranism,* p. 293.
67. Cf. Lindenmeyer, 'Regeneration', p. 6.
68. *UW, II,* pp. 465, 436, 439.
69. *Ibid.,* p. 568.
70. *Ibid.,* p. 287.
71. *Ibid.,* p. 460.
72. *UW, III,* p. 739.
73. Böhme, 'Christophia', p. 130.
74. *UW, I,* pp. 265, 203, 211, 252.
75. *UW, II,* p. 555.
76. *UW, I,* p. 252.
77. Goethe, *Gedenkausgabe,* Vol. V, p. 520; *UW,* p. 663.
78. Goethe, *Gedenkausgabe,* Vol. V, p. 151.

5. NOTES TO 'BERLEBURG YEARS — 1736–1740'

1. Maximilian Goebel, *Geschichte des christlichen Lebens in der rheinisch-westphälischen evangelischen Kirche* (3v. in 4, Coblenz, 1849–1860), Vol. III, pp. 104–130.

2. *ES*, pp. 186–187.

3. *Ibid.*, p. 217.

4. *Geistliche Fama* (2 vols., Büdingen, 1733–1736), XXI Stück, pp. 3–4.

5. Heinz Renkewitz, *Hochmann von Hochenau (1670–1721)* (Quellenstudien zur Geschichte des Pietismus, Breslau, 1935), p. 103.

6. Cf. Hirsch, *Geschichte der neuern evangelischen Theologie*, Vol. II, p. 256.

7. Nils Thune, *The Behmenists and the Philadelphians: A Contribution to the Study of English Mysticism in the 17th and 18th Centuries* (Uppsala, 1948), pp. 86–87.

8. Johannes Wallmann, *Philipp Jakob Spener und die Anfänge des Pietismus* (Tübingen, 1970), pp. 250, 253.

9. Goebel, *Geschichte des christlichen Lebens*, Vol. II, pp. 762–773.

10. Johann Adam, *Evangelische Kirchengeschichte der Stadt Strassburg bis zur Französischen Revolution* (Strassburg, 1922), p. 477.

11. Goebel, *Geschichte des christlichen Lebens*, Vol. III, p. 103.

12. *Die Heilige Schrift* ... (Berleburg, 1726–1742), Vol. I, Introduction.

13. *Die Berleburger Chroniken des Georg Cornelius, Antonius Crawelius und Johann Daniel Scheffer*, ed. Wilhelm Hartnack (Laasphe, 1964), pp. 148, 162; Friedrich Wilhelm Winckel, 'Die Berleburger Bibel', *Monatschrift für die evangelische Kirche der Rheinprovinz und Westphalens* (1851), pp. 1–33, 59–68; Josef Urlinger, *Die Geistes- und sprachgeschichtliche Bedeutung der Berleburger Bible,* diss. (Saarbrücken, 1969), p. 31.

14. This brief account follows Goebel, *Geschichte des christlichen Lebens,* Vol. III, pp. 193–233.

15. *ES*, p. 232.

16. Moritz, *Anton Reiser,* p. 11.

17. Ronald Arbuthnott Knox, *Enthusiasm: A Chapter in the History of Religion, with Special Reference to the XVII and XVIII Centuries* (Oxford, 1957), p. 332.

18. Jung-Stilling [Johann Heinrich], *Der Schlüssel zum Heimweh* (Marburg, 1796), p. 207.

19. Knox, *Enthusiasm,* p. 355.

20. 'Von einem Liebhaber der unpartheyischen Wahrheit.'

21. Pierre Poiret, *L'oeconomie divine, ou Principes et demonstrations des vérités universelles* (7 vols., Amsterdam, 1687), Vol. I, p. 2.

22. Poiret, *Die göttliche Haushaltung,* ... Vol. I, (Berleburg, 1737), p. 81.

23. Goebel, *Geschichte des christlichen Lebens,* Vol. III, p. 95.

24. Friedrich Wilhelm Winckel, *Aus dem Leben Casimirs* (Frankfurt, 1847), pp. 116–117.

25. *ES*, pp. 244, 229.

26. *Ibid.*, p. 242.

27. *Ibid.*, pp. 228–229.

28. J. J. Zentgraff, quoted by Urlinger, *Bedeutung der Berleburger Bibel,* n. 29.

29. *ES*, p. 248.

30. *Ibid.*, p. 250.
31. *Ibid.*, pp. 227–228.
32. *ES*, pp. 250, 245; for 'Tremblers', see *Oxford English Dictionary*.
33. Goebel, *Geschichte des christlichen Lebens*, Vol. III, p. 129.
34. Knox, *Enthusiasm*, p. 359.
35. Cf. *supra*, p. 99.
36. E. L. Gruber, *Historische Umstände*, quoted by Goebel, 'Geschichte der wahren Inspirations-Gemeinde', *Zeitschrift für die historische Theologie*, Vol. 24 (1854), p. 383.
37. Johann Conrad Dippel, *Sämtliche Schriften* (3 vols., Berleburg, 1747), Vol. III, p. 598.
38. *ES*, p. 259.
39. *Ibid.*, p. 278.
40. *Ibid.*, p. 274.
41. Wilhelm Bender, *Johann Konrad Dippel Der Freigeist aus dem Pietismus. Ein Beitrag zur Entstehungsgeschichte der Aufklärung* (Bonn, 1882), p. 224.
42. *ES*, p. 275.
43. Edelmann, *Sämtliche Schriften*, Vol. XI, pp. XIV—XV.
44. Johann Georg Schelhorn, *Ergötzlichkeiten aus der Kirchenhistorie und Literatur* (12 pts. in 3 vols., Ulm, 1762–1764), Vol. I, pp. 363–369.
45. *ES*, p. 275.
46. *Ibid.*, p. 297.
47. *Ibid.*, p. 298.
48. *Privilegia und Freyheiten ... Ernst Casimir Graf zu Ysenburg und Büdingen ... ertheilet hat* (Offenbach am Mayn, 1712).
49. *ES*, pp. 302–303.
50. Fürstlich Wiedisches Archiv, Schrank 66, Gefach 2, Fasci 7.
51. Richard Leineweber, *Salomon Jakob Morgenstern; ein Biograph Friedrich Wilhelm I*, diss. (Leipzig, 1899), p. 9.
52. Edelmann, *Sämtliche Schriften*, Vol. X, pp. 3–9.
53. Robert Reinhold Ergang, *The Potsdam Führer, Frederick William I, Father of Prussian Militarism* (New York, 1941), p. 50.
54. Friedrich Förster, *Friedrich Wilhelm I, König von Preussen* (5 vols. in 3, Potsdam, 1834–1835), Vol. II, p. 355.
55. *ES*, p. 64.
56. *Die Berleburger Chroniken*, p. 161; *ES*, p. 320.
57. *ES*, p. 336.
58. *Ibid.*, p. 362.

6. Notes to 'Moses mit Aufgedeckten Angesichte — 1740'

1. Cf. Hirsch, *Geschichte der neuern evangelischen Theologie,* Vol. II, p. 413.
2. *ES,* pp. 341, 350.
3. Johann Franz Buddeus, *Lehr-Sätze von der Atheisterey und dem Aberglauben mit ge-lehrten Anmerckungen erläutert …,* 2nd ed. (Jena, 1723), p. 144.
4. *ES,* pp. 274–275, 350–351.
5. Benedict de Spinoza, *The Chief Works,* transl. R. H. M. Elwes (2 vols., New York, 1955), Vol. I, 9; *ES,* p. 353.
6. Cf. Max Grünwald, *Spinoza in Deutschland* (Berlin, 1897), pp. 70–83.
7. Johann Gottfried von Herder, *Sämtliche Werke* (33 vols., Berlin, 1877–1913), Vol. VIII, p. 202; Goethe, *Gedenkausgaube,* XVIII, 851.
8. Karl Barth, *Die Protestantische Theologie im 19. Jahrhundert* (Zürich, 1952).
9. Hirsch, *Geschichte der neuern evangelischen Theologie,* Vol. III, p. 5.
10. Lutheran Church, Book of Concord, *The Book of Concord; The Confessions of the Evangelical Lutheran Church,* tr. and ed. by Theodore G. Tappert (Philadelphia, 1957), p. 464.
11. J. A. Quenstedt, *Theologia Didactico Polemica, sive Systema Theologicum* (Leipzig, 1702), quoted by Robert D. Preus, *The Theology of Post-Reformation Lutheranism: a Study of Theological Prolegomena* (St. Louis, 1970), p. 281. [For the discussion of the Orthodox views on the Bible the book by Preus and a study by Klaus Scholder, *Ursprünge und Probleme der Bibelkritik im 17. Jahrhundert* (Munich, 1966) have been of special help.]
12. Cf. M. Rue, 'Luther and the Scriptures', *The Springfielder,* Vol. 24, No. 2, (August 1960), p. 60.
13. Paul Tillich, *A History of Christian Thought,* 2nd ed. (London, 1968), pp. 244, 292.
14. *Ibid.,* p. 286.
15. *ES,* p. 217.
16. *Moses,* pt. I, p. 88.
17. *Ibid.,* pt. III, p. 112.
18. *Ibid.,* pt. II, p. 21.
19. *Ibid.,* pt. I, pp. 57–58.
20. John Dryden, *Religio Laici,* 11. 258–259.
21. *Moses,* pt. I, pp. 15–17.
22. *Ibid.,* p. 80.
23. *Ibid.,* pt. II, p. 8.
24. *Ibid.,* pt. I, p. 36.
25. *Ibid.,* p. 38.
26. *Ibid.,* p. 51.
27. *Ibid.,* p. 136.
28. *Ibid.,* p. 88.
29. *Ibid.,* pp. 99–100.
30. Spinoza, *The Chief Works,* Vol. I, p. 172.

31. *Moses*, pt. I, p. 106.
32. *Ibid.*, p. 108; pt. II, 45, 65.
33. Lucius Annaeus Seneca, *Ad Lucilium Epistolae Morales* (3 vols., Cambridge, Mass., 1917–1925), Vol. I, p. 273.
34. *Moses*, pt. II, p. 45.
35. Bruno Bauer, *Geschichte der Politik, Cultur und Aufklärung des 18. Jahrhunderts* (2 vols., Charlottenburg, 1843; repr. Aalen, 1965), Vol. I, p. 154.
36. The contemporary account, on which most information on Matthias Knutzen is based, is Johannes Musaeus, *Ableinung Der ausgesprengten abscheulichen Verleumbdung Ob wäre ... eine neue Secte der so genanten Gewissener entstanden ...* (Jena, 1674). The second enlarged edition was printed in 1675. Edelmann does not mention Musaeus but refers to a brief account in *Unschuldige Nachrichten ... Auf das Jahr 1703* (Leipzig, 1716), pp. 569–573. The most recent edition, the first since the 18th century, is *Matthias Knutzen, ... Ein deutscher Atheist und revolutionärer Demokrat des 17. Jahrhunderts*, ed. Werner Pfoh (Berlin, 1965).
37. *Moses*, pt. II, p. 34; Edelmann gives the following covering title 'Matthiae Knuzen/ Oldenswortha-Holsati/Epistola 1 Dialogi 2. Jenae 1672 apud Johannem Neugebauerum.' The date 1672 seems a copying mistake as reference in the first dialogue is made to Knutzen's preaching at Krempen December 1673.
38. Erhardt Albert, *Die Geschichte der Jenaischen Zeitung*, diss. (Jena, 1934), p. 24.
39. Musaeus, *Ableinung*, p. 2.
40. *Moses*, pt. II, pp. 38–40.
41. *Ibid.*, pp. 64, 41.
42. *Ibid.*, p. 59.
43. *Ibid.*, pp. 38, 53, 72. Luther's German translation reads: 'und nehmen gefangen alle Vernunft unter dem Gehorsam Christi.' The Revised Standard Version translates 'take every thought captive to obey Christ.' II Cor. 10:5.
44. *Moses*, pt. II, pp. 53, 75.
45. *The Interpreter's Bible* (12 vols., New York, 1951–1957), Vol. IX, p. 411.
46. *Moses*, pt. II, p. 72.
47. Corpus Juris Civil, Institutiones. *Imperatoris Iustiniani Institutionum libre quator*, 5th ed., ed. J. B. Moyle (Oxford, 1912), p. 98.
48. *Moses*, pt. II, pp. 49–50.
49. *Ibid.*, pp. 89, 59.
50. *Ibid.*, pp. 52, 61, 63.
51. Johann Wolfgang von Goethe, *Goethe: The Story of a Man; Being the Life of Johann Wolfgang von Goethe as told in his own words and the words of his Contemporaries*, by Ludwig Lewisohn (2 vols., New York, 1949), Vol. II, p. 407; Goethe, *Gedenkausgabe*, Vol. I, p. 515.
52. Georg Thomas Wagner, *J. C. Edelmann's Verblendete Anblicke des Moses mit aufgedecktem Angesicht, nach ihrer wahren Beschaffenheit forgestellt* (Frankfurt, 1747–1748), Vol. I, p. 26.

53. Friedrich Zucker, *Syneidesis–Conscientia* (Jena, 1928), p. 8; William Nickerson Bates, *Euripides: A Student of Human Nature* (Philadelphia, 1930), p. 205.
54. *ES*, pp. XI, 462.
55. Immanuel Kant, *Gesammelte Schriften* (Berlin, 1910–1970), Vol. II, p. 484.
56. H. A. Wolfson, 'Spinoza and Religion', *The Menorah Journal* (Autumn 1950), p. 147.
57. *Moses*, pt. I, p. 139.
58. Heinrich Heine, *The Poetry and Prose*, ed. Frederic Ewen (New York, 1948), p. 683.
59. *Moses*, pt. II, pp. 147–149.
60. *Ibid.*, p. 161.
61. *Ibid.*, p. 169.
62. *Ibid.*, pt. III, p. 7.
63. *Ibid.*, pt. II, p. 166.
64. *Ibid.*, pt. III, pp. 11–12.
65. Goethe, *Faust*, tr. C. F. McIntyre (Norfolk, Conn., 1941), p. 27; Goethe, *Gedenkausgabe*, Vol. V, p. 159.
66. Heine, *Poetry and Prose*, p. 682.
67. Ernst Bloch, *Das Prinzip Hoffnung* (2 vols., Frankfurt am Main, 1959), Vol. II, p. 999.
68. Cf. Jakob Böhme, 'Clavis ...', *Sämtliche Schriften*, Vol. IX, p. 100.
69. Benedict de Spinoza, *Ethic*, tr. from the Latin by W. Hule White (London, 1923), pp. 30, 32.
70. *Ibid.*, p. 48.
71. Heine, *Poetry and Prose*, p. 683.
72. *Moses*, pt. II, p. 150.
73. *Ibid.*, p. 123. 'Denn wann Gott dereinst in den Seligen Alles in Allen sayn wird, so muss er das fürwahr nur in den Spinozisten thun, die es nicht vor gefährlich halten, wenn Gott auch in ihnen alles ist und weset.'
74. *Ibid.*, pt. III, p. 5.
75. *Ibid.*, p. 27.
76. *Ibid.*, p. 90.
77. *Ibid.*, p. 29.
78. *Ibid.*, pt. II, p. 149.
79. *Ibid.*, pp. 124–125.
80. *Ibid.*, pp. 169.
81. J. C. Edelmann, 'Der unbekannte Gott' (1744), ms. in the Harvard Divinity School Library (Z. 110), p. 19.
82. *Moses*, pt. III, p. 99.
83. The name Hermes served as the author of a number of writings dating to the second and third century of Egyptian origin that were assembled as the Corpus Hermeticum. The title Poimandres belongs only to the first of the Hermetic treatises. The latest critical edition is: Hermes Trismegistus, *Corpus Hermeticum ...*, text established by A. D. Nock, tr. A.-J. Festugière, 3rd ed. (Paris, 1960), Vol. I.
84. Cf. Robert Fludd, *Mosaicall Philosophy: Grounded upon the Essential Truth or Eternal Sapience* (London, 1659), p. 41.

85. Robert Fludd, *Philosophia Moysaica* (Goudae, 1638), Sectionis Primae Lib., III, 20. Fludd's paraphrasing is most likely based on two different passages in the Piman- der. They read as follows: 'Paulo post umbra quedam horrenda, obliqua revolutio- ne subter labebatur ...' 'Lumen illud ego sum, mes, Deus tuus, antiquior quam natu- ra humida, quae ex umbra effulsit, mentis vero germen luces, Dei filius.' (Marsilio Ficino, *Opera omnia* (repr. Turin, 1959), Vol. II, pt 2, p. 837).
86. *Moses,* pt. III, p. 84; pt. II, p. 113.
87. Fludd, *Mosaicall Philosophy,* p. 42.
88. *Moses,* pt. II, p. 165.
89. Fludd, *Mosaicall Philosophy,* p. 45.
90. *Moses,* pt. II, p. 157.
91. Goethe, *Gedenkausgabe,* Vol. V, p. 250.
92. Pratje, *Historische Nachrichten Edelmanns,* p. 116.
93. *ES,* p. 350.
94. *ES,* p. XXIV.
95. François Marie Arouet de Voltaire, *Œuvres* (13 vols., Paris, 1835–1838), Vol. II, p. 561; *Stats- und Gelehrte Zeitung des Hamburgischen unpartheyischen Corresponden- ten, Anno 1740,* p. 129 (August 12, 1740).
96. *Moses,* pt. II, p. 61.
97. *Ibid.,* pt. III, pp. 157, 154–155, 150.
98. Cf. Friedrich II, der Grosse, *Œuvres de Frederic le Grand ...* ed. J. D. Preuss (31 vols., Berlin, 1846–1857), Vol. II, p. 119; Vol. XXIII, p. 123; Vol. XXV, p. 276.
99. *Publikationen ... des Preussischen Staatsarchivs* (1881), Vol. X, pt. 2, No. 723.
100. Friedrich II, *Œuvres,* Vol. XXIII, p. 114.
101. G. E. Lessing, *Gesammelte Werke,* ed. P. Rilla (10 vols., Berlin, 1954–1958), Vol. IX, p. 327.
102. *Briefwechsel zwischen Gleim und Ramler,* ed. Carl Schüddekopf (2 vols., Tübingen, 1906), Vol. I, p. 98.
103. *ES,* pp. 355–356.

7. Notes to 'Confession of Faith — 1741–1749'

1. *650 Jahre Stadt Hachenburg* (Hachenburg, 1964), 17. In his autobiography Edel- mann erroneously gave the year 1742 as the date of Count Casimir's death, instead of June 5, 1741. His account supports the date of early winter, 1741, for his move to Hachenburg rather than 1742 which he mentions. When Edelmann records these events a decade later, in the spring of 1753, he notes his confusion on dates. *EA,* p. 395.
2. *Die Berleburger Chroniken,* p. 161; *EA,* p. 368.
3. *EA,* p. 406.
4. *650 Jahre Hachenburg,* p. 73.
5. *EA,* pp. 398, 423.
6. *650 Jahre Hachenburg,* p. 66.

7. *EA*, pp. 395, 398; Zisterzienster-Abtei Marienstatt, Abtei Marienstatt, n.d. 9.
8. *EA*, pp. 423.
9. *Ibid.*, p. 343.
10. Manfred Schlosser, *Genossenschaften in der Grafschaft Ysenburg vom 16. bis zum 19. Jahrhundert* (Kallmüntz, 1956), p. 168.
11. Among the manuscripts were other such 'Sendschreiben'; the one of June 2, 1749 has been lost with other manuscripts (cf. p. 199). The other of November 3, 1749, a discussion of the concept of the immortality of the soul, is now included in Volume X of Edelmann's works.
12. *Begierde*, p. 4.
13. *Ibid.*, p. 199.
14. *Ibid.*, p. 14.
15. Cf. p. 170, *supra*, pp. 137–139.
16. *Begierde*, pp. 88–89.
17. Cf. *supra*, p. 136.
18. *Begierde*, pp. 93–94.
19. *Ibid.*, pp. 94–95.
20. *Ibid.*, p. 187.
21. Ernst Bloch, *Atheismus im Christentum* (Frankfurt a. M., 1968), p. 17.
22. *Begierde*, pp. 10–11.
23. *UW*, *XV*, p. 93.
24. *Moses*, pt. II, p. 54.
25. *EA*, p. 429.
26. *Begierde*, pp. 239, 237.
27. *Begierde*, pp. 242, 243.
28. *EA*, p. 429.
29. *Ibid.*, p. 432.
30. *Kayserliche und Gräffliche Wiedische /Privilegia/ Den Orth und Platz/ Neuenwiedt/ Zu einer Statt Zumachen und zu befestigen* (Herborn [1663]).
31. *EA*, p. 208; *300 Jahre Neuwied, 1653–1953, ein Stadt und Heimatbuch* (Neuwied, 1953), p. 384.
32. *Glaubens-Bekentniss*, p. 3.
33. The documents are kept at the Fürstlich Wiedische Archiv, 'Acta Johann Christian Edelmann et sons Secte zu Neuwied', MS. [Schrein 66, Gefach 2, Fasci 7].
34. *Ibid.*, p. 20.
35. For a detailed account based on the *Acta* see my article 'Edelmann in Neuwied', *Glaube, Geist, Geschichte, Festschrift für Ernst Benz* (Leiden, 1967), 207–216.
36. *G* 243.
37. *G* 313.
38. *G* 250.
39. *G* 93. Edelmann follows Spinoza. Cf. B. de Spinoza, *Opera*, ed. J. van Vloten (2 vols., Hague, 1882), Vol. I, p. 383. Edelmann has described the influence of the *Tractate* on his own thoughts in the *Selbstbiographie*, p. 350.

40. *G* 101, 255–256.
41. *Moses,* pt. III, p. 102.
42. *G* 142, 318.
43. *G* 110.
44. *G* 206, 90, 117, 121.
45. *G* 44.
46. *G* 142, 169, 164, 43.
47. *G* 308, 38; D. F. Strauss, *Das Leben Jesu* (2 vols., Tübingen, 1837), Vol. I, p. 30.
48. *G* 90.
49. *Moses,* pt. II, p. 92.

8. Notes to 'Refuge in Berlin — 1749–1767'

1. *ES,* pp. 1, 193, 389.
2. 'Bürgermeisterbuch 1750'. MS., fol. 137, 144, 149, Stadtarchiv Frankfurt a. M.
3. *Begierde,* p. 159.
4. Edelmann, *Schriften,* Vol. XI, pp. 334, 349; *ES,* pp. 114, 115.
5. Cf. *supra,* Chap. 6, n. 101.
6. Carl Mönckeberg, *Hermann Samuel Reimarus und Johann Christian Edelmann* (Hamburg, 1867), p. 184, and Pratje, *Historische Nachrichten Edelmanns,* p. 29.
7. *Ibid.,* p. 29 n. 32.
8. Bauer, *Geschichte der Politik,* Vol. I, p. 225.
9. Johann Peter Süssmilch, *Die Unvernunft und Bosheit des berüchtigten Edelmanns* (Berlin, 1747), pp. 2, 147; Bauer, *Geschichte der Politik,* Vol. I, p. 225.
10. Pratje, *Historische Nachrichten Edelmanns,* 32; *Acta Historico-Ecclesiastica,* pt. 76 (Weimar, 1748), p. 147.
11. Süssmilch, *Unvernunft,* p. 2; Herder, *Sämmtliche Werke,* Vol. V, p. 21.
12. Edelmann, *Schriften,* Vol. XI, pp. 285, 282; *ES,* p. 356.
13. Edelmann, *Schriften,* Vol. XI, p. 513. A reference to Voltaire's poem written on the occasion of Frederick's ascension to the Prussian throne.
14. Edelmann, *Schriften,* Vol. XI, p. 15.
15. *Briefwechsel zwischen Gleim und Ramler,* Vol. I, p. 92.
16. *Sechs Briefe von Johann Christian Edelmann an Georg Christoph Kreyssig,* ed. Philipp Strauch (Halle, 1918), p. 22.
17. *Ibid.*
18. *Ibid.,* p. 24.
19. Cf. *infra,* p. 199.
20. Edelmann, *Schriften,* Vol. X, p. XV; *ES,* p. 453.
21. *650 Jahre Hachenberg,* Vol. II, p. 165*f.,* 243*f.*
22. *Sendschreiben,* pp. 19, 7.

23. Hermann Samuel Reimarus, *Apologie oder Schutzschrift für die vernünftigen Verehrer Gottes,* ed. Gerhard Alexander (2 vols., Frankfurt a. M., 1972); cf. also Karl Ludwig Voss, *Christianus Democritus, das Menschenbild bei Johann Conrad Dippel* (Leyden, 1970), p. 82*f.*

24. *Bibliothèque Raisonnée des Ouvrages des Savans de l'Europe,* 41 (1748), p. 477.

25. Marianne Constance Couperus, *Un Periodique français en Hollande, le glaneur historique (1731–1733)* (The Hague, 1971), p. 221. Mme. Couperus has, in her recent publication, proved the authorship of La Varenne, and thus the fabrication of Vernede's account of the document has been borne out (*Ibid.,* p. 66*f.*).

26. *Sendschreiben,* p. 59.

27. *Ibid.,* pp. 4, 5. The reference is to Ludwig Holberg, *Moralische Gedanken,* transl. Elias Caspar Reichard (Leipzig, 1744).

28. It is impossible to say whether Edelmann was already acquainted with La Mettrie's works. The first direct reference to him is in the 'Siebenter Anblick' of *Moses,* which remained unpublished but was written around 1753. 'Moses mit Aufgedeckten Angesicht 7ter Anblick', p. 13, Ms. 2059.32, Andover-Harvard Library.

29. *Sendschreiben,* p. 26.

30. *Ibid.,* p. 53.

31. *ES,* p. 441.

32. Albrecht Kirchhoff, 'Zur Geschichte der kais. Bücher-Commission in Frankfurt a. M.', in *Archiv für Geschichte des deutschen Buchhandels,* Vol. 4 (1879), p. 98.

33. Cf. Johann Goldfriedrich, *Geschichte des deutschen Buchhandels (1698–1740)* (2 vols., Leipzig, 1908), Vol. II, p. 456.

34. Haus-, Hof- und Staatsarchiv Wien, Bücherkommission im Reich, F. z. 8:1743–1750 [Kaiserl. Bücherkommissariat in Frankfurt], fol. 238v./239v., 243v.

35. *Ibid.,* fol. 273v., 242v.

36. *Ibid.,* fol. 239v.

37. *Sechs Briefe von Johann Christian Edelmann an Kreyssig,* p. 27.

38. 'Bücher Kommission im Reich', MS., fol. 255v.

39. These documents that were part of the archive of the Predigerministerium were lost in World War II. Letter of April 9, 1964, Stadtarchiv Frankfurt am Main.

40. 'Bürgermeisterbuch 1750', MS., 137v, Stadtarchiv Frankfurt a. M.

41. Richard Grabau, *Das Evangelisch-lutherische Predigerministerium der Stadt Frankfurt a. M.* (Frankfurt a. M., 1913), p. 285.

42. Goethe, *Gedenkausgabe,* Vol. X, p. 167.

43. 'Bürgermeisterbuch 1750', *f°.* 149v.

44. Pratje, *Historische Nachrichten Edelmanns,* pp. 34, 40.

45. *Des berichtigten Johann Christian Edelmanns, Leben und Schriften* (Frankfurt 1750).

46. Pratje, *Historische Nachrichten Edelmanns,* pp. 22–23.

47. Moses Mendelssohn, *Gesammelte Schriften,* Vol. XI (Berlin, 1932), p. 21.

48. *ES,* p. XXVI.

49. Quoted by Karl Guden, *Johann Christian Edelmann* (Hannover, 1870), p. 62.

Notes to 'Conclusion'

1. Cf. *supra,* Ch. VI, note 13.
2. Hermann Samuel Reimarus, *Apologie oder Schutzschrift für die vernünftigen Verehrer Gottes,* ed. Gerhard Alexander (2 vols., Frankfurt am Main, 1972), Vol. I, p. 16.
3. D. F. Strauss, *Gesammelte Schriften* (12 vols., Bonn, 1877), Vol. V, p. 233; Strauss, *Das Leben Jesu,* Vol. I, p. 15; D. F. Strauss, *Die Christliche Glaubenslehre* (2 vols., Tübingen, 1840), Vol. I, p. 199.
4. Cf. Albert Schweitzer, *Von Reimarus bis Wrede. Eine Geschichte der Leben Jesu Forschung* (Tübingen, 1906).
5. Reimarus, *Apologie,* Vol. I, p. 286.
6. *Ibid.,* pp. 23, 11; Friedrich Wagner, *Der sich selbst verurtheilende Democrit, oder Wiederlegung seines Lehrbegrifs von dem Mittleramt Jesu,* parts 1 and 2 (Breslau, 1732–1733).
7. For a discussion of Dippel, cf. Voss, *Christianus Democritus,* p. 82*ff.*
8. Reimarus, *Apologie,* Vol. I, p. 104.
9. *Ibid.,* Vol. I, p. 29.
10. *Ibid.,* Vol. II, p. 482.
11. *Ibid.,* Vol. I, p. 35.
12. A. Schweitzer, *The Quest of the Historical Jesus* (London, 1954), p. 15.
13. Reimarus, *Apologie,* Vol. I, pp. 129–130.
14. Strauss, *Gesammelte Schriften,* Vol. V, p. 249.
15. Edelmann, *Schriften,* Vol. IX, p. 12.
16. Reimarus, *Apologie,* Vol. II, p. 365.
17. *Ibid.,* Vol. I, p. 41.
18. *Ibid.,* p. 15.
19. F. Jacobi, *Spinoza-Büchlein,* ed. F. Mauthner (Munich, 1921), pp. 65–66, 67, 201.
20. I. Kant, *Kritik der reinen Vernunft,* ed. Th. Valentiner (Leipzig, 1913), p. 39.
21. G. Lukacs, *Die Zerstörung der Vernunft* (Neuwied, 1962), p. 89.
22. *J. C. Edelmann's Abgenöthigtes, jedoch Andern nicht wider aufgenöthigtes Glaubensbekentniss* (Leipzig 1848); *Der neu eröffnete Edelmann* (Bern, 1847). Ernst Barnikol, *Das entdeckte Christentum im Vormärz* (Jena, 1927), p. 59.
23. Friedrich Engels, *Werke und Schriften bis Anfang 1844* (Marx–Engels Gesamtausgabe), Erste Abt., II (Berlin, 1930), p. 256.

Sources and Selected Bibliography

C.R.W. Klose gave an account of the Edelmann manuscripts in the Stadt-bibliothek at Hamburg in the introduction to his edition of Edelmann's *Selbst-biographie*, dated February 1848. He does not relate how and when these manu-scripts were accessioned. Christian Petersen in his *Geschichte der Hamburgischen Stadtbibliothek* (Hamburg 1838, pp. 79, 80) mentions that in 1761 the Hamburg Senate purchased 135 manuscripts from the estate of a Dr. Lossau. The purchase, prior to auction, is explained on the grounds of the rarity of the manuscripts and the wish of the Senate to prevent those of anti-Christian sentiment from becoming publicly available. Among these, Petersen mentions, were books and manuscripts by Cherbug, Servet, and Edelmann.

Not all the manuscripts Klose lists are still in existence. Losses occurred during the Second World War. The manuscripts presently available in the Staats- und Universitätsbibliothek, Hamburg, are listed below. Some appear to be in Edel-mann's own hand, others are copies. Among the manuscripts is an interleaved copy of J. H. Pratje's *Historische Nachrichten von Joh. Chr. Edelmanns ...* (Hamburg, 1753) with Edelmann's own comments (Cod. ms. theol. 2164).

Selbstbiographie. Cod. ms. theol. 1867.

Moses mit aufgedeckten Angesicht. Erster, zweiter, dritter, sechster, siebenter, achter Anblick. Cod. ms. theol. 1868.

Drittes Sendschreiben an seine Freunde, darinnen er seine Gedanken von der Unsterblichkeit der Seele eröfnet. Cod. ms. theol. 1874.

Eine Abhandlung, einer Gesellschaft vorgelegt, über metaphysische Begriffe. Selbstbiographie. Dritter Theil. Moses mit aufgedeckten Angesicht. Achtundzwanzigster Anblick. Über die Sibylle und Sibyllinischen Weis-sagungen. Cod. ms. theol. 1875.

The originals of Edelmann's letters to Georg Christoph Kreyssig are preserved at the Universitäts- und Landesbibliothek Sachsen-Anhalt, Halle. In Professor Harold Jantz's collection is the only extant manuscript copy of *Die Andere Epistel St. Harenbergs an Johann Christian Edelmann ihrem vornehmsten Inhalt nach von demselben beantwortet ... Anno 1748* – the copy formerly at Hamburg being now lost. A manuscript copy of *Die Göttlichkeit der Vernunft* is at the Library of the Harvard Divinity School. It may be identified as the collection of writings from which the printed work of the same title derived.

Klose as early as 1848 cited among the most regrettable losses a book in manu-script, begun by Edelmann at Lauban in 1715 and continued until 1759, in which he recorded his readings and commented on them. This manuscript was acquired by the geographer-historian Anton Friedrich Büsching who described it in the journal he edited (*Wöchentliche Nachrichten*, Berlin, July 24, 1775: Vol. 3, pp. 233—235).

Pratje used as frontispiece an etching portraying Edelmann. He himself doubted its likeness, and Edelmann in his own comment also disavows it when he states that 'his true friends do have a portrait *en Miniature* as well as in oil' (Pratje, *Nachrichten,* p. 42). Edelmann recalls that while on the way to Berleburg he visited his younger brother at Gotha and it was then that Schneider painted him 'en Miniature' (*Selbstbiographie,* p. 217). This 'miniature' and the 'oil painting' I have been unable to locate.

The following bibliography is highly selective. Whenever reference has been made to a work, the full bibliographical citation is in the notes. I have not attempted to list the numerous writings against Edelmann. Pratje and Trinius have documented these extensively. The bibliography is divided into primary and secondary material. The works of Edelmann in their chronological sequence, with the abbreviations used, and some major related works by contemporaries are included among the primary material. The secondary part lists major general works of the period, indispensable to this study. Also included in the bibliography are a few relevant monographs on persons and on movements, not specifically alluded to in the text. To keep the bibliography short rather than comprehensive was my preference.

Primary Materials

Works of Johann Christian Edelmann

Sämtliche Schriften in Einzelausgaben, ed. Walter Grossmann. Vols. I–VI, VII/I, IX, X, XI. Stuttgart-Bad Cannstatt, 1969—.

Disputatio Philologica qua ad quaestionem de Paschate Christi ... in Academia salana ad diem XXVI. Febr. MDCCXXIV ... a praeside M. Carolo Adolpho Jantzen gedan. et respondente Ioanne Christiano Edelmann ... Jena, [1724].

UW I—XIV: Unschuldige Wahrheiten. (*Erste bis Vierzehende Unterredung*). [Leipzig], 1735—1738, facs. in *Sämtliche Schriften,* I—V.

Bereitete Schläge auf der Narren Rücken. [Berleburg], 1738, facs. in *Sämtliche Schriften,* XI, 1—30.

Moses: Moses mit Aufgedeckten Angesichte, ... Erster, Zweyter und Dritter Anblick. [Frankfurt], 1740, facs. in *Sämtliche Schriften,* VII/I.

Christus und Belial, wie solche zusammenstimmen, in einem Theologischen Brieff-Wechsel zwischen unten benannten Auctore und Bruder Ludwig von Zinzendorff. (Neuwied), 1741, facs. in *Sämtliche Schriften,* XI, 31—272.

Die Göttlichkeit der Vernunfft, In einer kurtzen Anweisung zu weiterer Untersuchung der ältesten und vornehmsten Bedeutung des Wortes LOGUS, Nebst einigen, in diese Materie einschlagenden Briefen, Und Einem Anhange Von der Vernunfftmässigkeit des Christenthums. [Neuwied, 1743].

UW XV: Unschuldiger Wahrheiten Fünfzehendes und Letztes Stück, In Vier Gesprächen. [Neuwied], 1743, facs. in *Sämtliche Schriften,* VI.

G: Abgenöthigtes Jedoch Andern nicht wieder aufgenöthigtes Glaubens-Bekentniss. [Neuwied], 1746, facs. in *Sämtliche Schriften,* IX.

Die Begierde nach der vernünfftigen lautern Milch. [Neuwied], 1747, facs. in *Sämtliche Schriften,* X, 173-258.

Schuldigstes Dancksagungs Schreiben an den Herrn Probst Süssmilch. [Berlin], 1747, facs. in *Sämtliche Schriften*, XI, 273—303.
Die Erste Epistel St. Harenbergs an Johann Christian Edelmann, ... von demselben beantwortet, 1747, facs. in *Sämtliche Schriften*, XI, 413—578.
Das Evangelium St. Harenbergs, 1748, facs. in *Sämtliche Schriften*, XI, 304—312.
Send–Schreiben an seine Freunde den Vorzug eines Freygeistes vor einem armen Sünder zeigend, 1749, facs. in *Sämtliche Schriften*, X, 77—172.
ES: Selbstbiographie. Ed. Carl. Rudolph Wilhelm Klose. Berlin, 1849, facs. in *Sämtliche Schriften,* XII.
Sechs Briefe von Johann Christian Edelmann an Georg Christoph Kreyssig. Ed. Philipp Strauch. Halle a.S., 1918.

Other Works

Anon. *Edelmann mit aufgedecktem Angesicht oder Zu–verlässige Nachricht von des Herrn Edelmanns Aufenthalt in Berlin.* Frankfurt and Leipzig, 1747.
Arnold, Gottfried, *Unparteyische Kirchen- und Ketzer–Historie, von Anfang des Neuen Testaments biss auf das Jahr Christi 1688.* 2 vols., Frankfurt, 1699.
[Berleburger Bibel] *Die Heilige Schrift Altes und Neues Testaments nach dem Grund-text aufs neue übersehen und übersetzet.* 7 vols., Berleburg, 1726—1739.
Buddeus, Johann Franz, *Historische und theologische Einleitung in die vornehmsten Religions-streitigkeiten, aus Hrn. Johann Francisci Buddei Collegio herausgegeben, auch mit Anmerckungen erläutert und vielen Zusatzen vermehret von Joh. Georg Walchen.* Jena, 1724.
Lehr-Sätze von der Atheisterey und dem Aberglauben mit gelehrten Anmerckungen erläütert. ... 2nd ed., Jena, 1723.
Dippel, Johann Conrad, *... Sämtliche(n) Schriften Christiani Democriti.* 3 vols., Berleburg, 1747.
Geistliche Fama, 3 vols., [Berleburg], 1733—1736.
J. J. J. *Aufrichtige und wahrhafftige Extracta Aus dem allgemeinen Diario Der wahren Inspirations-Gemeinen.* VIII. Sammlung. 1742.
Pfaff, Christian Matthäus, *Institutiones Historiae Ecclesiasticae.* Tübingen, 1721.
Pratje, Johann Heinrich, *Historische Nachrichten von Joh. Chr. Edelmanns, eines berüchtigten Religionspötters, Leben, Schriften, und Lehrbegrif, wie auch von den Schriften, die für und wider ihn geschrieben worden.* 2nd ed., Hamburg, 1755.
Trinius, Johann Anton, *Freydenker Lexicon.* Leipzig, 1759; reprint, Turin, 1960.
Unschuldige Nachrichten von alten und neuen theologischen Sachen, Büchern, Urkunden ... Wittenberg and Leipzig, 1701—1719. Superseded by: *Fortgesetzte Sammlung von alten und neuen theologischen Sachen.*

SECONDARY MATERIALS

Barth, Karl, *Die protestantische Theologie im 19. Jahrhundert.* 2nd ed., Zurich, 1952.

Bauer, Bruno, *Geschichte der Politik, Cultur und Aufklärung des 18. Jahrhunderts,* I. Aalen, 1965.

Beck, Lewis White, *Early German Philosophy. Kant and His Predecessors.* Cambridge, Mass., 1969.

Becker, Karl Wolfgang, 'Die Wahrheit nach meinem besten Vermögen zu bekennen. Johann Christian Edelmanns Autobiographie', pp. 168–208 in *Goethe–Almanach auf das Jahr 1970.* Berlin, 1969.

Bender, Wilhelm, *Johann Konrad Dippel; Der Freigeist aus dem Pietismus.* Bonn, 1882.

Benz, Ernst, *Nietzsches Ideen zur Geschichte des Christentums und der Kirche.* Leiden, 1956.

Bertolini, Ingo, 'Und Gott war die Vernunft zu Joh. Chr. Edelmanns Autobiographie 1749–1752', pp. 289–318 in Istituto Universitario Orientale *Annali,* Sezione Germanica, 14 (Naples, 1971).

Beyreuther, Erich, *Studien zur Theologie Zinzendorfs.* Neukirchen, 1962.

Bornkamm, Heinrich, *Mystik, Spiritualismus und die Anfänge des Pietismus im Luthertum* (Vorträge der theologischen Konferenz zu Giessen 44. Folge). Giessen, 1926.

Elert, Werner, *The Structure of Lutheranism,* I, trans. Walter A. Hansen. St. Louis, 1962.

Goebel, Max, *Geschichte des christlichen Lebens ...,* III. *Die niederrheinische reformierte Kirche und der Separatismus in Wittgenstein.* Coblenz, 1860.

Guden, Karl, *Johann Christian Edelmann. Ein Beitrag zur deutschen Cultur- und Kirchengeschichte im achtzehnten Jahrhundert.* Hannover, 1870.

Hazard, Paul, *La pensée européenne au XVIIIème siècle.* 3 vols., Paris, 1946.

Heise, W., 'Johann Christian Edelmann: Seine historische Bedeutung als Exponent der antifeudalen bürgerlichen Opposition', diss. Humboldt University, Berlin, 1954.

Hettner, Hermann, *Geschichte der deutschen Literatur im achtzehnten Jahrhundert,* 5th rev. ed., 3 parts, Braunschweig, 1909.

Hirsch, Emanuel, *Geschichte der neuern evangelischen Theologie,* 4th ed., 5 vols., Gütersloh, 1968.

Krauss, Werner, *Studien zur Deutschen und Französischen Aufklärung* (Neue Beiträge zur Literaturwissenschaft XVI), Berlin, 1963.

Kümmel, Werner Georg, *Das Neue Testament. Geschichte der Erforschung seiner Probleme,* Munich, 1958.

Langen, August, *Der Wortschatz des Deutschen Pietismus,* 2nd ed., Tübingen, 1968.

Mauthner, Fritz, *Der Atheismus und seine Geschichte im Abendlande, III: Aufklärung in Frankreich und in Deutschland,* Stuttgart, 1922.

Mönckeberg, Carl, *Hermann Samuel Reimarus und Johann Christian Edelmann.* Hamburg, 1867.

Philipp, Wolfgang, *Das Werden der Aufklärung in theologischer Sicht,* Göttingen, 1957.

Schweitzer, Albert, *Von Reimarus bis Wrede. Eine Geschichte der Leben-Jesu-Forschung,* Tübingen, 1906.

Seeberg, Erich, *Gottfried Arnold die Wissenschaft und die Mystik seiner Zeit. Studien zur Historiographie und Mystik,* Meerane i. Sa., 1923.

Stiehler, Gottfried, ed., *Beiträge zur Geschichte des vormarxischen Materialismus,* Berlin, 1961.

Stolzenburg, Arnold F., *Die Theologie des Jo. Franc. Buddeus und des Chr. Matth. Pfaff,* Berlin, 1926.

Tillich, Paul, *A History of Christion Thought,* ed. Carl E. Braaten, London, 1968.

Urlinger, Josef, *Die geistes- und sprachgeschichtliche Bedeutung der Berleburger Bibel,* diss., Saarbrücken, 1969.

Wieser, Max, *Der sentimentale Mensch,* Gotha, 1924.

Williams, George, ed., *Spiritual and Anabaptist Writers,* Philadelphia, 1957.

Winter, Eduard, *Frühaufklärung. Beiträge zur Geschichte des Religiösen und Wissenschaftlichen Denkens,* Berlin, 1966.

Wolff, Hans Matthias, *Die Weltanschanung der deutschen Aufklärung,* Bern, 1949.

Wollgast, Siegfried, 'Johann Christian Edelmann, Abgenöthigtes Jedoch Andern nicht wieder aufgenöthigtes Glaubens-Bekentniss', in *Deutsche Literatur Zeitung,* 92 (Berlin, July 1971), no. 7, 560–562 [Review].

Index

Alexander, Count of Neuwied *see* Johann Friedrich Alexander
Allix, Pierre 39
Allut, Jean 99
Altdorfer, Albrecht 24
Altdorfer, Erhard 24
Aristophanes 126
Aristotle 123
Arndt, Johann Christian 64, 65
– *Wahres Christentum* 12, 62
Arnold, Gottfried 15, 43, 63, 64, 70, 73, 74, 77, 78, 94
– *Kirchen und Ketzer Historie* 14, 47, 48, 49, 62, 66
Auersperg, Anna Christine Caroline 37
Auersperg, Count Maximilian 37
Auersperg, Count Wolf Augustin 36, 37, 44, 45
Auersperg, Count Wolf Reichard 36, 38
August II (August der Starke), elector of Saxony 54

Bach, Johann Sebastian 1
Bauer, Bruno 177
Bauer, Georg Lorenz 153
Baxter, Richard 47
Bayle, Henri (Stendhal) 40
Bayle, Pierre 15, 61, 120, 137
Beckmann, Friedman 13
Benz, Ernst 73
Bethlen, Gábor 26

Betke, Joachim 43, 63, 64, 65
Birckenstock, Conrad von 166
Böhme, Jakob 64, 65, 80, 81, 83, 89, 90, 94, 130
Bloch, Ernst 130, 145
Bourignon, Antoinette 90, 93, 95
Boyle, Robert 39, 40
Brockes, Barthold Heinrich 24, 40, 56, 71, 143, 156
– *Irdisches Vergnügen in Gott* 23, 84
– *Der Patriot* 61
Brunner, Otto 27, 40
Buchner, Georg Balthasar 141
Buddeus, Franz 10, 11, 12, 13, 14, 15, 16, 17, 18, 22, 47
Bülow, Johanna Sophie von 94
Büsching, Anton Friedrich 169, 199
Buonaiuti, Ernesto 80
Buttler, Eva von 90, 93

Callenberg, Count August Heinrich Gottlob 46
Callenberg, Countess Charlotte Catharina 51
Callenberg, Christiana Sofia (Countess Zinzendorf) 50
Callenberg, Countess Clara Elizabeth 93
Calvin, John 80
Carl, Johann Samuel 90, 96, 98
Casimir, Count of Sayn-Wittgenstein–Berleburg 53, 89, 90, 91, 92, 94, 96, 100, 140, 155, 159

Chemnitz, Martin 4, 30
Christian II, elector of Saxony 3
Christian of Sachsen-Weissenfels 2, 3
Cicero 7
Cranach, Lucas 24, 29
Cyprian 30

Danton, Georges Jacques 177
Derham, William 39
Descartes, René 16, 95, 133, 137
Dippel, Johann Konrad 43, 53, 63, 90,
    95, 100, 102, 110, 162, 172, 173, 175
Dober, Leonhard 59
Dryden, John 116

Edelmann, Christian 2
Edelmann, Dorothea Magdalena 2
Edelmann, Dorothea Sophia 3
Edelmann, Gottfried 4, 6
Edelmann, Gottlob 1, 2, 4, 8
Edelmann, Heinrich Gottlob 3, 10, 43
Edelmann, Moritz Rudolph 3
Eichhorn, Johann Gottfried 153
Eisler, Tobias 92
Engels, Friedrich 177
Euripides 126

Ferdinand III, Emperor 26, 33
Ficino, Marsilio 134
Firmian, Leopold Anton, Archbishop
    of Salzburg 44
Fischer von Ehrenbach, Friedrich 32
Fleischbein, ... von 93
Fludd, Robert 128, 131, 133–135
Franck, Sebastian 48, 64
Francke, August Hermann 11, 34, 35
    39, 52, 89
Frederic II, Emperor 25, 26
Frederick II (King of Prussia) 88, 112,
    113, 137, 138, 139, 144, 156, 160, 164,
    176

Freud, Sigmund 147
Friedrich III, Count of Neuwied 148
Friedrich August II, elector 54
Friedrich Wilhelm I of Prussia 15, 108,
    109
Friese, Friedrich 7

Gaudliz, Gottlieb 47
Gelt, Robert 94
Georg Friedrich, Count of Kirchberg
    and Sayn-Hachenburg 141, 159
Gersdorf, Henriette Katharina von 52
Gichtel, Johann Georg 132
Gleim, Johann Wilhelm Ludwig 139
Goebel, Max 99
Goethe, Johann Wolfgang 48, 85, 94,
    112, 125, 129, 130, 135, 136, 146,
    167, 177
Goeze, Johann Melchior 176
Gottsched, Johann Christoph 61
Gross, Andreas 87, 88, 92, 97, 107
Gruber, Eberhard Ludwig 99, 100, 101
Gundolf, Friedrich 49
Guyon, Madame Jeanne Marie de la
    Motte 90, 92–94, 98, 129

Haberland, Moritz Wilhelm 6, 7
Händel, Georg Friedrich 1
Harenberg, Johann Christoph 161
Hasse, Adolf 160
Hasserodt, Johann Ehrhard 19, 22
Haug, Johann Friedrich 87, 90–92, 94,
    97–99
Haug, Julianne Charlotte 93
Haupt, J. B. 143, 149, 166
Hedwig-Sophie, Countess of Sayn-
    Wittgenstein–Berleburg 89
Heer, – –, Rector at Lauban 5
Hegel, Georg Wilhelm Friedrich, 146,
    177

Heimburg, Johann Kaspar 15
Heine, Heinrich 128, 130
Heinrich Albert, Count Sayn-Wittgen-
    stein–Hohenstein 89, 90
Henneberg, – –, Rector of Sangerhau-
    sen School 3, 4
Herder, Johann Gottfried 49, 94, 112,
    158, 177
Heyde, Blasius 25
Hirsch, Emanuel 39, 82, 89
Hobbes, Thomas 15
Hochmann von Hochenau, Ernst Chris-
    toph 89, 90
Hölderlin, Friedrich 146
Holl, Karl 65
Horche, Heinrich 89
Huber, Wolf 24
Hunnius, Aegidius 4
Hunnius, Nikolaus 39
Hutter, Leonhard 3, 7

Jacobi, Friedrich Heinrich 176
Jantz, Harold 199
Johann Adolf of Sachsen-Weissenfels
    1, 2, 4
Johann Friedrich Alexander, Count of
    Neuwied, 147, 149, 150, 156, 159
Johann Georg of Sachsen-Weissen-
    fels, 2
Johann Georg I of Saxony, elector 1
Johann Georg II of Saxony, elector 2
Joseph II, Emperor 26
Jung-Stilling, Johann Heinrich 94

Kant, Immanuel 177
Khlesl, Melchior 25
Kinzing, Christian 148
Klose, Carl Rudolph Wilhelm 168, 199
Knox, Ronald Arbuthnott 94

Knutzen, Matthias 112, 115, 120–126,
    136–138, 146
Kornfeil, Count Andreas III 25
Kornfeil, Count Ferdinand Friedrich 29
Kornfeil, Countess Franziska Isabella
    29
Kornfeil, Count Hector 26
Kornfeil, Count Hector Wilhelm 27,
    28, 32, 38, 40, 44
Kornfeil, Count Johann 25, 26
Kornfeil, Countess Maria Josepha 28
Kreyssig, Georg Christoph 160, 199
Krieger, Johann Philipp 1

La Mettrie, Julien Offroy 163, 164
La Serre 162
Lange, Joachim 16
Leade, Jane 89
Lee, Francis 89
Leibniz, Gottfried Wilhelm 16, 137
Leopold I, Emperor 31
Lerche, Christian 32, 36, 38–40, 44, 45
Lessing, Gotthold Ephraim 119, 139,
    151, 156, 168, 171, 176, 177
Locke, John 67
Löscher, Valentin Ernst 11, 44
– *Unschuldige Nachrichten* 61, 62
Logau, Friedrich von 65
Ludwig Ferdinand, Count of Sayn-
    Wittgenstein–Berleburg 140
Lukács, George 177
Luther, Martin 4, 7, 11, 12, 57, 74, 75,
    76, 77, 80, 82

Malthus, Thomas Robert 158
Marion, Elie 99
Marperger, Bernhard Walther 47, 80
Marsay, Carl Hector von 90, 93–95
Meier, Georg Friedrich 162
Melanchthon, Philipp 4, 76

Mendelssohn, Moses 168, 169, 177
Möllenhof, Christian Nicolaus 36
Morgenstern, Solomon Jakob 108
Moritz, Karl Philipp
– *Anton Reiser* 33, 35, 94
Müntzer, Thomas 64
Musaeus, Johannes 121

Neumeister, Hermann 40
Nock, Arthur Darby 79

Petersen, Christian 199
Pfaff, Christian Mattheus 13, 14
Philipp, Wolfgang 39
Pilgram, Johann Sigmund 31, 32
Pinell, – –, 107, 110, 112, 156–158
Pöttinger, Wolfgang 25
Poiret, Pierre 95, 98
Pordage, John 89, 90
Pratje, Johann Heinrich 9, 14, 40, 43,
    111, 136, 155, 167, 168, 199, 200

Quenstedt, Johann Andreas 113

Ramler, Karl Wilhelm 139
Reimarus, Hermann Samuel 151, 171–
    176
Reitz, Johann Heinrich 89, 97
Rock, Johann Friedrich 53, 96 99–101,
    103, 104, 106, 148
Rosenbach, Johann Georg 96
Rothe, Richard 53, 56
Rousseau, Jean Jacques 20
Roux, – –, Secretary of the Weimar
    Court 19, 20, 22
Rudolf II, Emperor 25, 165
Rückenbaum, Anton von 31
Rus, Johann Reinhard 17, 18

Scheffer, Johann Adam 92
Schein, Johann Hermann 1

Schneemelcher, – –, Rector of Sanger-
    hausen School 3
Schelling, Friedrich Wilhelm Joseph
    146
Schütz, Heinrich 1
Schumann, Johann Michael 9
Schweitzer, Albert 171, 174
Schwenckfeld, Kaspar von 64
Seebach, Christoph 92, 95, 110
Segner, Adam 45
Seneca, Marcus Annaeus 119
Serpilius, Samuel Vilmos 31, 32
Simon, Richard 116
Spalatin, Georg 6
Spangenberg, August Gottlieb 54, 58
Spener, Philipp Jakob 11, 34, 52, 64,
    65, 74, 76, 89
– *Pia Desideria* 10
– *Theologische Bedenken* 66
Spinoza, Benedict 15, 16, 112, 118, 127,
    128, 130, 131, 133, 135, 136, 150,
    161, 163, 173, 176, 177
Stendhal *see* Bayle, Henri
Stockhorner, Maria Franziska Rosina
    38
Strauss, David Friedrich 153, 171
Süssmilch, Johann Peter 139, 157, 158,
    159

Thomas à Kempis 93
Thomasius, Christian 16, 61, 62
Tillich, Paul 114, 115, 171
Trinius, Johann Anton 200
Tuchtfeld, Victor Christoph 110

Varenne, Jean-Baptiste de la 62, 162,
    163
Vergil 7
Vernède 162, 163
Voltaire 17, 137, 138, 144, 177

Wagner, Friedrich 172
Wagner, Georg Thomas 126
Walch, Johann Georg 10, 13
Walther, Samuel Benjamin 62
Watteville, Friedrich von 50, 52
Weber, Alfred 106
Weigel, Valentin 48, 64
Wernsdorf, Gottlieb 11
Wilisch, Christian Friedrich 6–8, 44, 47
Williams, George Huntson 64

Winckel, Friedrich Wilhelm 92
Wolff, Christian 15, 16, 108, 137, 158

Zinzendorf, Countess Erdmuthe 52
Zinzendorf, Count Friedrich Christian 50
Zinzendorf, Count Nikolaus Ludwig 44, 50–58, 90, 102, 104, 143, 148, 151
– *Der Dresdnische Socrates* 52, 55
– *Teutsche Socrates* 61, 62